# ADULT CHILDREN WHO WON'T GROW UP

# ADULT CHILDREN WHO WON'T GROW UP

Dr. Larry V. Stockman
Cynthia S. Graves

**CB**

**CONTEMPORARY BOOKS**

CHICAGO · NEW YORK

**Library of Congress Cataloging-in-Publication Data**

Stockman, Larry V.
    Adult children who won't grow up / Larry V. Stockman and
Cynthia S Graves.
        p.   cm.
    Bibliography: p.
    Includes index.
    ISBN 0-8092-4503-5
    1. Young adults—United States—Psychology.    2. Adult
children—United States—Psychology.   3. Parenting—United
States.    4. Dependency (Psychology)   I. Graves, Cynthia S.
II. Title.
HQ799.7.S75    1989
306.8'74—dc19                         89-30973
                                                       CIP

HQ
799.7
.S75
1989

Copyright © 1989 by Dr. Larry V. Stockman and Cynthia S. Graves
All rights reserved
Published by Contemporary Books, Inc.
180 North Michigan Avenue, Chicago, Illinois 60601
Manufactured in the United States of America
Library of Congress Catalog Card Number: 89-30973
International Standard Book Number: 0-8092-4503-5

Published simultaneously in Canada by Beaverbooks, Ltd.
195 Allstate Parkway, Valleywood Business Park
Markham, Ontario L3R 4T8 Canada

To my parents, Marcella and Victor,
whose caring about and for all people
taught me the discipline of love.
L.V.S.

To my husband, Ben.
Without your love, encouragement,
patience, and hard work,
this book would not have been possible.
C.S.G.

# Contents

# Acknowledgments

The authors wish to acknowledge the many people who helped to make this book possible. We thank the clients of Dr. Stockman who allowed us to discuss their cases in these pages and volunteered their time for interviews. They were unselfish in their time and in their willingness to share their own struggles and triumphs.

Dr. Stockman specifically thanks his spouse, Laura, for her loving advice, and for teaching him about independence, and his son, Ben, for providing firsthand lessons in parenting. He also expresses his heartfelt thanks to Dr. Albert Ellis, who taught him how to "rational-emotively" challenge and teach his clients.

Ms. Graves is deeply appreciative of her husband, Ben's, support and hard work. From the first draft of the proposal to the final draft of the manuscript, he read every page and offered insight and constructive advice. She also offers love and thanks to her stepdaughters, Beth and Leigh, and her daughter, Jessica, for their love and for providing insight into what really matters most in this world. She thanks her parents, Marjorie and Chuck, for love, encouragement, and being role models of personal commitment to owning their own choices.

We are also deeply indebted to our agent, Jeff Herman, for encouraging us to submit a proposal for this book, and to Stacy Prince, our editor, for her patient assistance in restructuring and rewriting the original drafts.

Finally, we wish to acknowledge our readers. Without parents trying—the best they know how—to be healthy and loving parents, this book would have no purpose.

# Introduction

An adult adolescent is a child over the age of eighteen who is capable of self-sufficiency and independence, but who (for some reason) is choosing not to be fully self-sufficient. Adult adolescents cling to at least one significant facet of their dependency on their parents. They may still live at home or have returned home, or they may live in an apartment or own their own home. They may live down the street or across the continent. They are adults chronologically but are still childish in terms of their extended dependency. It is in the context of this dual nature, an "adolescent" in an adult body, that we use the term *adult adolescent*.

Extended dependency in a young adult manifests itself in innumerable ways. These include showing low self-esteem, depression, self-pity, excuse making, refusal to take responsibility for anything, anger with the world in general, refusal to accept any form of authority, financial dependency, "clinging" behavior, poor decision making, job-hopping or chronic unemployment, verbal abuse of the parent, rudeness or "ungrateful" behavior, a sense of entitlement ("you *owe* it to me"), an inability to make commitments, creating one crisis situation after another, and running home every time there's a problem.

This book concentrates on the extended dependency of young adults on their parents, taking a broad view rather than focusing on a narrow cause (like alcoholism) or a narrow manifestation (like living at home). It's essential not to overlook the dependent adult who is living away from home or whose parents have no chemical addiction. And there are millions of such adult adolescents.

The case studies discussed in this book represent actual cases Dr. Stockman has seen in his twenty-seven years as a counselor. At times, we have taken some liberties with dialogue or details of the story to make the situation clearer for the reader. In some cases, the genders are reversed or ages altered slightly to guarantee anonymity. In all cases, the names and identifying details were changed to protect the clients. Many of the cases are composites of two or more similar cases. However, nothing has been changed that would detract from the central issue . . . the problem of adult adolescents.

Also, we have made two simplifications for ease of reading. The first is in regard to the problem of gender. The English language limits us to a choice of a masculine or a feminine pronoun (he/she, him/her). Since to say, "he or she," repeatedly would be cumbersome, we have elected to use the masculine most of the time, but to occasionally insert *she* or *her* to remind you that by the masculine we also mean the feminine.

Second, in these days of blended families, natural or adoptive parents are frequently not the only kind involved in a relationship with an adult adolescent. The term *parent* is used generically and includes stepparents unless otherwise noted. We will occasionally remind you that we are including both by saying, "parent or stepparent." We appreciate your patience with these limitations of the language.

Finally, any book, by limitation of its topic, cannot address all the types of dysfunctions that can occur in families—nor all the solutions to these problems. We have provided a bibliography, which lists books we have found particularly helpful in cases of codependency. Also, an appendix lists agencies and organizations that may be helpful. In any situation of family dysfunction, you should examine the options available for help (books, support groups, government agencies, charitable or religious organizations, and mental health professionals) and determine which one or several is best for the particular situation. (Chapter 11 gives advice on selecting a good mental health professional.)

If you have an adult adolescent or know someone who does, this book will be an important first step in understanding and addressing that situation.

# ADULT CHILDREN WHO WON'T GROW UP

# 1

# A Parent's Rights

There is no more amazing moment in a parent's life than the first seconds of holding a newborn son or daughter still damp at his birth. You wonder how such a miracle could occur and envision all the fun times, and all the things you will teach your child. Unfortunately, parenting has another side as well—the times when you can't sleep and you ask yourself questions like, "Where did I go wrong?" as though you and you alone were responsible for all your child's successes and failures.

If you are the parent or stepparent of a child eighteen or older who is capable of being independent but for some reason "can't seem to grow up," then this book can help. We call these offspring "adult adolescents" because they are old enough to be adults—but still retain some or many of the dependencies typical of adolescence.

The situation may be as simple as the son who brings his laundry home for Mom to wash or the daughter who asks you to balance her checkbook. Or it may be far more serious—like the son who pawns his mother's jewelry whenever he wants money to impress a girlfriend on a date, or a daughter who attacks her mother with a frying pan for not giving her what she asked for. Any number of adult parenting issues can cause concern. You may recognize your child in a few of the examples of common adult adolescent problems that follow.

## ADULT ADOLESCENTS
## WHO WON'T LEAVE HOME

Anne Marie was in her early fifties and had four children. The oldest was a daughter, Stephanie, who graduated from college, got a job, and got married. Stephanie and her husband owned their home and seemed to be doing well. The same could not be said for her other three children, all sons. All in their twenties, they were still at home and seemingly at a loss for any direction or purpose in their lives.

Anne Marie and her husband, John, both had good jobs with a large company. They had a nice home and had provided well for their children from a material standpoint. After years of tension, however, relations among the family members were poor. The boys were belligerent, and John would lose his temper with everyone in the family at the slightest provocation. He and the three sons fought constantly. Anne Marie, who was also coping with the terminal illness of her mother, had withdrawn into a shell of quiet, hopeless misery.

Raised in a strictly disciplined environment, she didn't know how to cope with sons who talked back and always seemed to be getting into some sort of trouble, or with a husband who lashed out at her with verbal abuse. In the office her life was orderly and controlled—she was self-confident, almost cocky. But at home she felt out of control. She was everyone's emotional punching bag.

Anne Marie first came to see Dr. Stockman in 1987. Long the stoic, she showed her tension only through her clenched jaw and nervous laughter. She had buried tears a long time ago.

"I can't stand it any longer," she said in desperation after she explained her story. "Tell me what to do to fix it. Tell me how I can make John less mean. Tell me how I can make my sons less insecure. How can I help them get a start on their lives? You know, Rose Kennedy said, 'Raise the first one right, and the rest will follow.' She was wrong. Stephanie turned out fine, but these boys . . ."

"Do you think you're a bad mother?" Dr. Stockman asked.

After a lengthy pause, she replied in a whisper, "Yes, I guess so."

## ADULT KIDS WHO "CAN'T DECIDE"

There are adult adolescents who, while they may appear competent to the rest of the world, cannot make the simplest decisions without help. Amy was such a case. In high school, she had expected her parents to choose her courses, her clothes, and her extracurricular activities. When she was invited to a dance, Mom would have to choose a dress for her. When it came time to choose a college, her parents had to do that as well.

Amy didn't do well at college and eventually dropped out and came home. She finally got a job in another town (not too far away) and moved into her own apartment. She was so insecure about the move that her parents helped her choose the apartment and the furnishings. From that day on, Amy was on the telephone to home.

When she was invited to a party, she would call home and beg her mother to come visit to go to the beauty salon and select her new hairstyle. When her car needed to be replaced, she called her father and asked for help. Amy believed herself *incapable* of making a decision. Both parents were convinced that, for whatever reason, Amy was right. So Mom would help her pick a hairstyle, and Dad went out and selected a good used car for her to buy. At the age of thirty, she was wearing on their nerves.

The problem was more serious than just asking for *advice*. Amy was asking other people, primarily her parents, to take responsibility for decisions affecting her life.

For most of us, it's tiring enough making all the decisions that affect our own lives. Having the additional burden of making them for someone else is wearisome. Amy's parents came to see Dr. Stockman out of exhaustion as well as concern for Amy.

"I don't know why she can't grow up," her father said. "We've tried to be good examples for her. Her mother and I are competent people. What's wrong with Amy?"

"I can hardly sleep for worrying about her," Amy's mother added. "She's thirty years old and has no romantic prospects at all. Every time a fellow gets interested in her, Amy somehow manages to mess things up. I think she does it because she's scared, although I can't understand why. Then she figures it's all her fault and asks me what she should do to get Joe, or Tom, or whomever back again. I feel like I'm living in a badly written soap opera. I know Amy's not happy. And I'm exhausted."

"Yeah," the father agreed, "and this whole business is not good for our marriage. We never have time for each other. We're always talking about Amy. I love my daughter, but I'm damned tired of this."

## THE ADULT ADOLESCENT WHO FEELS "ENTITLED"

Derek was thirty-two years old and unemployed again. He had attended college briefly many years ago, leaving to enlist in the Army. When his tour of duty ended, he drifted from one job to another. He was always fired or "forced to quit" by circumstances that were "not his fault." Frequently he came home for months at a time to enjoy a rent-free existence until he left again. Each time he was home, he was a financial drain. But, more importantly, he emotionally exhausted his parents.

Feeling free to ignore their wants and needs, Derek abused every privilege. He lied habitually. In addition, he verbally harassed his parents whenever they tried to stand up to him. The last time he showed up, they allowed him to spend one night but then told him he was on his own.

Derek's response was to wait until his parents left the house. He then took his parents' shotgun and shot up the interior of the house. After that he took off for a few hours. When his parents returned, they bolted the front door. Derek was livid to find himself locked out.

Shouting obscenities and still carrying the shotgun, Derek broke in the front door while his parents escaped out the back door. Derek screamed after them, "You can't lock me out! This is as much my house as it is yours!"

At thirty-two years of age, Derek believed that he had a

divine right to everything his parents owned. By virtue of being their offspring, he thought he was *entitled* to take, use, and abuse their property (and even them) as he saw fit. He was a sixth-grade bully in a grown-up body.

The parents phoned Dr. Stockman, terrified to return to their own home. Eventually the police had to be involved and the son given a restraining order. Such an order stated that if he ever trespassed on their property again he would be arrested.

## THE SAD CHILD

Dana's parents felt so guilty. Their daughter was thirty-seven years old and miserable. Not in the hand-wringing, tearful way—at least not all the time. Mostly it was just a quiet, sad way that she had, as if there were no hope of ever being happy. As if the best she could hope for was to go to her job each day, bring home a steady paycheck, and pay all her bills.

On the surface it was hard to see what the problem was. She was slim, attractive, and well dressed. She worked out regularly and took care to fix her hair and makeup nicely. All the men she worked with said she was good-looking. But Dana didn't perceive herself as attractive. In fact, she couldn't imagine why anyone would want to date her. As a result, she remained aloof, withdrawn, seemingly unapproachable. For her part, Dana would never *dream* of approaching a man she found interesting and asking him out.

So she went on with her life. Her coworkers had no idea that she was unhappy. She occasionally shared her sadness with her parents—her desire to be married, to have children, and to "just have a little fun." But since she saw how worried they got about her and how earnestly they tried to help, she usually figured it was best just not to bother them. So she would clam up.

But her silence was just as bad for her parents. They could still see her unhappiness. They wanted to see her happy, but they had no idea where to start.

Dana didn't believe herself to be lovable. She did not know how to give love freely, nor to receive it joyfully. She could stay in this depressed pattern for the rest of her life. Or, perhaps with her parents' help, she could begin to change.

## THE CRISIS CREATOR

Ted was twenty-eight. Ted's parents, while only in their late fifties, felt as if they were much older than that. They had never thought parenting could go on and on for so long, or that it could be so exhausting. Sometimes they wished that God would intervene and "just straighten him out."

After five years at college, Ted had accumulated only enough credit hours to be considered a sophomore. He had failed courses, dropped out of courses, and otherwise just been unable to succeed. This was in spite of nearly a straight-A record in high school.

Every semester of college was a battle. Ted was involved in one crisis situation after another. He was in trouble with the dormitory adviser, or a teacher, or the administration, or even the police. He got in fights, got traffic tickets, and bounced checks. He went away for spring break with some friends and gambled away the money for his hotel bill. There seemed to be no end to the "emergencies" that came up.

Each emergency wore his parents down a little more. By the time they came to see Dr. Stockman, they were exhausted and blaming each other for the problems with Ted.

"I don't know what else to do," his mother moaned. "We've given him everything. We've always tried to be there for him. But no matter what we do, Ted is always in trouble."

Finally, after seven years, Ted dropped out of college and came home. He got a job and eventually moved out. He moved into a condominium that his parents helped him get by cosigning the mortgage. When Ted lost his job, the mortgage fell to his parents to pay. Due to a downturn in the economy, the parents' business was suffering, but they couldn't sell the condominium because of the poor market. They felt compelled to keep up the mortgage payments to protect their credit history, yet it required more belt-tightening than they'd had to suffer anytime since their early years of marriage.

Since they were nearing retirement, they were angry and resentful at the financial insecurity their son was causing them. What was the next crisis going to be? When would the parenting end? Or would it ever?

## DO YOU HAVE UNREASONABLE EXPECTATIONS?

Whatever the degree of the problem, you as the parent are probably concerned. "When is Johnny going to learn how to run his life?" "When is Mary going to stand on her own two feet?" "Why does Tom keep getting into trouble?" Your worry may be mild, or it may be desperate.

You may also be concerned about yourself. You may feel trapped in a role you no longer wish to play. You may be tired of being the laundromat, accounting service, or bail bond company. You may feel that your son only comes to visit when he's in trouble or that your daughter only calls when she wants something. The strain may be telling on your physical or mental health—or even on your marriage or your ability to do your job.

At what age do you have the right to expect your adult adolescent to get on with his life and let you live yours? When should he be financially independent? What can you do to help an adult adolescent who can't seem to make decisions? Or one who runs home every time life presents an obstacle? How do you wean an adult adolescent from the "mothering" he still clings to? How do you handle an adult adolescent who engages in "parent abuse" as Derek did?

How do you know when you've done enough? When is your obligation to "parent" over? When can you say, *"Stop!* I have rights, too"?

These are basic parenting questions. When your child was a toddler, you were happy to hold his hand. But at eighteen, or twenty-five, or thirty-eight years of age, your son or daughter needs to know how to walk on his own. That's the true joy of parenting . . . seeing your child mature into a self-sufficient, self-confident, responsible adult. But in large numbers, today's young adults are balking at making that final step. That balking may be as minor as wanting help with unexpected expenses or as serious as moving home every time a small obstacle appears.

You have a responsibility as a parent. But when does it end? How do you draw the line?

While no one can force another person to grow up, you can help your child by not always being the safe harbor. In the process, you will also be helping yourself. You will feel better about yourself as a parent—that you are doing the best thing for your adult adolescent. And you will feel better about yourself as a separate person, with rights of your own that are finally being respected.

## A PARENT'S FUNDAMENTAL RIGHTS

For many parents it's a radical concept to imagine that they have any rights in a parent/child relationship. Being a parent is a responsibility. It carries *obligations*. But we forget that we don't cease to be people when we become parents. And as people living in a democracy, we have certain rights that we call inalienable.

In addition to the inalienable rights, we have certain rights that can be summarized as the right to be healthy. While another person may want us to be unhealthy in our relationship with him, to further his own purpose, we have a right not to participate in his dysfunction. We can choose to be healthy, no matter how he chooses to relate to us.

These inalienable rights and the right to be healthy can be narrowed down to those that are crucial in a parent/young adult relationship. If you are to have a healthy adult/adult relationship with your adult sons and daughters, you should assert six fundamental rights:

1. The right to love your adult son or daughter
2. The right to "let go" of your adult offspring
3. The right not to feel unreasonable guilt about the past, and not be controlled by the guilt others would place on you in the present
4. The right to say no to requests
5. The right to be free of verbal abuse
6. The right to feel physically safe from harm by your adult offspring

Unless you are able to assert these rights with your adult adolescent, his extended dependency on you will probably continue. Such an extended dependency is not healthy for your adult adolescent or for you.

Let's examine these rights in more detail.

## The Right to Love Your Adult Adolescent

Some adult adolescents are difficult to love. In an effort to retain their relationship to you in a child/parent mode, they may constantly do things that require you to rescue them. They may do things that make you "discipline" them. Or they may be so determined to stay "on the payroll" that they verbally or physically abuse you.

They may seem to reject any love you give them that does not take the shape they want (money, discipline, and so on). Yet you want to love them in a healthier way. You want to hug your daughter and say, "I love you." You want to have heartfelt conversations over hot chocolate and popcorn. You want to tell your son so many things that are in your heart. And you want to hear what is in his. In the very best sense, you want to love your adult adolescent . . . even though he may sometimes make you furious.

But love is tricky. It scares us. We're all afraid that if we give it, it might be rejected. And that means rejecting "us." We fear that possible rejection more than anything else. It can cause our sense of self-worth to crumble.

So we wait for clues from the *other* person that indicate that he wants our love. All the while, we are also wanting love from the other person. But do we let the other person *know* that we want his love? Isn't he as scared as we are of rejection?

It's easy to see how a pattern of not expressing love develops. Everyone's too scared to say it first.

But what if you feel a lot of love for someone and you're in a situation—like with an adult adolescent—where you always seem to be at odds? How can you express your love? Should you bother trying?

Expressing your love is critically important for your own emotional health. Have you ever been to a funeral where the bereaved said, "I wish I'd told him how much I loved him"? Time is fleeting. If we don't express our love when we have a chance *today*, we may not have a chance tomorrow. And knowing we lost the opportunity will make our grief greater in the future.

But even more than the potential grief in the future is the pain in the present. What pain? Think of a beautiful clear-water spring that gurgles happily out of the ground. That's how most of us begin our lives. We give love freely. As soon as we feel it in our hearts, we express it . . . whether that's with a baby's smile and gurgle or a two-year-old's kiss on Daddy's cheek. Unfortunately, very early in life, we learn to control the spring. We dole out its waters carefully, lest we look foolish. We don't kiss Daddy in front of his boss. We don't hang on to Mother's neck when she wants to talk on the phone. And sometimes we seal off the spring altogether.

This is frequently what happens in a relationship with an adult adolescent. It gets harder and harder to say, "I love you," when the adult adolescent is seemingly always causing trouble. What happens to a well that's capped? The pressure builds up behind the lid. It causes us pain. But chances are good that the well's been capped for so long that we've accepted the pain as normal—as how we're "supposed" to feel. For each of us, our love is a pressure within that should be released for our own good health.

What happens when we overcome our fear of "not being loved back" and release our love toward others? First, we feel a tremendous sense of relief. The "headache" we have had for so long that we forgot how it felt not to have it is suddenly gone. We feel light-hearted and joyful. And the more we uncap the spring, the more love is available to express. We get emotionally more and more healthy.

Second, given some time, there is a great likelihood that our continual expression of love to the adult adolescent may uncap his own well. He may begin to say, "I love you, too." Thus, he too can feel the joy of relief.

As parents and adult adolescents begin to be comfortable expressing love for each other, parents no longer have to enforce the next five rights. They will seem natural. After all, can you abuse someone you love? Can you refuse to respect him? Can you burden him with guilt? Or refuse to "let go"?

Remember, giving love is your privilege. We cannot control anyone other than ourselves. We can't expect guarantees that we'll be loved back or that the other person will be glad that we love him. What we can expect, and demand, from ourselves is that we uncap our feelings. So what if he rejects our love? The joy (and the health) is in the giving.

## The Right to "Let Go" of Your Adult Adolescent

"Once a parent, always a parent." True or not? Biologically speaking, yes. As long as you are alive, you will have as part of your personal history the fact of parenthood. Does that mean that for as long as you both live, you have an obligation to "parent" your adult adolescent?

Do you have to be intimately involved in every single decision the adult adolescent makes (as in the case of Amy mentioned earlier)? Of course not. Are you obligated to keep the adult adolescent "on the payroll" for the rest of your life? Naturally not. Yet this is what some adult adolescents would have you believe. They use an incredible array of techniques, which we will discuss later, to manipulate you into playing parent to them. But you have the right to stop playing the game.

What does letting go mean? First, it means allowing your child to be an adult. Stop thinking of your adult adolescent in the familiar way, the way he wants you to. Stop thinking of him as your son or daughter that you have to "take care of." Think of him as a young adult who needs to make his own choices and live with the consequences. Think of yourself as a loving, older and wiser friend who can act as a teacher or mentor. The best teachers do not lecture or give "advice." They listen when their younger friends talk. They challenge their students with questions, getting them to think their own way through problems. They don't give answers. They help the students find their own.

So letting go begins with two things: letting go of your image of yourself as "the parent" and letting go of your image of your adult adolescent as a "child."

Letting go of the parent in ourselves is tough. When our child was three years old, we knew better than he did that stoves can burn, that cars can hit you, and that good food and vitamins are needed for healthy bodies. We felt comfortable making choices for him as he grew. ("Yes, you really do have to learn arithmetic.") But now he's an adult. Can we still know what's best all the time?

How many of us can say that we never made a bad choice? Probably none of us. Yet we learned from our mistakes. So will Johnny or Mary. Thus, letting go also means forgetting any notion that you know what is best for your son or daughter. He will have to answer that for himself. It's the only way he'll learn.

Letting go means letting your adult adolescent make mistakes and learn from them. It means releasing him, freeing him to live his own life. His life will not be your life. He lives in a different time. He is a different person. His choices may not be to your liking. But you will love him and listen to him whenever he wants to talk. You may ask him questions to make him think. But that is all.

*This doesn't mean that you don't care* or don't love your adult adolescents anymore. It means that you love them and care about them too much to enable their dependency. You will still be there to encourage their efforts to grow, to listen, to help out in a *true* emergency. But your communications and your support will be healthy and growth-producing, not growth-retarding.

What happens when you let go? You are telling your adult adolescent that you believe he has the ability to handle his own life. This is a great gift to him—your faith in him. But you are also giving yourself something. You are relieving yourself of an unhealthy burden—"playing parent"—and giving yourself a chance for a totally new relationship with your adult adolescent: that of an adult to an adult. Such a relationship can contain a great depth of love and affection. It can also contain something very important: respect for each other as competent people.

Your adult adolescent may not want you to let go of him. He may fight the change in your relationship. He has spent all his life relating to you in a child/parent mode. But remember, you can both be happier in the long run if you, as the parent, exercise your right to let go of your adult adolescent.

## The Right Not to Feel Guilty

Guilt is a powerful weapon. We use it against ourselves constantly. We say things like, "If I'd spent more time with Tommy . . . ," or, "If we hadn't made Mary move during high

school . . . ," or, "If I hadn't been so sick when she was little . . . ,"
and then go on to excuse all sorts of irresponsible behavior. The
logic is that somehow we are to blame, not the adult adolescent.

The problem lies in determining what is reasonable. There is
no doubt that most of us did things as parents to contribute to
our adult adolescent's extended dependency. Some of us may
have made serious mistakes that were partially or largely responsible for our child's dysfunction. But what is past is past. It
cannot be changed. Dwelling on guilt, however real the mistakes, is unhealthy. When we carry the past as a burden, or
when we blame ourselves for things that are not our fault, we are
contributing to the problem of extended dependency.

What happens in our relationship with our adult adolescent
when we feel this unhealthy degree of guilt? We are taking
responsibility for what our child does. That means that Johnny
or Mary is *not* responsible for his or her actions, whether that
means getting a good job or stealing a car. Does this make good
sense? Of course not. And it's unhealthy.

If we accept responsibility for our adult adolescent's misbehavior, then he doesn't have to change. After all, it's our fault,
not his! We're saying that he's powerless to control himself. He's
the product of his upbringing—of his past—with no option for
the future. We, as his parents, become a convenient excuse. And
he will probably encourage us to continue in our beliefs, since it
takes the pressure off of him to grow up.

As parents we must remember that the past is *not* the future.
If Johnny had a tough few years while you moved him around,
that is a shame. But that doesn't predestine him to remain
trapped in adolescent misery forever. He can choose to overcome.

We must shed the unreasonable burden of guilt we would
place on ourselves. We can acknowledge our mistakes, make up
for them in a healthy way, and let them go. We must refuse to
allow the adult adolescent to make us carry the past as his
excuse for the present. And we must stand up to friends or
relatives who try to make us feel unreasonable degrees of
responsibility for our adult adolescent.

Learning to do this is difficult. It actually takes a good deal of "unlearning." Chapter 4 will discuss how to deal with the guilt you place on yourself. Chapter 12 will address coping with the guilt others try to make you carry.

## The Right to Say No to Requests

Stemming from their feelings of guilt, many parents feel trapped into saying yes to all their child's requests. Here's a possible conversation between this type of parent and Dr. Stockman:

> PARENT:    Poor Mary had such a difficult time. She had a speech impediment when she was young. All the kids teased her about it terribly. She never got over it. I have tried to make it up to her by giving her as much attention as possible, but nothing seems to work. She's twenty-four now and positively horrible to me. She ignores my birthday. She "forgets" to give me a Christmas present. But she never forgets me when she needs something.
>
> DR. STOCKMAN:    And what do you do when she needs something?
>
> PARENT:    Well, I tell her that I wish she'd call me once in a while just to talk to me, and that I think she's not being very responsible.
>
> DR. STOCKMAN:    And then you give her what she asked for?
>
> PARENT:    Uh . . . well, yes.
>
> DR. STOCKMAN:    And why do you do that?
>
> PARENT:    Because she needs my help.

The parent is giving in, not because it's *really* best for Mary, but because Mary had such a tough childhood. The parent feels responsible and is trying to make it up to Mary by continuing the parenting role beyond where it is healthy. But giving money or bailing Mary out of trouble will not change the past. And it will never really satisfy the parent or the adult adolescent. The making it up goes on and on. Mary is in an ideal situation here. She can now manipulate the parent to get whatever she wants.

This parent has also convinced himself that he's doing these things because "Mary needs my help." The implication is that Mary, because of her speech impediment in early childhood, is permanently and irreparably impaired. She *cannot* function as an adult. "Daddy" or "Mommy" has to rescue her all the time. The parent is in a trap that will be very hard to get out of. As soon as he tries, Mary will say something to bring up the guilt: "But, Daddy, you *know* how hard it is for me. . . ."

There may be other reasons, besides guilt, that make it difficult for a parent to say no. We may also become convinced, in our own minds, that Johnny or Mary *cannot* make it without us, that our participation in their lives is essential. In addition, most of us enjoyed parenting to some degree. We liked being needed, being depended upon. Saying yes allows that dependency to continue.

In the example, Mary's father clearly feels all three motives: he feels guilt, he believes she cannot get through life without his help, and he likes protecting Mary. Together, these motives make it tough for him to say no.

Later we will deal with our subconscious needs that encourage us to parent when we shouldn't. Those needs are challenges for us to overcome. But they are not rights for us to enforce with our adult adolescents. What we do have the right to is freedom from manipulation by guilt. And we have the right to say no. "Yes" is not the morally required answer to every demand— although some adult adolescents may believe otherwise.

Adult adolescents are not used to hearing no. They will rebel when they hear it. The second half of this book will show you how to say no and deal with the aftermath. At this point, however, it's important that you understand that you are not *obligated* to give your adult adolescent everything he asks you for. Even if his childhood was exceptionally difficult, hardships are part of life, and the past is the past. Dealing with today is the challenge. By saying no to your adult adolescent, you can help him face that challenge.

## The Right Not to Be Verbally Abused

More common than physical abuse is verbal abuse. The most obvious form of this transgression is angry, hurtful, frequently obscene statements. These can sound like:

- "I hate you."
- "You're the worst excuse for a father I've ever seen."
- "You f———g asshole . . . you give me that money right now!"
- "You're nothing but a whore. You'll sleep with anyone. You don't have the right to call yourself my mother."
- "You're nothing but a damn loser. Everybody talks about you. I'm embarrassed to be your kid."

The primary characteristics of verbal abuse are that it's deliberately hurtful; it occurs repeatedly (not just once during a heated disagreement, but anytime there's a slight provocation); the statements are disrespectful and frequently (but not always) contain foul or obscene language; and it is designed to "keep you in your place"—submissive to the will of your adult adolescent.

Verbal abuse can also occur more via the tone of voice than in the words themselves: "I'm sure this is the *best* you could do," or, "I *suppose* this will *have* to do," said disparagingly and accompanied by rolled eyes or a disgusted sigh is also disrespectful and hurtful. Such a put-down places the parent on the defensive (the adult adolescent's intent) so that the parent will "try to do better" at meeting the adult adolescent's demands.

What is the result of a relationship where the adult adolescent continually harasses his parent in this way? Is any love present? Is anyone happy? The adult adolescent may be getting his way by browbeating you, but is what he asks for what he really *needs*?

While the bullying adult adolescent may seem to get what he wants, he's not opening himself to receive your love. (Bullies generally don't think anyone really loves them.) He's also not growing into a self-confident, considerate adult. So the harassment hurts him as well as you.

The second half of this book will show you how to cope with the fears the adult adolescent uses to make you feel helpless—as though you have no choice but to accept the abuse. You do *not* have to take the abuse. You have the right to stop it!

## The Right to Feel Physically Safe

It goes without saying that we should all have the right not to constantly be in fear of physical abuse from another person. But what do you do when you fear your own child?

There are two important places to turn. First to friends, and second to the police or social service agencies. Chapter 11 will discuss how to establish a support network. Such a group of friends (and this may include relatives) can be invaluable. They can help you expand your options and think through the advantages and disadvantages of each one. And a support network can help you in whatever choice you make about handling this physical abuse.

There are many ways to handle situations of physical abuse. What's important is to realize you are *not* obligated to put up with physical abuse. You have the right to physical safety. You do *not* have to tolerate it. *You have a choice!*

## THE RIGHTS OF THE YOUNG ADULT

Parents sometimes expect certain things from their children to which they are, in fact, not entitled. It is important for a healthy relationship that we, as parents, not only demand our rights but acknowledge the rights of our offspring. These include:

1.  The right to love us
2.  The right to let go of us as parents
3.  The right not to feel unreasonable guilt about the past and not to be controlled by the guilt we or others would place on him in the present
4.  The right not to live up to our expectations
5.  The right to disagree with our choices in life
6.  The right to be free of verbal or physical abuse

Let's look at each of these rights briefly.

## The Right to Love Us

If a parent is dysfunctional, choosing to encourage dependency (or otherwise demonstrating unhealthy forms of "love"), the young adult may still choose to be healthy. He may choose to give healthy love to the parent, adult to adult. If we are clinging to him, he has the right to love us without allowing us to hold onto him like a dependent vine.

Conversely, we can all choose *not* to exercise our right to love. Although we need to love others in a healthy manner in order to be emotionally healthy, we can choose to be unhealthy. Thus, if our adult adolescent chooses *not* to give healthy love, we cannot force him to be healthy. Nor can we "earn" his love.

Some parents get caught up in believing (through their feelings of guilt or inadequacy) that if they just do "a little more" for Johnny, maybe he'll love them back. But is it love if it's bought this way? Isn't real love something another person gives to you just because you are there and he is choosing to love you? Don't let yourself feel unlovable if your adult adolescent chooses not to love you. That is his choice. It is based on something within him. It is not proof that you haven't "done" enough, or that you're not lovable.

### The Right to Let Go of His Parents
Just as we have the right to let go of our role as a parent, the young adult has the right not to "play child" anymore. Sometimes, without even realizing it, we parents project the role of a child onto our adult offspring. We encourage them to act "cutesy" or to "come to Mamma/Papa." Old behavior patterns are hard to break. But our young adults have the right not to fit the mold we might want them to fit.

They don't *have* to keep coming home for every Thanksgiving or Christmas. They don't *have* to let us buy their clothes, or cook their meals, or tell them what medicine to take or whom to date. They have the right to exclude us from their decision making, to keep certain things in their lives private. Even if we don't want to let go of the role of parent, they have the right to let go of the role of child.

### The Right Not to Feel Guilty
Lots of comedians have made fun of how guilty their parents make them feel. "Mrs. So-and-so's son does this for his mother," and so on. The cartoon strip *Momma* derives most of its humor

from a mother who brilliantly uses guilt—and adult offspring
who demonstrate extended dependency. We laugh because it's
so familiar. There's a grain of guilt in the relationship we all had
with our parents.

And there's also at least a grain of guilt in our own parenting.
Have you ever heard yourself saying or thinking, "That ungrateful kid! After all I've done for him . . ."? There are plenty of guilts
we foster in our children.

Some of these guilts are reasonable. Just as our culture expects
parents to feed, clothe, shelter, educate, and nurture their
children, children are expected to meet certain minimal standards of behavior. These would include respecting the privacy,
property, and physical safety of the parents. Social norms also
include a belief that adult offspring should help their parents
when they are sick, elderly, or otherwise in need. These kinds of
social responsibilities enable us to live together fairly harmon-
iously. They also foster the continuation of and, one would hope,
the social evolution of the human race.

But our adult sons and daughters have a right to be free of
unreasonable guilt, just as we do. When guilt becomes irrational
and an adult adolescent's life is spent trying to meet an unreasonable model of a "good child," then he's making his choices
based on the unhealthy reasons. He has taken his parents' words
("After all I've done for you . . .") as an obligation that can *never*
be satisfied. He is trying to be "a good boy" as defined by his
parents. He is not growing as a unique and healthy individual.

When we believe that our children owe us endless gratitude
for the sacrifices we made on their behalf, we are fostering
unreasonable guilt. When we say things like, "I'd never have
stayed married to your father if it weren't for you kids," or,
"Putting you through college cost us most of our retirement
savings," we are out of line. Such statements become heavy
harnesses for children—requiring them to forever "make it up"
to Mom and Dad. Whatever we want, they "owe us."

This is just as unhealthy as a parent who is always trying to
make up for exaggerated guilt. As parents, we must beware of the
inappropriate or unreasonable guilt we may try to foster in our
children.

## The Right Not to Live Up to Our Expectations

In thousands of ways, we give our children messages as they grow up about what we expect of them. When they are young, we teach them to say thank you when they receive a present. We expect them to brush their teeth. We try to instill in them the social and personal sense of responsibility that makes it easier to get along in the world.

We also usually expect a lot of other things. We may expect our young adult to go to college, marry "a nice girl/boy" (as we define nice), or lead a particular type of lifestyle. We may have a road map of his life laid out and expect him to follow it. We may believe it is appropriate for him to do certain things to prove his respect or love for us. The list can be endless.

But such excessive expectations are unhealthy. We are making rules about another person's life choices. We do not have that right. We may say to an adult son, "Johnny, I'm sad that you and Mary are divorcing. I like her, and it may make it harder for me to see the grandchildren." This is a statement of feeling. But when we say, "Johnny, you should reconcile with Mary. She's a good wife for you. And I want to be sure I can spend lots of time with my grandkids," we are making a statement of expectation. This is close to giving orders: "Do this if you want to be my good little boy/girl."

Other unreasonable expectations could include: "You should go to church on Sunday"; "You should vote for so-and-so"; or "You need to find a job with a bigger company." (Notice that all these statements begin with the word *you*—especially using the phrases *you should* and *you need to*.) Such expectations are not necessary for societal peace. They do not foster the evolution of the human race or the personal growth of the young adult. In fact, they inhibit individual growth.

As parents, we need to be very careful about the expectations we communicate. If we are unreasonable, we will not be able to have a healthy adult/adult relationship. We will be carrying the parent role beyond its healthy limits and attempting to constrain the independence of our adult sons and daughters.

## The Right to Disagree with Us

The right to disagree goes beyond not meeting our expectations.

It can be a disagreement with our personal belief system. It may mean that our adult son or daughter finds our chosen lifestyle or religion or politics distasteful or shallow. Or that, for whatever reason, he chooses to lead his life in a way that is quite different from ours.

For many parents, disagreement is synonymous with disrespect. If we're Protestant and our child becomes Catholic or Jewish, that's disrespect. If we're Democrats and our child becomes a Republican, that's an affront. When our children choose to follow a different course than our own, we sometimes view that as a rejection of our chosen lifestyle. And such a rejection must mean our way is "not good enough." This can be seen as an insult.

While it's a perfectly *human* reaction to take offense when someone disagrees with us or rejects our choices, it's not a *healthy* response. Our children are unique individuals. If we bear children so that we might make clones of ourselves, we are guaranteed to fail, for each of us is unique. Our children see things differently. They have different goals. Just as we are not clones of our parents, our children are not clones of us. They have the right to make choices that are very different from ours. The choices may be well thought out or impulsive. But the choices themselves are not disrespectful.

What can be disrespectful is how they handle or communicate their disagreement with our chosen values. For example, it is disrespectful to say, "Mom, I can't believe you're *stupid* enough to believe that!" But disagreement itself is a healthy and important part of being an individual. It's a right we must strive to allow our adult adolescents.

### The Right to Be Free of Verbal or Physical Abuse

As with the parents' rights, young adults have the right to be free of abuse by their family. This is a right they should enforce in their relationship with you, just as you should enforce it with them. Since this is a fairly obvious right, we will not dwell on it here.

## THE RIGHTS OF ALL ADULTS

You may have recognized the large amount of overlap between

the fundamental rights of parents and the rights of the young adult. You may have also noticed yourself identifying with the rights of young adults as they apply to your relationship with your parents. ("Yeah, my dad never forgave me for not joining his firm"; "Mom still makes me feel guilty about marrying Harry.") This is because, although we are parents, we are also somebody's child. If we remember that, and remember the difficulties we had separating ourselves from our own parents— establishing our own identities—it can help us in our dealings with our adult adolescents.

While we need to remember our rights as parents and insist that they be respected, we also need to release our adult adolescents. We need to give them their freedom, their rights, and all the responsibilities that go with them.

We might do everything we possibly can to establish a healthy relationship with our adult adolescent, and he may choose not to reciprocate. We must say, "That's OK . . . that's her decision." We have control over no one but ourselves. And we can go on being egalitarian, parenting and giving healthy love. Because *giving* healthy love is our right. Demanding it in return is not.

# 2

# What's Going On?

The burgeoning awareness of the problem of extended dependency in young adults is creating the same kind of confusion among parents that Woodstock and the hippie movement did in the late sixties. We were all going happily along, "parenting" as best we knew how . . . and suddenly things started going askew.

The "formula" we believed in isn't working. Our kids aren't growing up. Why is this happening? Is our child unique? How big is the problem?

## HOW BIG IS THE PROBLEM?
Your child is definitely not unique in this regard. The U.S. Census Bureau estimated that 52.6 percent of young adults ages eighteen to twenty-four were living at home in 1986. This was up from 48.4 percent in 1980. Young adults ages twenty-five and up are also still living at home in increasing numbers, although these are more difficult to quantify. The majority of these young adults are physically and mentally capable of self-support. But they are choosing, for whatever reason, to remain at (or return to) home.

But living at home is only one way to remain dependent. Young adults are living in apartments, condominiums, and single-family dwellings and still being subsidized by their parents to "make ends meet." Others may be financially independent but emotionally dependent. This problem may demonstrate itself, as in the case of Amy, in an inability to make simple decisions without the parents. Or it may show itself through crisis creation (as with Ted), through prolonged or recurrent physical ailments (always having a cold or the flu), or in various other methods that cause the parent to continue parenting.

Based on Dr. Stockman's clinical experience, it would not be unreasonable to estimate that at least 40 percent of the current group of young adults (eighteen to forty years of age) are excessively dependent. This would mean that approximately 36 *million* young adults are taking an unhealthy length of time to sever the ties of adolescence. If there are two parents or stepparents for every case of extended dependency, approximately 78 *million* parents are faced with this issue.

The total potential impact, 114 million affected individuals, is about half of the total population of the United States. This is without even considering the effect on healthy sisters and brothers, employers, or the spouses and children of the dependent young adults. The scope of the problem is enormous, and the need to cope with it is urgent. For if we have a generation of unhealthy and overly dependent young adults beginning to raise their own children, they are unlikely to be able to teach their children how to be independent. And the problem will snowball.

## HOW DID THIS HAPPEN?

Some causes of the sudden increase in the extended dependency of young adults have nothing to do with the specific family relationships. These are sociological pressures that increase the likelihood that children will respond to their family structure with adult adolescent behavior patterns. While it is difficult to alter such broad influences, it's helpful to understand them. As a parent, you can learn what you're up against. Understanding these influences is not enough, of course. If there is to be a change in our relationships with the adult adolescents in our lives, we will have to change how we relate to them one on one.

The rest of this chapter will outline ten of these sociological pressures. Later chapters will address the family dynamics that also contribute to the problem (what we call the three behavior traps) and how to correct them.

## Postwar Prosperity

What parent doesn't want "the best" for his child? How often have you heard a parent say, "I want my son to have it easier than I did?" Such statements are usually followed by stories about how tough that parent had it when he grew up.

Most of us, as parents of adult adolescents, were raised either during the Great Depression or World War II, or close in their shadow. Times were tough, and hardships were an expected part of life. Many of us gave up childhood toys early for paper routes or other jobs to help the family make ends meet. We stepped out of high school (or college, if we were lucky) expecting to have to support ourselves. There was no chance of asking Mom or Dad for a new car—they probably only owned one old clunker themselves.

Most of us really struggled to build up our financial resources. With our spouse, we may have started out renting a tiny apartment and limiting our social life to walks in the park and an occasional pizza. With hard work and a lot of budgeting, we bought our first car, bought a house with a thirty-year mortgage, and slowly filled it with furniture.

The memories of the Depression and the rationing of World War II were close enough to affect us. We knew how easily "the good life" could disappear.

So we decided that things would be "better" for our children. And economic prosperity and the lack of another world war helped us make things better. We saved and gave our children the best education we could afford and all the material things we felt they needed. But was all that really "better" for Johnny or Mary? Probably not.

The problem is not that more education isn't good for them, or that material things are necessarily bad. The problem is that Johnny or Mary got these things just because they were living and breathing. There were no demands on them. Maybe a few chores had to be done . . . but our children were insulated from the sacrifices being made (giving up a vacation, not buying a new car, taking money out of the retirement fund) to provide these things. Out of desire to protect them and keep them from feeling guilty about the sacrifices we made, we in fact created the illusion that there were no sacrifices—that life is supposed to be easy.

We sheltered our children from the fear as well—our fears about how easily things could all fall apart. With no real economic hardship besetting the country as a whole, a safe fantasy world became reality in the minds of a generation of children. Things would always be wonderful . . . it was their right as Americans.

The nature of this cultural delusion is more apparent if you compare our lifestyle in the United States to that of any Third World nation. A majority of the world's population considers hot and cold running water a luxury—and owning a television set an impossible fantasy! But here we take such things for granted. And the children of this postwar prosperity have come to *expect as their due* a lifestyle that their parents struggled to provide and that most of the world envies. This false expectation—that the easy life will be there for them without any exertion on their part—comes face to face with harsh reality when they leave home.

The result is shock and disbelief, even a feeling of betrayal. How could the world treat them so unfairly? So they go back to Mom or Dad and expect this gross injustice to be corrected. Mom and Dad either have to take the adult adolescent back into the home (where bills are paid and life is relatively worry-free), or they are expected to help pay the adult adolescent's expenses or make his decisions. And Mom and Dad, for the first time in middle-class history, can *afford* to do this.

This is not to say that every child born after 1945 is incapable of hard work, responsibility, and independence. What it does mean is that those born after 1945 were not forced, as previous middle-class Americans were, to fend for themselves. They had the *option* to let Mom and Dad deal with the world. And a large number of them are still taking that option.

## The Breakdown of the Extended and Nuclear Family

The extended family is the one that goes beyond Mom, Dad, and the kids. It includes grandparents, aunts and uncles, and cousins. When family mobility was limited, most children grew up in the same town all their lives, surrounded by relatives.

These extended families were a wonderful support system for parents struggling through the trials of their child's adolescence, and for the child trying to become an adult. When the parents became overwhelmed with guilt, a friendly aunt or loving grandparent might have stepped in to say, "You let that boy fend for himself. I never mollycoddled you." Without such a support network, parents are more vulnerable to a child's manipulations. They are more prone to feel guilty (especially if there's been a lot of moving around) and to let the growing child off the hook too easily. When the son or daughter becomes an adult adolescent, the pattern of not being held accountable frequently continues.

All of this is further complicated by the breakdown of the nuclear or "traditional" family (Mom and Dad raising their own children). With many young adults having lived through the divorce and remarriage of their parents, they have a handy guilt tool to use against their parents. They also have additional parents, where stepparents are involved, to manipulate. This makes playing one person against another a fairly easy game. Eventually, the adult adolescent can find at least one soft-touch parental figure to go to anytime he needs something.

## Pop Psychology

Popular (or "pop") psychology has played a role in the growing problem of extended dependency in young adults. During the sixties and seventies, many theories were propounded about the "correct" way to raise children. This created the first of two problems: the presumption that there was only one correct way to raise children, and that if parents didn't adopt the one correct way, then any maladjustment in the children was the parents' fault.

As parents heard more and more of how they were "supposed to" raise their children, they fell further and further into the trap of believing that everything their children did was their fault.

The danger in this is that it absolves the adult adolescent of any responsibility for his own decisions. If Johnny decides to steal $1,000, it's because Mom and Dad weren't perfect parents. If Mom and Dad believe this, then they accept the blame for the crime and will try to do everything in their power to be sure that Johnny suffers no consequences for his action. As we will discuss later, this is a very dangerous path to follow.

The second problem is the flip side of the coin. Kids learned quickly that if you told the school guidance counselor you had "problems at home," you could get out of all kinds of trouble. If your parents were having marital difficulties, you were expected to be traumatized, and it was OK if your grades fell. The pattern of excuse finding was being officially sanctioned. Not only did Mom and Dad believe that Johnny's misbehavior was their fault, so did the school and popular magazines. Johnny, being no dummy, soon figured out that the way he got what he wanted, or got out of trouble, was to blame it on his "tough childhood."

The problem for Johnny (or Mary) is that when he gets out of school and into the grown-up world, the mortgage company doesn't care that his parents got a divorce. His employer is unimpressed, when he misses yet another deadline, by his tales of woe. The old surefire method of getting what he wants isn't working out there. So he either returns home (where it does work), or he gets the money or emotional support he wants by exercising the childish routine he's comfortable with on Mom and Dad.

It's a pattern that's tough for all parties to break. But it can be done.

## "Spockian" Permissiveness

Dr. Benjamin Spock has been erroneously blamed for the permissive style of parenting and teaching that became popular in the sixties. In fact, his writings never promoted such a philosophy. Nonetheless, many of us think of that period as a time of lax parenting promoted by Dr. Spock.

As the students of the sixties rebelled against authoritarian structures, a new concept of child rearing became popular. The permissive parenting philosophy believed that a child should be allowed to set his own pace. Rigid educational or developmental structures should not be imposed on him. Telling him, "You have to finish your homework before you can watch TV," was not healthy. Such structuring, the belief went, squelched a child's natural desire to learn. It stifled his creativity and imagination. Such a child would not be able to reach his full potential. Instead, we were to give Mary enough time and latitude to choose for herself when the right time was to work on things. Eventually, her natural desire to learn and to achieve would motivate her to do her math homework.

This philosophy spilled over into the schools and colleges, where large numbers of elective courses became not only available but fashionable. The three Rs became less important as students were allowed to take fewer hours of these core courses and given the freedom to take "more interesting" electives.

While it is true that too rigid a family life or education can diminish creative expression and, in severe cases, result in neurotic children, too permissive an upbringing carries no less danger. Take the example of Tammy. Her mother read a lot of books and listened to speakers who told her to let her child make her own decisions about everything. Her father left the parenting up to Mom, so Tammy was raised by the book. Although it took a long time for Tammy to understand it, she now sees that she didn't respect her parents. They were "too soft." She used them for whatever she could. Her life after leaving home was one problem after another, none of them "her fault." She first met Dr. Stockman when she was in jail for possession of an illegal drug.

At that time, Tammy believed that society owed her everything. She felt she was being treated unjustly. Through therapy, Tammy came to accept more responsibility for her life. She learned that the real world is a place where you are held accountable for your actions. She later had children of her own and has been a good mother to them. But it was a hard road for her.

When we expect children to make good choices, we need to be sure they have the tools with which to choose. In the sixties and seventies, children like Tammy were allowed to make

choices without the necessary maturity to understand the consequences. Now, as adult adolescents, they may still be making
impulsive, poorly considered choices. But because they are
adults, the world is no longer listening to their excuses.

Unaccustomed to the structure of the working world and the
rigid rules about "paying your bills," such adult adolescents
usually continue to rebel. And their behavior may grow increasingly antisocial unless they manage to grow up.

## Love and Money

"If you love her," the advertiser says, "buy her diamonds."
What does such a statement do to the man reading it? It puts
him on the defensive. If he doesn't buy her diamonds, then he
must not love her.

While we cannot blame advertisers for our behavior (after all,
they tell us what we want to hear), such ads do reflect our values.
In the last two decades of prosperity, *things* have become evidence of love. Our children grew up in a world where it was
easier for a parent to give a child a bike than to take him fishing.
With two incomes, parents had more money than time, so giving
things was easier. It also seemed to be what the child wanted.

Johnny's friends didn't go fishing with their dads. Mary's
girlfriends didn't fingerpaint with Mom. What they did was get
together and play with their new toys. So, as parents, we tried to
love them and meet their needs at the same time. We saw their
need to go bike riding with friends and bought the bike. We saw
Mary's desire to play dolls with her friends (who all had the
latest Barbie doll), so we bought her the newest Barbie and the
clothes and accessories to go with it. The children seemed
happy. It all seemed to work.

But it was an insidious kind of addiction. The inexpensive toy
that makes the two-year-old happy becomes out of style. What
is needed is a more expensive toy, and then an even more costly
one, until it costs the parent more and more for the child's
addiction. No one is really satisfied, not the parent or the child,
because in our subconscious we know the truth: money and
things are not the same as love.

Jeremy is a case in point. His parents were loving but aloof.

They showed their love through things. Jeremy went with them on expensive vacations, got to go to exclusive summer camps, and got a car when he left for college. But these things were not what he needed . . . and he grew increasingly wilder with time. He drank more and more, and got into fights. He left college and moved back home. He abused his parents' property with the attitude "they can get another one." Although he had received everything materially he could want, he was rebellious and unhappy. And he was unwilling to grow up.

Not only wealthy parents have this problem—although it's most obvious when the child grows up in wealth. Frequently, divorced parents will play the "I can buy you more than your mommy/daddy" game to try to win a child's loyalty and love. And parents of almost any income bracket can substitute a toy for a kiss.

But if this has been the history, how can you put the adult adolescent through "withdrawal"? Won't he feel unloved?

For a while, he might. But in his heart he knows that money and love are not the same. That is why he needed more and more expensive "toys" to feel loved. The reward, the high, was a temporary delusion—a cheap substitute. The real high is love that feeds the soul—the kind of love that is expressed in words, in a look, and in a hug. It's the kind of love that respects another person as a whole and separate being, valuable in his own right. It's the kind of love that says, "I'm willing to share my hurts, my anger, and my joys with you. I hope you'll share yours with me."

How do you wean an adult adolescent from his unsatisfying need for things and teach him that you really love him from your heart? It's not easy. All change is tough; we have a natural urge to resist it. In addition, this kind of an addiction creates symptoms of withdrawal when the "drug" is withheld. Anger, hurt, and feelings of betrayal will probably surface quickly when the adult adolescent is denied a material request. But a little force-feeding of healthy love can diminish the unhealthy need.

That is why the right of a parent to love an adult adolescent is so important. If you give healthy love, then, no matter what words an adult adolescent returns to you (and they can seem hateful), the love gets through. If you keep giving it, eventually almost all adult adolescents will learn to receive it and enjoy it. And the false belief that a parent's love is shown in *things* will fade.

The important point to remember is that just because your adult adolescent may hold such a false belief right now, he is not predestined to hold that belief forever. And if you yourself held the belief that presents were the best way to show your love, you can grow past that. There is potential for change. And we'll show you how to help make it happen.

## Instant Gratification

"Why wait?" the television advertiser pleads, "easy credit terms available." That one sales pitch says a lot about the changes in American society. With consumer debt climbing ever higher, we've become a population accustomed to getting things when we want them. Like the two-year-old who stomps his foot and demands his ice cream *"now!"* we are losing the art of delaying gratification. The joy of saving up for something and paying for it in cash has become secondary to the fun of having it now.

Young adults are more vulnerable to this phenomenon than their parents, since the younger generation doesn't have a memory of how things "used to be." All their lives, today's young adults have lived in a world of "buy now, pay later." They have learned to "love" themselves in the same false manner they expect "love" from their parents . . . with things.

But there is a deeper and far more dangerous consequence of the desire for instant gratification. It is the inability to delay gratification.

Delaying gratification means delaying pleasure. It means postponing doing something you want to do (like buying a TV or going to the beach) to do something you'll enjoy less (like saving your money or mowing the lawn). It is one of the most important skills of adulthood. It is the foundation of responsible behavior.

If we cannot delay gratification, we cannot work through a problem and learn from it. If we have a fight with our spouse, the "instant gratification" is an instant fix . . . to make it all go away. We'll kiss and make up regardless of whether the problem is truly rectified, just to avoid the present discomfort of the estrangement. The healthy response would be to delay gratification (the making up) and spend time suffering through the problem, working it, struggling with it until it is truly resolved and we've grown past it. The long-term result of constant quick fixes is a marriage where no real communication takes place. And that's a recipe for misery.

This is true in any mature relationship between adults. Delaying gratification is essential for the long-term health of the relationship.

This brings us back to the beginning. An adult adolescent who is addicted to instant gratification is inherently unwilling to delay gratification. Without delaying gratification, he will choose not to accept the responsibility to work through a problem. It's too unpleasant. The more pleasant (i.e., gratifying) solutions to any problem are to blame it on someone or something else ("it's not my fault"), to decide it's incapable of solution (choosing helplessness), to deny that it exists (maybe it'll disappear on its own), or to get someone else to make it go away (asking someone to "play parent"). The adult adolescent wants the instant gratifications of adulthood—coming and going on his own schedule, spending his money as he chooses, enjoying sexual relations in the privacy of his own apartment—without the responsibilities, the pain, that go with it.

As a person being asked to play parent, you can control your reaction to the adult adolescent. You cannot force him to delay gratification. And you cannot eliminate the pressures in our society that encourage him to instantly gratify himself. But you can choose not to be an active participant in his "instant fix" lifestyle.*

## Economic Expectations

Along with postwar prosperity came a series of expectations. These include the previously mentioned expectation that, as Americans, our adult adolescents feel it is their right to expect

---

*For more information regarding the dangers of not delaying gratification, the authors highly recommend the first section of *The Road Less Traveled* by M. Scott Peck, M.D. (New York: Simon & Schuster, Inc., 1978).

peace and plenty as a society. On a personal level, the ease of their upbringing (from a material perspective) led them to expect new clothes and a nice home as the way it's supposed to be. Along with a refusal to delay gratification comes another manifestation: unwillingness to reduce their lifestyle.

You can see the problem. How many of us, the first year we were out on our own, were able to replicate the life we'd enjoyed at home? Very few, if any! And we didn't *expect* to replicate it. After all, our parents had worked many long, hard years to buy a home, furnish it, and provide the material comforts we'd enjoyed while we lived there. We, too, expected to suffer and work hard to accumulate those things.

Somehow that message got lost on a lot of young adults now in their twenties to forties. They move out, discover how much things really cost, and decide that "something has to be done" about their discomfort. Since they can't imagine delaying gratification, they find quick fixes. This could be a credit card (until they've reached the limit of their credit) or, better still, a "free" source of supply for their lifestyle.

If you believe love equals money, then the logical place to turn to support your lifestyle expectations is to your parents. Thus, the adult adolescent challenges his parents to "prove" their "love." And the parent, who wants the best for the adult adolescent, and "hates to see him struggle," gives the support. That may mean allowing an adult adolescent to move home and live rent-free, or it may mean subsidizing his lifestyle in other ways.

The problem lies in expectations. The adult adolescent expects to rapidly attain the standard of living he had at home. Where we might have worked many years to buy our first home, he expects to equal our lifestyle in just a few years. When that doesn't seem possible, he gets frustrated. He is not being instantly gratified. He feels cheated by forces beyond his control. It never occurs to him that his own expectations are out of line with reality, and that maybe *he* needs to change, not the rest of the world.

The problem is exacerbated by the popularization of the concept of the yuppie (young upwardly mobile professional).

Better educated than any previous generation, and with access to more white-collar jobs as the service sector of our economy grows, many of our adult adolescents have earned "professional" jobs. Their preoccupation with instant gratification and the easy availability of credit lead them to spend their money readily. Advertisers love them and have targeted them heavily. The high-consumption yuppie lifestyle, much written about in the popular press, fuels the belief among adult adolescents that this is normal, reasonable behavior.

In fact, it is not. What is reasonable is for a young adult to suffer a drop, frequently a severe drop, in economic status when he first moves out into the world on his own. This is not only normal, it's character-building. It's an opportunity for a young adult to prove he can make it on his own, that, like generations before him, he can scrape and save and (eventually) provide a secure living for himself and his mate and offspring. When deprived of the obstacle, he is deprived of the pride that comes from overcoming it. He is deprived of growing up.

As a culture, we need to learn to value difficulties, not to be outraged by them. For in order to walk tall, we all need to fall down a few times and learn how to pick ourselves up.

## Downward Mobility

A new catch phrase has recently become popular: *downward mobility*. It refers to a difference between the status of the current generation of young adults and that of their parents. Young adults, the logic goes, are faced with a terrible dilemma. Where their parents were able to buy bigger and nicer homes and have an easier lifestyle than their grandparents, young adults will be hard-pressed just to *equal* the lifestyle their parents enjoy.

The support for this logic is demographic and socioeconomic. The former argument is that there are so many baby-boom children in the same age group filling up the job market that there is less money for each to take home. The socioeconomic view is that the economy is not growing as fast as it did in the sixties, so the current work force cannot expect to see its net pay increase the way its parents' did.

The underlying presumption is that this is a shocking and painful realization—that somehow, as Americans, we had the right to expect that each generation would continue to exceed the material acquisitions of the preceding generation. This constant "bettering" was not only expected, but considered to be good.

Now this "American dream" is proving false. This appears to be an occasion for wringing of hands and railing against the unfairness of it all. One adult adolescent complained to Dr. Stockman that she had been born "at the wrong time," that she *couldn't* make it in the economy she had to deal with.

What does this sound like? It sounds like hopelessness. It sounds like an excuse. "I can't ever *hope* to achieve my parents' lifestyle through my own hard work, no matter what I do." When you put an "it's not my fault" concept like this together with an "I deserve to have the same lifestyle now as I did growing up" belief, what is the result? It is a group of young adults who believe that somebody (but not themselves) has to fix their discomfort by helping them to maintain their accustomed lifestyle. That somebody is a person willing to "play parent" to their "child" and take care of him.

Now, we do not contest that there *may* be validity to the downward-mobility theory. It may, in fact, be more difficult for the current generation of young adults to exceed the lifestyles of their parents. The future will tell. What we do disagree with is the hopeless feeling this seems to generate. Is it *impossible* to exceed our parents' accomplishments? Of course not. There are those who will exceed and those who will do worse in every generation—no matter what the socioeconomic environment.

But what if the theory is correct, and the current generation of young adults as a group does *not* exceed its parents' incomes? Is this terrible and unfair? We do not believe it is. It is a *difficulty* ... but that only means it's an opportunity to grow and learn. It need not be a disaster or even an embarrassment.

With the high level of material comfort enjoyed by most of the United States, it's no great tragedy to have to learn to survive with a little less. It is *not* a humiliation. Yet we act as if it is. If we could visit any location in the Third World, we'd see for ourselves just how rich we are. Maybe then we'd be embarrassed that we thought it such a great tragedy to do without a VCR, a second car, or a bigger house.

## Peer Pressures

None of us is immune to the expectations of our peers. When we were children, we were terrified to stand out. We knew what happened if we did. If we were the tallest, we got teased. If we were the fattest, we were taunted. If we were teacher's pet, we were hated. Being different is painful. So we tried not to be, even when being the same wasn't good for us. Being accepted by our peers was everything.

As adults we still care what our peers think and say about us. And so do our adult adolescents. Each generation has some characteristics that are its own. Each age group has expectations that are its own rules of normal behavior. What are the expectations of young adults today?

Much has been written about the materialism of the eighties. Young adults today do seem quite concerned about money and possessions. We make fun of materialism through characters like Alex Keaton on the television show "Family Ties." We glorify and despise it through characters like Gordon Gekko in the hit movie *Wall Street*. But laugh or cry about it, like it or hate it, as a nation we are more concerned with money (and the power and things it buys) than we have been in recent history.

Adult adolescents are not immune to this interest in money. In fact, some of them are significantly more interested than the bulk of the population. How to get it and how to spend it can become a preoccupation. One comedian joked that a yuppie sits on a plane reading the catalog (you know the one; it contains every conceivable electronic gadget and every possible "travel convenience") and tries to find something he *doesn't* already own.

The eighties have also brought with them a high level of consciousness of self. This is not the same as the self-awareness that is enlightenment . . . the kind of introspection that leads to wisdom. No, this is the reverse. It is an awareness of self in the selfish sense. "What do I want?" "What is good for *me*?" It demonstrates itself not only through greed (the desire for material comforts), but also through complacency. The problems of others (poverty, racism, violations of civil rights) are of concern only when they impinge on the self. In the sixties and early seventies many young adults were at least conscious of social issues. But by the eighties young adults had become preoccupied with issues of self.

The result is a generation of young adults who like comfort. They have been well taken care of materially and had opportunities for more education than any prior generation. They have not lived through a Great Depression or a World War, through slavery or the Holocaust. They see nothing wrong with "taking care of number one."

This is not to say that there are not plenty of hard-working, ambitious young adults out there. There are. And plenty of them are responsible, mature people who understand that sacrifices come before rewards—and that they should learn how to stand on their own two feet. But many of those hard workers are still adult adolescents. How can this be?

We, as parents, have learned that it takes more than just hard work to make a mature, responsible adult. Hard work may earn you a paycheck. But managing that paycheck to pay obligations first and to buy discretionary purchases second shows financial responsibility. Making decisions with forethought and accepting the consequences show emotional responsibility. Being willing to suffer the downs as well as the ups of interpersonal relationships shows maturity. In these areas, adult adolescents are weak, and so are the peers they select.

We seek out those most like us. An adult adolescent is likely to choose a peer group composed of young adults also suffering from extended dependency. What kind of pressure do your adult adolescent's peers place on him? Although generalities do not always apply to the individual, there are definite norms or beliefs among adult adolescents.

So what are the beliefs of the current generation of adult adolescents? It may be easier to say what they don't believe. They do not believe that it is wrong to have your parents subsidize your living arrangements. They do not believe it's a sign of personal weakness to live on credit and live "beyond your means" (it's a sign of how hard the times are). They do not believe that suffering and hardship are normal, healthy parts of life.

Those who are financially dependent do not value someone who chooses to work hard, live a Spartan lifestyle, and save carefully for unexpected expenses and future discretionary purchases. Such a person might be referred to as neurotic, a structure freak, dull, uptight, a grind, a nerd, or a geek. A person who knows how to delay gratification is certainly not their choice to "party with."

More important, the emotionally dependent do not find fault with excuse making. And adult adolescents are highly skilled excuse makers! Anything and everything can be someone else's fault. They are not really accountable for their decisions, because "that's what so-and-so told me to do," or "I had no other choice," or "so-and-so didn't understand (or do his part or whatever)."

These nonbeliefs can be summarized as *a belief in the value of extended dependency as a lifestyle.*

What's the impact of this kind of peer pressure on our adult adolescents? It means that it's tough for them to choose to be responsible, delay gratification, and generally be self-sufficient. Such behavior is not valued by their peer group and may even be looked at with dislike. It's easier not to be different. So, the adult adolescent has created a self-perpetuating situation. The adult adolescent *chooses* friends who reinforce the rightness of remaining dependent.

For an adult adolescent to break free of this peer pressure, he will have to believe that the rewards of adulthood exceed the rewards of being accepted by those peers or, at a minimum, that the method of dealing with life that he and his friends have believed in doesn't seem to be working. He will have to want to try a new approach. And he will need to find new friends who will not mock him for trying to control his own life—for trying to be responsible. Those people *are* out there, and they can be found.

## The Entitlement Syndrome

The final and perhaps most disturbing sociological pressure

contributing to the increase in young adult dependency is something we call "the entitlement syndrome." Some of it was evident in the other pressures discussed so far. Adult adolescents feel entitled to peace, prosperity, and a rapid equaling of their parents' lifestyle (or even a bettering of it). But the entitlement syndrome goes beyond this.

To explain, think of the world through the eyes of an eighteen-month-old sitting in his playpen. Assume he's an only child. All the toys in the playpen are his. He knows this. No one else attempts to claim them or play with them. They are his exclusive territory. Even at this age, he knows the word *mine*. All these toys are "mine" in the most exclusive sense.

Now imagine he stands up in the playpen and surveys the rest of the house. He knows that everything out there is used by other people . . . particularly his parents. But he also knows that he can play with those things as well. He can bang on pots and pans. He can climb on chairs. He may have to share, but in his understanding of the world, all those things are "mine" as well. He will cry and have a tantrum if someone wants to use the pot he's banging on, because at that moment the pot is exclusively his. Mom or Dad can use it when it's not "mine."

As the child grows, typically he comes to understand the property and privacy rights of others. He expects that no one will read his diary. She knows not to read other people's mail. He learns not to take Dad's fishing pole without his permission. She understands that Mom's clothes are not to be "borrowed" without asking first. This could be paraphrased to say that the child learns that "what's mine is mine, and what's yours is yours."

Adult adolescents suffering from the entitlement syndrome haven't really learned this. Their belief is more like the two-year-old's: "What's mine is mine, and what's yours is mine!" Heaven forbid that you should violate his privacy, take his belongings, or expect him to take care of you. Yet he feels free to violate your privacy, take or use your property without asking, and expect you to support him.

Take the example of a young woman we'll call Becky. She was twenty-six and lived in a town an hour away from her parents. One weekend Becky's parents decided to rearrange their house and use some furniture that was stored in the attic. They went into the attic only to discover a piece of furniture was missing, and they saw a lot of boxes up there they hadn't seen before. Upon opening the boxes, they found Becky's clothes, old tennis rackets, books, and other belongings. They called Becky immediately. Here's the conversation:

MOM: What are all these boxes doing in our attic? They seem to be yours.

BECKY: I needed someplace to store some stuff.

MOM: And you couldn't ask us first?

BECKY: You were out of town. I knew you wouldn't mind.

MOM: The last time we were out of town was three months ago. You should've waited till we got back. And why didn't you tell us what you'd done when we got back?

BECKY: I guess I forgot.

[*Mom pauses to collect her temper.*]

MOM: Did you take the old oak dresser?

BECKY: Yeah. It looks really great—I cleaned it up.

What happened here was that Becky violated her parents' privacy, used their attic for her storage without permission, took the oak dresser without asking, and then failed to tell them what she'd done when they returned. She just waited for them to find out on their own. When confronted with her actions, she made excuses: "You were out of town," "I knew you wouldn't mind," and, "I guess I forgot." She didn't apologize or feel any remorse. She even expected her parents to be happy that she "cleaned up" the old dresser.

Yet you can imagine what her response would be if her parents had entered her apartment when she was out of town, used it to entertain friends, and then taken home as a souvenir a piece of her furniture. She would have been livid!

When questioned about this type of behavior by Dr. Stockman, a young adult will answer with other excuses. These include: "They don't need it," "They can afford it," "They've got the space," "They owe it to me," and the one that reveals the most: "That's what parents are for."

Adult adolescents will twist the words they've heard from

others to place obligation on the parents: "It's an investment in my future," and, "Parents are supposed to help their kids get started." This logic gives them a license to help themselves to their parents' resources, to impose on them at will. And the license doesn't expire. They continue to exercise their "privilege" at twenty-five, or thirty-five, or even older. (Some adult adolescents are still doing this in their fifties.)

The entitlement syndrome takes away from the parent the right to say no. And the adult adolescent's peer group, who are likely similar to him in disposition, reinforce him in his belief that parents should be silently agreeable when the adult adolescent "needs" something.

What if a parent does say no to such an adult adolescent? The response will vary. In its most severe form, the reaction can be violent. Remember the case of Derek breaking into his parents' house with a shotgun? His words were: "This is as much my house as it is yours!" In most cases, fortunately, the reaction is not physically violent. Anger, however, is inevitable the first time an "entitled" adult adolescent hears a no from his parent. Chapter 10 will show you how to cope with it.

The key point to remember is that you should not allow yourself to believe that you have no options. The entitlement syndrome can create a belief in the parents that maybe they *do* owe it to their adult adolescent. After all, "we *can* afford it." But you do *not* have to let the adult adolescent have his way. You do have a healthier option. You can tell the "entitled" adult adolescent no.

## THE IMPORTANCE OF THE FAMILY

All of the sociological pressures just discussed have increased the likelihood that a young adult will choose not to grow up. There is less embarrassment now than ever before for an "average" young adult (one not from a wealthy family) to keep letting Mom or Dad make his decisions and/or subsidize his lifestyle. Being adolescent at twenty-five or thirty is no longer something to hide.

But another crucial factor is involved in young adults choosing this extended dependency lifestyle. That is, of course, their relationship with their parents. Parenting is a difficult job at best. All of us do or say things that may not be helpful for our children when they are struggling to become adults. But parents of adult adolescents are more prone than others to fall into one (or more) of three common behavior traps. These traps we call authoritarian, overprotective, and permissive/insecure behavior. Chapters 4, 5, and 8 will define, explain, and show examples of these traps.

## GROWING TOWARD HEALTH

Chapter 1 introduced you to some families in crisis. Each has taken steps toward becoming healthy.

Anne Marie, the wife of the "rageaholic" with three dependent sons, has learned that she was not a bad mother. Her daughter is perfectly healthy. She was also not the sole influence over her sons; her husband played a crucial role. What she has been is an enabler—encouraging her husband and her sons to keep doing what they were doing to her by not demanding that her rights be acknowledged.

Anne Marie has learned that while she was not always healthy in her parenting, she did the very best she could as she was raising the boys. She cannot change the past, and she cannot change her husband. She has been learning to stop feeling trapped by exaggerated guilt. As long as she believed she was a "bad mother" and responsible for her sons' problems, she removed all responsibility for their behavior from them. And they allowed, even *encouraged* her to do this. For if things were not their fault, they didn't have to take any action.

Anne Marie, whom we will discuss further in Chapter 6, has begun learning to express her feelings instead of bottling them up. She has been learning to set limits on what she will do for her sons. She has been learning that she has rights too, and that when she asserts them with love and gentleness, her sons will respect her more. They will also begin to let go of her.

Derek, the son who broke down his parents' front door, was confronted by the authorities and given a restraining order forbidding him to set foot on his parents' property. Three years later, Derek settled down with a steady job and a steady girlfriend. He made no more efforts to bully his parents. They asserted their rights and *refused to be abused*. And Derek has begun to grow up.

Amy, Dana, and Ted all made progress as well, although at varying speeds. In each case, the growth of the children followed a change in the status quo by their parents. These changes weren't easy. They required careful thought and perseverance by the parents. But once the parents chose to be healthier, things began to improve.

## CAN ANYTHING BE DONE?

Something absolutely can be done. As these and other case studies will show, extended dependency situations can get better. As the parent or stepparent of an adult adolescent, you are a player in the game of extended dependency. You can learn how to alter the rules so that you will not contribute to the problem. As you will see in Chapter 7, when the parents refuse to play parent anymore, it's hard for the adult adolescent to keep playing child.

If you are not a parent, but another interested person . . . a spouse or sibling or employer of an adult adolescent, this book will still be helpful. It can teach you to recognize techniques the adult adolescent uses to remain dependent on others. You may learn what you might be doing to enable, or encourage, the dependency. If you are the parent of younger children, the three behavior traps described in Chapter 4 may be of particular interest. And, as we show the parents who have worked through these traps in later chapters, you may learn how to avoid falling into one altogether. While this book is addressed to parents, the more all of us understand the motivations and needs of an adult adolescent, the more easily we can address that behavior in those we care about.

# 3

# The Goals of Parenting

Before we can say what we, as parents, might do to improve our relationship with an adult adolescent, we need to understand what the goals of our parenting are. Once goals are defined, then we can examine what we are doing that might help or hinder us in achieving them.

Most parents, if asked to state in one sentence what they wish for their children, would probably answer something like, "I want them to be happy and healthy." This seems to be a reasonable goal. How can we help our children achieve it?

## TEACHING THEM TO FISH

Let's address the question of health first. In the context of being happy and healthy, it refers to physical health. As parents, almost all of us did our best to meet our children's physical needs. These efforts included providing food, clothing, shelter, and medical care. We fed them vegetables. We might have given them vitamins. We saw that they got their vaccinations, and we taught them to brush their teeth and otherwise take care of themselves. Other sources of disease (genes, the environment) we had less or no control over. But we tried to protect their health as best we could.

As young adults, how can they remain healthy? By taking care of those same physical needs: food, clothing, shelter, and medical care. How can they do this? Usually by earning a paycheck.

You've probably heard the saying, "Give a man a fish, and he eats for a day. Teach a man to fish, and he eats for a lifetime." So it is with children. All children who are capable (that is, not severely handicapped or retarded) should be taught, as they develop, "how to fish." They need to be able to support themselves by a reasonable age (typically eighteen to twenty-two in our society). Not in any fancy manner. They should just be able to rent an apartment (or a room in someone's home), buy groceries and clothes, and get medical help when it's needed. So the first goal of parenting could be said to be *to have my child learn a way to make a living*.

Most parents do this without thinking. We teach our children to read and write. We teach them basic survival skills.

If your adult adolescent is over eighteen, how do you know if he's got the skills to make a living? Does he have a high school diploma? If the answer is "yes," then he can certainly find some type of employment. If the answer is "no," ask yourself if he is capable of some lesser-skilled form of employment (like yard work). Most likely the answer to this is "yes, but. . . ."

"But," you might say, "my daughter tries to find a job. She just can't find one that pays enough." There are two words in here that jump out at anyone doing a lot of counseling in the area of adult adolescents: *can't* and *enough*.

Exercise care when using the word *can't*. Usually we use *can't* to make excuses. It means, "It's totally impossible." Very few things are *totally* impossible if we put our minds to it.

The other word is *enough*. Ask yourself, "Enough for what?" If the answer is, "Enough to live on," then ask yourself, "Does anyone in the whole United States manage to get by on the money my daughter can earn today?" The answer is almost invariably yes. In fact, many people can live comfortably on very small incomes *if* they budget well. So *enough* is really just an excuse. It means she can't make "enough" that she can live the lifestyle she prefers, or enough to compensate for her lack of budgeting.

All this is not to say that your adult adolescent might not *want* to earn more money. Nor is it to state that you can't *want* that for him also. And you may choose to assist him in efforts to acquire the skills to earn more. Just remember that "wants" are choices we make . . . unlike "can'ts," which are impossibilities imposed from outside.

The chances are disproportionately large that your adult adolescent *can* make *enough* to support himself if he *wants* to. It may take sacrifice and budgeting, but he *can* do it. He knows enough "to fish." This brings us to the question of desire.

## WANTING TO FISH

Let's assume your adult adolescent can work. Does he choose to work? If he's unemployed and living off the resources of others, he is making a choice. He is choosing not to work at the jobs that are available. They may be "too menial," "too boring," or "not paying enough." Or he may have determined his "field" so narrowly—say he only wants to be a concert violinist—that his chances for employment in that field are very slim. Yet, while he searches for a job in his field, he may refuse to "compromise himself" by taking some other job—like flipping hamburgers— to support himself.

The excuses are myriad. But the real problem is that some adult adolescents *choose* not to be employed. They try to get their parents involved in their alibi, so that the parents begin repeating the same excuses to other family members or friends. ("Poor Johnny, he just can't find a job. . . .")

The problem is simple. Johnny knows how to "fish." If he is unemployed, he is *choosing* not to cast his line. Why? He may be lazy. He may be scared of adulthood. Or there may be other motives. (We'll discuss these further in Chapter 5). But his behavior demonstrates something he doesn't have: a belief in the importance of self-sufficiency.

So if knowing how to earn a living isn't enough, we could say that a second goal of parenting is *to instill the desire for self-sufficiency.*

How does a parent instill this desire? In two ways. First, by modeling self-sufficiency. A parent who does not expect others to provide his living for him and who is happy and proud of his self-sufficiency teaches a child that being self-sufficient is good. Yet many of us are self-sufficient, and our kids still don't think it's important for them. Why? Well, there are the sociological pressures mentioned in Chapter 2, which may be working against parental efforts in this area. But there is another problem: parents tolerate too much.

What does this mean? It means that parents accept shoddy excuses. They provide a constant safety net for the irresponsible adult adolescent. Parents "loan" money that is never paid back. They allow their adult adolescents to move home "just one more time." They help them make "one more decision" or get them out of jail "one more time."

A wise person once said, "Necessity is the mother of invention." We could take that one step further and say, "Necessity is the mother of desire." When parents stop compensating for the adult adolescent's choice not to be self-sufficient, and when the adult adolescent gets hungry enough, he will suddenly (and perhaps with great reluctance and anger) develop the desire to be self-sufficient. When no safety net is available, adult adolescents are much more careful to be successful in walking the "tightrope" of self-sufficiency.

So if your efforts to be a good role model have not been enough, there is hope. Chapters 7 and 8 will show you how to step back and let necessity instruct your adult adolescent. Then he will have both the ability to work and the desire to be self-sufficient.

## TEACHING THEM TO "COOK"
Learning the skills to be employed and wanting to be self-sufficient are necessary first steps. But what if the fisher catches the fish but can't clean or cook it? What if your adult adolescent is employed and brings home a paycheck, but has no sense of financial responsibility? Eventually he'll lose his apartment, his car, and just about everything else. He still won't be able to provide for his physical needs. So a third goal of parenting could be said to be *to have my child learn to be financially responsible*.

How do you instill financial responsibility? It can begin when a child is quite young. Other books have addressed ways to do this (such as careful management of an allowance, having a paper route, and so forth). But assuming your child is now eighteen or more years old and *not* yet financially responsible, is it too late for him to learn? Absolutely not. In the second half of this book, you'll see ways to help him attain financial responsibility—or at least to not stand in the way of his learning process.

## EMOTIONAL HEALTH AND HAPPINESS

Assume the first three goals of parenting are accomplished. Your adult offspring is "catching his fish" and "cooking them" quite well. He is meeting his own physical needs. He is physically healthy.

What about the happy part of the parent's desire for the child? Is he happy?

Taking care of one's physical needs is, for most of us, a prerequisite for happiness. It's hard to be cheerful when you have no place to live and your belly is empty. But having all your physical needs met does not guarantee happiness. Even if you have an abundance of material things, money, as the saying goes, doesn't buy happiness.

If your adult adolescent is a crisis creator like Ted, or unwilling to make decisions like Amy, she is not happy. She may seem to have everything, like Dana, and still be miserable. If she seems to like nothing better than having a good sob story to tell you ("poor, poor pitiful me"), she is not happy. And if she is always saying angry, hurtful things to you, she is definitely unhappy. But what is necessary for happiness?

Volumes have been, and will continue to be, written on this subject. But for our purposes, we can summarize it this way. Emotional health is necessary if we are to feel the emotion of happiness, and there are three things in addition to physical health that are necessary for emotional health. They are *the receiving of love, the love of self,* and *the giving of love to others.*

### Receiving Love

As soon as we're old enough, at about six months, to perceive ourselves as separate from our parents, we develop something called "separation anxiety." We have a fear of being abandoned—that Mommy or Daddy will go away and never come back. We know, in our childish mind, that we need them very badly. If they don't come back, if they abandon us, we cannot survive.

Eventually, given the consistency of their attention to our needs, separation anxiety eases. We come to take for granted that they will be there when we need them. We come to assume that we are cared for. And that "caring" is not just physical. Our parents love us.

We need that love desperately. It defines us. Without any larger perspective, we cannot see ourselves except through the eyes of our parents. We need their love to feel worthwhile—to feel lovable. We need reassurance frequently that they "still love us" even though we broke a glass, or got a D in algebra.

As we reach adolescence, we begin to feel a need to separate from our parents. If we have been loved and feel lovable, this separation is easier. We believe in ourselves.

But we never lose the need for love. No one is too old to feel joy at being loved by a parent, a friend, a lover, or his own children. We all have "bad days," or moments when we feel insecure. Times when we need someone there to hug us and say, "I love you. I believe in you."

As the parent of an adult adolescent, how can you meet this need for your adult adolescent? You can't go back to his infancy now and try to give extra loving. The past is gone forever. But what about the present? Doesn't he know that you love him?

Yes, he probably does. But did you tell your spouse, "I love you," at the wedding, and then assume you never had to say it again? No. You say it many times over. If said with feeling and accompanied by loving behavior, this statement is an essential ingredient in a healthy marriage. The same is true in any relationship between people. Love has to be given repeatedly— in words and, more importantly, in *actions*. Chapter 9 tells you more about how to express healthy love for an adult adolescent.

If you are expressing healthy love for your adult adolescent, is he receiving it? On some level, yes. The subconscious misses almost nothing. He'll feel it if you give it. But fully receiving love, and enjoying receiving it, requires that it be received not just by the subconscious mind, but by the conscious mind as well. It means being able to say, "Thanks, Dad, that means a lot to me," when your father shows his love. And it means feeling joy and peacefulness upon receiving that love.

This is tricky because you get into a chicken-and-egg dilemma. You can't consciously accept love if you don't feel lovable. ("It must be a mistake. He can't really love me . . . I'm not worth it.") And you can't feel lovable if no one has ever loved you. Can this be resolved? The answer is yes, but slowly, tentatively, and *repeatedly*.

We learn to receive love—to trust it—*slowly*. Believing that we are lovable doesn't happen all of a sudden. It is a process that begins in early childhood and continues until our death. It is a cumulative process. We don't wake up one day and say, "Gee whiz, I'm *totally* lovable." Rather we start by thinking ourselves "not all bad" and then build on that. We grow to believe we're "a little bit OK," then "a pretty nice person." But it takes time.

The process is *tentative*. Like a mouse coming out of our den, we are easily scared back into our hole. We'll take one step forward, and then we might take two steps backward. But, for most of us, the overall direction during the course of our lives is forward.

The learning is *repetitive* because we never fully believe it. Something will happen to even the most self-confident person to shake him. What we hope to learn is to stop needing other people to always tell us, "It's OK, you *are* a good and worthwhile person." Ideally, we learn to tell ourselves. And that brings us to self-love.

### Self-Love
The second of the three things necessary for emotional health and happiness is self-love. Self-love has nothing to do with selfishness. Selfishness is the child refusing to share his toys; it is the adult who will give nothing of himself. Self-love is a belief deep within our being that we are worthwhile. Not that we are worthwhile because of what other people say or for the actions that we take. It is a faith in ourselves that, no matter what the world thinks, we are important.

And what do you do with something that's important? You

take care of it. You nurture it. *You help it to grow.*

Thus, when we love ourselves, we cannot abuse ourselves. We cannot destroy our lives with chemicals. We cannot commit suicide. We believe in our own ability to handle problems and to cope with life's difficulties. Obstacles may be appearing all around, but a person with self-love doesn't panic. He says, "This is tough, but I'll get through it."

When we love ourselves, we take time for ourselves. We take the time that is needed for introspection. We give ourselves that time to get over something, to work through a problem. We forgive ourselves for our mistakes, and pick ourselves up and try to learn from them. We nurture ourselves like a beloved garden . . . pulling out the weeds and fertilizing the flowers.

Self-love is not an undying affection. We have to give our relationship with ourselves the same attention we give to any love relationship. It needs our time and our energy. We need to learn how to love ourselves the first time, and then keep relearning. We all grow and change. The person you loved at sixteen is a different person at twenty-six or seventy-six. We need to keep loving an evolving personality.

And we all have "bad days" when we feel like hating ourselves. But the skill of self-love allows us to work through the bad times—to get past the negative feelings and feel good about ourselves again. And we get past the bad times by telling ourselves, "I *am* worthwhile." We don't need someone else to tell us all the time because we can tell ourselves.

So if an adult adolescent must have self-love to be happy, yet his behavior is saying that he doesn't love himself, what can you do? First, don't despair. We all need some improvement in this area—even us parents! What can we do to help our children develop this skill? The answer is twofold: *love our children* and *love ourselves.*

Healthy love needs to be given repeatedly, especially to adult adolescents who are, by definition, still not emotionally mature. Healthy love teaches a child of any age that he is "lovable." Loving ourselves teaches him a model for self-love. We learn about these things intuitively. A child, adult or otherwise, learns by observing the way his parents treat themselves. Showing self-respect, not berating ourselves for being "inadequate" or "a jerk," can teach our children that *making* a mistake and *being* a mistake are two entirely different things.

So if your adult adolescent is immature and short on self-love, ask yourself if you are short on it as well. If you are, get busy! You can change yourself. It is within your power, but it'll take work. You may need to read some books on the subject (some are listed in the Bibliography). You may want to find a self-help group, a religious leader, or a mental health professional to help you. Or you and your mate may want to tackle it together . . . both of you working on understanding and developing self-love.

Whatever your method, your efforts to work on self-love will have a positive effect on your adult adolescent. Although only he can make the decision that he wants to change, he can learn from watching you. As you grow, he'll have a model for growth himself! And there are two rewards in this for you: the joy of loving yourself and the joy of helping your adult adolescent.

## Loving Others
The final item in our list of prerequisites for happiness is giving love to others. As mentioned in Chapter 1, love is like a spring. It bubbles out of us naturally when we're very young. But early in our lives, we learn to be cautious about expressing how we feel. We might be rejected. We might get hurt.

One of the most beautiful by-products of self-love is the ability to love others *without* fear of rejection. This doesn't mean that the possibility of rejection is eliminated—it is not. What it means is that we cease *worrying* about whether our love will be rejected. All we care about is giving it. As in handing a rose to a stranger, the joy is in the giving, regardless of whether the stranger throws the rose on the ground or treasures it. It would be nice to have him receive our gift with joy. But because we want to give it, we will give it regardless.

And the spring of love is miraculous. The more you draw on it, the more there is bubbling forth. You won't run out. It doesn't have to be rationed. And the more you give, the better you feel about yourself. Your self-love increases. It's a tremendously energizing cycle to get into. As you love yourself more, you're even more confident in the giving out of your love. And on and on it goes!

The wonder of all this is that the more love you give, the greater the likelihood that it will be returned. And your joy in receiving it will be great, because your self-love has grown through the giving of it. You believe you are worth the love, so you can receive it and enjoy it.

This cycle isn't something you get into once and, presto, you're happy forever. It takes effort to sustain it. There will be days when it just doesn't seem to work. But with a little effort, we can get back into it. On the days it does work, we will be deeply happy. And on the days it doesn't, we won't feel anxious, because we'll know that we can get back on track. We'll be peaceful, knowing that the joy of loving is just a little effort away.

How can we help our unhappy adult adolescent to tap into this cycle? Again, the place to start is with ourselves. If we give love freely, joyfully, and healthily to our adult adolescent, without expecting anything in return—just for the sheer joy of giving it—we will be a model of happiness for him. He will observe how delighted we are to give love. He will sense the peace we feel as a result. And it will make him curious. On some level, either conscious or subconscious, he will want to know what our "secret" is. And as we continually show him our love, he may gain the courage to express a little himself.

As a parent, you need to be watchful for those first signs of love being expressed. Chances are it's been a long time since the adult adolescent showed, through words or actions, that he loves you. He's afraid of rejection. He'll rush back into his "hole" if he's not reassured. Expressing your joy upon receiving his love, however tentative and small its expression, is something you'll learn how to do in Chapter 10.

## GROWING INTO SELF-SUFFICIENCY

We've outlined the six goals of parenting. Those are the objectives. But what about the process? Is there a normal pattern of development into adulthood that might reveal where our adult adolescent got off track? Is there an ideal pattern of parenting that might help us see where we fell short? Yes, there is a normal process of five steps that children go through to become adults. And there is an "ideal" pattern of parenting, which we call egalitarian.

Understanding each of these is helpful as a reference point. It allows us to understand where our adult adolescent is in his development, and what steps he still has to go through. It also allows us to see areas where we can improve our parenting behavior.

## The Five Steps to Adulthood

Just as there are no perfect parents, there are no perfect children. The process of growing from a totally dependent infant into an independent adult capable of making decisions and assuming responsibilities does not follow a straight path. Such growth is composed of fits and starts—advances followed by retreats. It is a difficult period of change for both the child and his parents. But in the normal process of separating from his parents, a child shows more advances than retreats and is generally prepared to take on the world somewhere between the ages of eighteen and twenty-two.

The growth process itself can be broken into five stages, as outlined by Michael V. Bloom.* Stage 1 begins when the child first begins to rebel against the established parent/child routines. Both parent and child have been comfortable with the behavioral patterns established during the child's early years. At approximately age twelve, this begins to change. The urges of adolescence create alternating needs for freedom and restraint. One minute the child seems to desire the old ways of behaving, only to be screaming for more independence a few moments later. It is a time of stress for parents and child, as routines are gradually altered. This stage ends when the family no longer tries to maintain the old ways of relating and accepts that eventual separation between parent and child is inevitable.

Stage 2 is when the adolescent tries to prove that separation

---

*Michael V. Bloom, "Leaving Home: A Family Transition," in *The Psychology of Separation and Loss: Perspectives on Development, Life Transition, and Clinical Practice* (San Francisco: Jossey-Bass Publishers, 1987).

exists. Household rules become the subject of many arguments, as do politics, sex, or any other controversial topic. Peers become the focus of the child's life, and proof of her separateness. This is the most difficult time for parents, for they must maintain some control while not stifling the child.

Stage 3 sees the child "moving on." This may be to college or into an apartment for the first time. The transition is marked by feelings of sadness on both sides, although these feelings may not be openly expressed. The child may get homesick for cookies and tender loving care. The parents may miss the nurturing role they played for so long. Gradually these feelings dissipate as both parties accept their new roles.

Stage 4 is the time when each family member redefines his goals or self-image. The parents with an "empty nest" find other means of fulfillment. The young adult is able to objectively accept or deny his parents' values in a way he could not during the fight for separation. As each builds a new distinct self-image, the family moves into Stage 5.

Stage 5, the final stage, is the development of a new relationship among the family members. These are adult/adult relationships. Each person is recognized as separate and worthy. The young adult may ask advice as one would ask a friend or other relative. But the parent may seek the young adult's advice on matters in his area of expertise as well.

## Where Does the "Ideal" Development Break Down?

In most cases, the breakdown occurs at Stages 2 and 3. At Stage 2, the problem involves one of several "parental traps"—modes of behavior that you and your child establish that do not allow normal separation. We will outline these in detail in Chapter 4, and discuss them further in Chapters 6 and 8. For now it is sufficient to know that these traps result in a continuation of the parent/child roles instead of an evolution into an acknowledgment that the child is a separate person, responsible for his own decisions and responsible (eventually) for caring for himself.

No family in history could honestly boast that they encountered no difficulties going through Stage 2. The teen years are notorious for the stress they place on the parents and the child.

What is different in the case that results in an adult adolescent is that the unhealthy behavior patterns become dominant, and the efforts to move to Stage 3 are unsuccessful. The adult adolescent cannot break away. He will do whatever is necessary to keep returning home. That may mean dropping out of college or being evicted from an apartment. Or, if a physical return home is not the goal, the adult adolescent may try to remain emotionally in the nest by using various tactics to keep the parent(s) closely involved in his life. This might mean creating one crisis after another. Or it might be as simple as having Mom and Dad make every decision (via "advice"), no matter how minor, for the adult adolescent.

In these cases, since the adult adolescent cannot complete Stage 3, the growth into an independent adult with a distinct ego and value system is impossible. Nor is there a chance for an adult/adult relationship between parents and offspring.

This does not mean that once the normal development goes awry, there is no hope for ever getting it back on track. On the contrary, Dr. Stockman has seen many cases where the normal growth process resumes and an adult adolescent evolves into an independent adult. These success stories occur most often when the parents learn a new mode of behavior.

## Egalitarian Parenting

The ideal method of parenting is what we call egalitarian, or democratic, parenting. While no parent can be an ideal parent all the time, the parent who is egalitarian *most* of the time will be doing everything in his or her power to help a child mature.

What is egalitarian parenting? The word *egalitarian* means to value equally. Thus an egalitarian parent values his own needs and feelings as no less and no more important than his child's. An egalitarian parent knows exactly how much freedom to give a child and when to give it. He knows this because he listens carefully to his adolescent. He observes the adolescent's behavior closely. Because he gives so much time to knowing his child, it is easier to know how much freedom to give—and when to give it.

The egalitarian parent teaches a child to make decisions by not jumping in too quickly to tell the child what to do. Instead, this parent asks leading questions, helping the child see the options available, and the advantages and disadvantages of each. This parent teaches a child to be responsible for his own decisions by not eliminating all negative consequences of the child's choices.

An egalitarian parent is loving and supportive but expects the adolescent to move on steadily toward adulthood. This parent provides reassurance whenever the teen hits an obstacle, and lavishes praise when the obstacle is overcome. This parent never uses ridicule and guilt.

If the child is typical, he will become secure, self-confident, and capable of independent thought. He will move into greater and greater levels of self-sufficiency. He will be able to care for his physical needs by the age of approximately eighteen to twenty-two.

Obviously, in a pure form, this parent doesn't exist. It is doubtful that any parent could truly say that she never lost her temper with a child, that she never answered a whine of "Why?" with a curt, "Because I told you to!" There are times when all of us are too tired to be good listeners or too sick to ask all the right questions. When two (or more) parents are involved in raising a child, they always have some disagreement on how to respond to various situations. This can create opportunities for the child to manipulate his parents. In short, there is no perfect child-rearing environment.

What we can ask ourselves, however, is how we fall on a sliding scale of behavior patterns. Are we egalitarian most of the time? Or do we tend toward one of the parental traps: authoritarian, overprotective, or permissive? The next chapter will explain these three traps and provide you with a self-diagnostic quiz that will help you identify which trap (or traps) you are most susceptible to.

## CHANGING THE FAMILY DYNAMIC

Assuming, since you have an adult adolescent problem, that you are prone to behave in one of the three behavior patterns that is not egalitarian, is there any hope for change? Most certainly. Most of us are unaware of the parenting trap we are falling into until someone points it out to us. But once we see what we are doing, and make a conscious effort to watch ourselves, we can relearn how to parent fairly quickly. Twenty or thirty years of ingrained habit can be modified in as little as a few months of practice. The second half of this book will show you how to create different and healthier habits.

The key principle of changing your unhealthy relationship with your adult adolescent is to remember that it is a *relationship*. Two (or more) people are involved in the "game" that the adult adolescent is playing. The adult adolescent is not sick, and neither are you. What is unhealthy is the way you relate to each other. Either player can decide it's time to change the rules of the game (that is, the way you interact).

Usually it is the parent who decides the change is due. This could be because the parent is older and wiser, or it could be because the parent is tired of playing parent. Whatever the reason, it is usually the parent who initiates the change in the relationship with an adult adolescent.

## The Wrong Way to Start

From reading this book, you may gain sufficient knowledge and understanding that you feel comfortable in tackling a new relationship with your adult adolescent. Or the book may be just the beginning. You may feel a desire to have support as you go through the period of change. You may take the advice we give in Chapter 11, and either find or start a support group. Or, if things are really tough, you may want help from a professional.

Chapter 11 provides specific advice on choosing a mental health professional. If you take this route, we strongly encourage you *not* to let someone tell you that the only way to fix the problem is to "fix" your adult adolescent. That is, don't buy in too quickly to the notion that it is your adult adolescent alone who is ill and that the problem can be corrected if you can get your adult adolescent into analysis or on medication.

A lot of mental health hospitals are advertising now. "If you or someone you love has this problem," they say, "come to XYZ Hospital." The hospitals do provide an important service. But it's not usually the best place *to begin* when an adult adolescent problem exists.

In some cases, long-term psychoanalysis, medical treatment

to correct a chemical imbalance, or inpatient care may be the best solution. But most adult adolescent problems can be dramatically improved by working on the family relationships. To single out the adult adolescent alone for therapy is to say it is "his problem." This would deny the parents' role. For the adult adolescent to "play child," someone must play parent. In-depth psychoanalysis can be very expensive and is frequently not effective. Family therapy, on the other hand, can be much less expensive, and (since it recognizes that more than one person is involved in the behavioral dysfunction) it can result in rapid improvement.

For these reasons, we recommend beginning with a family therapist if you feel a need for professional help. A family therapist can be a psychologist, a social worker, or a trained religious leader or lay person. A competent family therapist can tell you if the problem is so severe (as in the case of drug addiction, suicide attempts, or psychosis) that inpatient or outpatient treatment with a psychiatrist is advisable as a first step. Usually it is not. Thus, if you use a therapist at all, you can begin working with a therapist who uses a family dynamics model (working on the parent/child interaction). If you see no improvement after a reasonable period of time, you may seek other, more expensive options.

### It's Not Your Fault Either

Just as we need to be careful not to label the adult adolescent as the problem, we need to be careful not to blame everything on ourselves either. Each participant in the extended dependency is to some degree "at fault." Determining the extent of your contribution to the current problem, dealing with your feelings of guilt, and then letting go of the past are the subjects of the next chapter.

# 4

# Is It My Fault?

You may be feeling that you failed at parenting. You thought that you were teaching your child how to be financially independent and emotionally healthy, but he or she grew into an adult adolescent. The tendency is to blame yourself. But are you at fault? And are you solely to blame?

In a logical world, all things have a cause. There is action and reaction, cause and effect. When we try to understand things, this is generally the approach we take; in order to "fix" the effect, we must eliminate the cause. So if the effect is an overly dependent young adult, what is the cause? This is a simplistic approach, and emotional problems are rarely simple.

Two easy cop-outs can result from a cause-and-effect approach to this question. The first is to blame the problem on society. The second is to blame it on the parents. Neither is completely correct. The real answer is that lots of factors contribute to the creation of an adult adolescent problem. And parents are one important factor.

"Ah," you might say, "I knew it was my fault!" Not so fast. Being an important factor is one thing ... but things being "all your fault" is quite another. This is a question of shades of gray, not black or white. Learning to determine the shade of gray— the degree of guilt—and then learning to cope with it, is critical both to your emotional health and to your adult adolescent's.

It's important to point out that guilt is not all bad. If people *never* felt guilt, they would not go to work, or study in school, or show up for appointments on time. Feelings of social responsibility are directed by a healthy desire to avoid being guilty of irresponsibility. Without reasonable feelings of guilt (or, said differently, the desire to be socially responsible), no one would stop at red lights, no one's property would be respected, and society as we know it could not function.

But guilt becomes dysfunctional when it gets out of control— when we make decisions based upon *exaggerated* guilt feelings instead of a well-balanced emotional and rational response to life. We have to learn to ask ourselves, "Is this a reasonable degree of guilt to feel in this situation?"

## BUT EVERYONE ELSE TELLS ME IT'S MY FAULT

We don't start inflicting exaggerated guilt on ourselves unassisted. Our culture helps, with its "feel good" mentality. We want instant gratification and no pain. If we have a headache, we take a pain reliever. If we have a cold, we take a cold medicine. If we are injured, we sue for "pain and suffering." If we are suffering . . . it should be *fixed.* If we are suffering, it's somebody's fault!

When we get angry about the things that go wrong in our lives, we are feeling "*mis*treated." In other words, for us to be treated properly, nothing should go wrong. Everything should go our way. When the world doesn't meet this expectation, most of us don't stop to examine the expectation. Rather, we lash out. We are not at fault for having an unrealistic expectation. Someone else, or some*thing* else, is at fault for not meeting that expectation.

The unrealistic expectation is that suffering is bad and that happiness is our due. Anyone (or anything) who denies us "our due" is therefore evil, and "at fault." If it is a person, he or she *should feel guilty* for violating our "right" to happiness.

Is this reasonable? Is happiness the norm, and suffering or hardship something inflicted on us by evil people or by unkind Fate?

Isn't there some fallacy in that logic? Somehow, it doesn't feel right. It doesn't make sense. Yet so many people every day will make statements like, "It's not fair . . . " and then proceed to tell you how their car broke down or their spouse just lost the best job she ever had. But if something doesn't sound right about this logic, what's wrong with it?

What's wrong is the underlying assumption that happiness is our due. Imagine the literal extension of this . . . heaven on earth. A famous writer once said he could imagine nothing so dull as heaven. He was speaking of heaven as it was commonly imagined: floating around on clouds, singing all day, and never needing to eat or work or struggle. He saw it as a vision of stagnation, like constantly being in the womb at nine months since conception . . . all your needs met, but unable to grow and learn.

Humans are creatures who thrive on overcoming. If there was no mountain to climb, no goal to achieve, no hurdle to overcome—what would there be? We could never gain the sense of self-worth that comes from accomplishment, from doing something that stretched us and really made us work.

One client told Dr. Stockman, "You know, I wasted a lot of years being angry with my parents. I blamed them for everything. I felt that they had ruined my life when they moved me here. I left all my friends behind in Ohio. And everything else bad that happened to me here . . . it was all their fault.

"Now I see how stupid that was. They had a choice to make: take the promotion and move or stay put. They did what they believed was best. If they'd stayed, there would have been other problems in my life in Ohio. Problems just happen. You have to cope."

A lot of wisdom and years of struggle went into that patient's realization. And he's way ahead of most of his peers. As long as we believe that all pain is someone's fault, we'll look for someone to blame. And parents are one of the easiest scapegoats of all.

So, if you feel that lots of people seem to be blaming your

adult adolescent's behavior on you, you're probably right. In our culture we're very quick to blame. Specifically, we blame the parents for the problems of their children. Many churches do this ("If the child had been raised in a more Christian [or Jewish or whatever] home . . . "). Some mental health professionals, guidance counselors, and teachers will also say, "These problems begin at home" (no matter what the problem is). Spouses, and especially ex-spouses, can tell you, "It's all your fault that Johnny or Mary acts this way." Friends and neighbors may imply that you're to blame. And most of all, the adult adolescent will be quick to reinforce your guilt . . . because it frees him from any ownership of his problem. It's easy to get caught into that and blame yourself. But no one is completely responsible for another person's behavior. Even if you did some things that you really regret, you were not the only influence on your child.

With all these people and institutions telling us parents that we're to blame, how do we avoid painting ourselves as the person in the black hat? Remember Anne Marie in Chapter 1? She had three adult sons who were living at home and letting her slave for them. None of them was aggressively working toward moving out. They were fighting with their father and working her to exhaustion. Yet she felt that it was her fault, that she was a "bad mother."

As Anne Marie worked with Dr. Stockman, she came to see the behavior patterns she had engaged in that made dependency easy for the boys. These patterns are called "enabling" behaviors. Yet she was not enabling their dependency deliberately. She was doing her best to love her sons. When it was obviously not working, she sought help. With that help she was able to improve her parenting techniques. That doesn't mean she had been a bad parent before. It means she hadn't been as effective and loving (in the healthy sense) as she was capable of being. It means that she had room to grow in her role as parent. But we *all* do.

Every single one of us can improve in our parenting behavior, just as we can all improve in our behavior as a spouse or as a friend. But does having room to improve make all of us bad? No. What makes us good parents is that we are trying: trying to love our children in the healthiest way possible, trying to love ourselves in the healthiest way we can, and trying to grow in our understanding of parenting.

If you are trying to do these things, you are unquestionably a *good* parent. This doesn't mean that your behavior as a parent didn't *help* to create the problem with your adult adolescent. It probably did. We are *to some degree* responsible for the creation of an adult adolescent behavior pattern.

As good parents, we can take inventory—determine what we've done and what we continue to do that enables the dependency. We can try to change those behavior patterns and stop enabling. This book will explain how to do that. But first, let's put into perspective how much we, as parents, influence the creation of an adult adolescent's behavior pattern, and the dangers of taking on exaggerated feelings of guilt.

## THE SOURCE OF AN ADULT ADOLESCENT'S PERSONALITY

An adult adolescent, like all young adults, is the sum of many influences on his life. There are two opposite schools of thought regarding the development of personality. The first is the theory of the "blank page" (or *tabula rasa*). This theory holds that children are born into the world as a blank page. Their parents and the world then "write" on the page, creating a personality out of nothingness.

The opposing school of thought is the "nature" theory of personality. This is a theory of predetermination based on genetics. At the moment of conception, the mother's genes and the father's genes merge and create a combination of personality factors. Nothing that the father or mother does, or that anyone else does, during the child's life can alter these fundamental characteristics.

Very few people today espouse either theory in the extreme sense they are portrayed here. Generally, the two theories are blended. We believe that children are born with a "baseline personality"—a sort of genetic predisposition to react in a certain way to the outside world. Genetic influences on personality have been demonstrated in studies of identical twins separated at birth. As they mature they may have startling similarities—even if raised in very different environments. Yet those twins do not behave *exactly* alike. Environment plays a role. And anyone who has seen the effect of severe abuse or neglect on a child knows that environment *can* take a predominant role in the behavior patterns a child develops.

So environment is a major factor in the development of a child's personality. What composes the environment? Is it solely the parents? What about the child's friends? His teachers? His religious leaders? The neighbors? The larger society he sees on television or reads about in the paper? Common sense says that all of these play a role. But how large?

The only honest answer is to say that we don't know, and that it varies from child to child. For one child, a grandparent or neighbor may have had a very large influence. For another, the father or mother may have been primary. But regardless of the varied weight each carried, the important thing to remember as a parent is that you are not single-handedly responsible for how your child turned out.

What you can be sure of is that you were a factor, and you weren't perfect (no one is). We'll talk more shortly about coming to terms with the things you did or didn't do which you now regret. But first we need to understand guilt, and its dangers, a little better.

## THE DANGERS OF GUILT

When a parent feels totally at fault for an adult adolescent's behavior, what is the adult adolescent learning? First and foremost, he's learning that his behavior is "not my fault." After all, if his parents are acting guilty (and we telegraph our feelings easily to our kids), then his problems aren't "his" anymore. The adult adolescent will give up ownership of the problem.

This is the essence of dependency. "I don't own my life . . . *you* do!" But life is full of problems and independence is growing *through* the problems, not moaning passively about "the unfairness of it all." So if the adult adolescent doesn't own his problems, he will take no responsibility for working on them. Without working on them, it is *impossible* for him to grow. In this mode, he will remain, like a needle on a scratched record, stuck in the same groove, going around and around in circles, repeating the same mistakes again and again.

As long as you feel this exaggerated guilt, as long as you feel responsible for his problems, you are taking ownership away from him. To the degree you do this, you are encouraging the dependency! This is not to say that you enjoy his dependency, merely that your behavior is stuck in an unproductive pattern, just as his is. You'll both keep "going around in circles," and you'll both be unhealthy. Your adult adolescent is not learning and practicing healthy self-love nor is he giving or receiving healthy love. Thus, such guilt works against three of the goals of parenting as explained in Chapter 3.

## WHAT CAN I DO ABOUT MY GUILT?
The first thing you can do about your guilt is to change your philosophical viewpoint. You must come to see your exaggerated guilt as a hindrance to a healthy relationship. Second, you must sort out and admit where you made your mistakes as a parent (and we *all* make them!). Third, you must accept and love yourself, in spite of your mistakes. Then, fourth and finally, you can learn how to acknowledge your mistakes to your adult adolescent, "make up" for them once and for all, and put them away.

### Changing Your Viewpoint
Changing your philosophical viewpoint is an important first step, because guilt is a great paralyzer. It's hard to exercise good judgment when you feel debilitated by responsibility for someone else's problems. So the first thing you can do is to take a piece of paper, and write on it in large print: HARDSHIPS ARE A HEALTHY PART OF LIFE—NOT A SIGN OF BAD PARENTING.

Now post this sign somewhere where you will see it frequently. The bathroom mirror or the refrigerator door is a good spot. If your adult adolescent happens to see it, that's fine. It may create an opportunity for you to explain your new philosophy.

Each time you look at the sign, remind yourself of the fallacies of the "happiness is our due" social outlook:

- *Fallacy Number 1—Parents owe their children a peaceful, untroubled childhood.* This is a recipe for failure. Can any parent prevent life from impinging on her child? No, of course not. Other kids will tease him. Teachers aren't always "fair." Physical ailments are inevitable. If we believe this fallacy, we are guaranteeing that we'll see ourselves as failures. We'll feel guilt, and we'll feel responsible for all the child's problems. We'll be taking away ownership of the problems. We'll deprive ourselves of self-love and the child of growth.
- *Fallacy Number 2—Hardships are unfair.* As we stated earlier, humans are creatures who thrive on overcoming. If there was no goal to achieve, no hurdle to overcome—what would there be? We could never gain the sense of self-worth (and self-love) that comes from accomplishment, from doing something that stretches us and makes us really struggle.

It is ironic, but moments of *unhappiness* are essential to achieving personal fulfillment. In a very real sense, misery is necessary for happiness. But turning each hurdle into an accomplishment is hard work. It requires that we quit blaming anybody for the problem and just accept that it's there. It's there just because it is—because that is the way life is. Finding "fault" is a waste of energy. It prevents us from overcoming. We must consciously decide that the problem exists and that we are responsible for overcoming it. No one else owes us an instant fix.

So hardships are not only *not unfair*, they are essential for personal growth, learning self-love, and ultimately, for happiness. Thus, hardships are part of life. They are unquestionably not a sign that you were a bad parent!

### Your Adult Adolescent's Viewpoint

In addition to changing your viewpoint about hardships, think about the viewpoint your feelings of guilt and responsibility can give your adult adolescent.

First, if you believe that hardships are unfair, so will your adult adolescent. It gives him the perception that the world owes him a life without hurdles, and that if he had better parents, his life would be hurdle-free. It leads to a feeling of having been wronged by his parents. He will blame you for his problems, further enhancing your own feelings of guilt. Thus a downward spiral of guilt can grow.

Such a perception will lead the adult adolescent to treat every mishap as a personal affront ("Why is this happening to *me?*") instead of as an opportunity to show what he's made of. Thus, he may be trapped in a pattern of always feeling angry or depressed with the world (and specifically with you, as his parent) for treating him so poorly.

The adult adolescent's anger or depression is a continuation of his refusal to own his own problems. He will never be able to cope with the world on his terms ... because those terms are not realistic. He must come to understand that life is full of problems that are no one's fault, but which he must learn to deal with. If he learns this, he has the opportunity to become a self-sufficient adult capable of self-love and happiness.

This is the philosophy we'd like our adult adolescents to learn. But we can't drill it into their heads. What we can do is to believe it ourselves and radiate it. We can stop our behavior patterns that encourage his self-defeating belief system.

Later in this chapter, we'll talk about the three behavior traps that guilt fosters. As you learn to recognize which trap (or traps) you fall into, you'll learn to identify the type of behavior that encourages the adult adolescent to relinquish ownership of his problems. Whether the problem is paying the rent, deciding on a type of car, or finding a mate, he owns the problem, not you. We'll show you how to encourage him in his efforts to conquer each hurdle and to overcome his dependency.

## Admitting Your Mistakes

The place to begin is with yourself. Take a quiet self-inventory. On a piece of paper, list the major things you wish you'd done differently as a parent. Then put a mark next to each thing you did because, at the time, you *believed* it was the best action to take (for example, taking a job transfer or working overtime to earn the extra pay). Make a different mark next to the things you did because you didn't "know as much then as you do now" (for example, you know now that you should have spent more time with the kids). Now, circle in red the items that you regret where your motive was to be *deliberately hurtful* to your children.

For most of us, there will be no red circles. Even if you were physically abusing your child, you were probably out of control. You were like an alcoholic. You had a disease. You did not wake up each day and say to yourself, "I'm going to make Johnny's life miserable today." What you could have done differently was to not *deny* that you had a problem. You could add that to your list of regrets. You could regret that you didn't get help—or get it sooner. But you didn't stay sick just to make your child unhappy.

This is both a humbling and an enlightening list to read. We can see our faults, but we can also see that they sprang from our immaturity and our lack of knowledge (or our own mental ill health). Our goals (such as "I want more money") may or may not have been wrong. But given what we understood about the world and the expectations we had of life and of ourselves, that's how we decided to act. *We* decided. We *accept* the responsibility for those decisions. Some of these choices, in retrospect, were flawed. That's the humbling part. The enlightening part is that we did not set out to make bad decisions. We are not evil or bad parents. We tried.

Now, to balance out this list, make a list of things you believe you did well. Remember the night you stayed up all night to sew Mary's Halloween costume? Or the hours you sat and rocked Johnny when he was sick? How about the times you had heart-to-heart talks over cookies and milk? Remember how you agonized with Johnny over how to ask Susan to the prom? And how you spent long hours discussing the problems of drug abuse with Mary?

Whenever we list our faults, we need to balance it with the things we did right. It helps to see that as we went along, we made decisions as best we could. Some things we did very well. Others we didn't. That makes us human.

So now that you have your two lists, the next step is to learn more about the behavior patterns that are the cause of your strengths and weaknesses as a parent. Three traps—authoritarian, overprotective, and permissive/insecure—are explained in the following sections. It is important to identify which pattern you fall into, and how often you operate out of that model. Chapters 6 and 8 will show you some examples of families caught in these traps.

### The Authoritarian Behavior Trap

The world is frequently an authoritarian place. There is a "right" and a "wrong" way to do most things. Obeying traffic laws is right; breaking them is wrong. Getting to work on time is right. Doing what the boss tells you is right. Most religions tell people the right way to live. In an authoritarian frame of reference, there is one right way to handle every situation.

To some degree, an authoritarian structure is necessary. We have to have laws (with their corresponding punishments) to preserve social order. Without some sort of structure, we would have total anarchy. Yet, for many of us, authoritarian behavior models are all we know.

*Most* of us were raised in an authoritarian household. Anyone who broke the rules got punished. School was an authoritarian place for those of us educated before the midsixties. Challenging the teacher was not allowed. And work is usually not a democracy . . . the boss tells us what to do and how to do it.

So, for many of us, when we became parents, we fell back upon the role model we'd seen the most of: the authoritarian. What kind of behavior are we talking about?

Let's start with a simple example. Think of a Marine Corps drill sergeant and his recruits. The sergeant gives orders, and the recruits follow them. Negotiation is not possible. A new recruit doesn't say, "Gee, Sarge, can't we skip the hike today?" He says, "Yessir!" to everything he's told to do. This kind of discipline is essential for maintaining effectiveness during combat. It is not so helpful in teaching a child to think for himself.

How does a parent fall into this trap? It's easy for those of us who had this kind of role model. It's also an easy trap for parents who are successfully managing their own lives. We know how to run a business, pay bills, and handle problems with the next-door neighbor. We are busy people with lots of responsibilities weighing on our minds. When a child comes home with a problem ("I got an F in math"), the authoritarian parent has the answer ("That's it, young lady. No more TV until that grade comes up. Every night after dinner, you'll do your homework . . . "). This parent does not ask the child for input ("Why are you having so much trouble in math?") or for suggestions.

When a child is very young, a gentle, moderately authoritarian response may be appropriate. The child honestly may not know what the problem is or have any idea how to resolve it. The parent might have to take control and go talk to the teacher. But as the child ages, such a pattern of behavior becomes an easy trap for both parent and child. For the parent, it means a quick solution to every problem. For the child, it means not being responsible for making any decisions. If Mom or Dad always tells the child what to do, then any negative outcome from those decisions is not the child's responsibility. A child who is fearful of responsibility (and who isn't sometimes?) has strong and frequently subconscious desires to maintain this pattern.

In addition to being in an order giver/order taker kind of relationship, the authoritarian parent has the disadvantage of operating out of a purely analytical mode. Have you ever seen a drill sergeant hold a recruit's hand and say, "I love you"? Can you imagine him crying as he hugs a recruit and saying, "I'm sorry you hurt. I hurt for you, too"? The authoritarian model is aloof and unemotional. The more time a parent spends in this mode, the harder it is for him to express a full range of emotions with the child. This makes it difficult to exercise the first right of parents, the right to love.

It's also difficult for the child of such a parent to express a full range of emotions. Just as the recruit doesn't let the sergeant see tears or joy, the child frequently learns to stifle his feelings around the authoritarian family. The only "allowed" emotion is usually anger. Thus children of authoritarian families are either totally and meekly submissive (which usually leads to depression) or angry and rebellious. The rebellion may be obvious, or it may be subtle—taking the form of lying or deliberately "failing" at responsibilities.

Since healthy love requires being able to share feelings, it's hard for healthy love to happen in an environment where the parent is authoritarian beyond the age where it is appropriate, and beyond a small percentage of the time. Adult adolescents may overachieve to win love from an overly stern parent, or may be crisis creators to vent their anger and get attention. They may be terribly insecure about making decisions, since Mom and Dad always made them. Some young adults grow through this kind of upbringing without becoming adult adolescents. Others, for whatever reason, react badly. They continue their emotional dependency. But authoritarian parents can learn to modify their behaviors to discourage the dependency and encourage independence.

### The Overprotective Behavior Trap

Do you remember the first time you allowed your child to cross the street without you? How many times you showed him how to do it, and then anguished as you watched him take it solo? You were desperately afraid he'd forget to look each way and that he'd be hit by a car. And if he died, there would be a hole in your life that nothing could fill. You would feel not only the pain of his loss, but the guilt—the belief that it was your fault, because you let him cross the road too soon.

Being protective is part of our responsibility as parents. Young children *need* us to watch out for them. They don't know all the dangers that the world holds. We are the ones who have to tell them not to take candy from strangers and not to touch the hot pan on the stove. Having a child causes you to look at life differently. As one of the authors says, "Parenting and paranoia go together."

Controlling the "paranoia," the belief that you must always be there to safeguard your child, is very difficult. But at some point Johnny has to learn to cross the street alone. Mary has to learn how to ride her bike to Susie's house without you beside her. They have to learn to go to and from elementary school, and then (eventually) to and from work without you holding their hand. This is the process of letting go.

Letting go takes cooperation by both the parent and the child. Some parents are very reluctant to let their child venture forth.

Some children are especially scared to venture. But for healthy development to take place, venture they must. The overprotective parent has trouble with this. For various reasons, the parent becomes convinced that Johnny or Mary "can't" make it without the parent's help.

Whether stated or unstated, this parent thinks of the adult adolescent as "my little baby." This is true even if the adult adolescent is forty or fifty years old. The natural desire to protect a young child from harm has carried over into a desire to prevent the adult adolescent from suffering any of life's hardships or disappointments. The parent may willingly make all the adult adolescent's decisions, to ensure that the "right choice" is made.

This parent will also do everything in his power to prevent the adult adolescent from suffering the consequences of any hardships the adult adolescent brings on himself. Such a pattern usually begins early in the child's life. The bad grade at school is either a result of a teacher who "doesn't understand Johnny" or the result of "poor Johnny" not being *able* to handle the subject. He's just not as bright as the other kids, or he's not good at math. This parent makes excuses for the child. The message to Johnny is either "don't worry, Mom will fix it" or "Dad doesn't think I'm very bright—I guess I'm not" or, worst of all, "my errors are not my fault."

Being overprotective is a fairly sure route to extended dependency in the young adult. The result can be an adult adolescent who is insecure and unable to make decisions, who feels that she is not in control of her life (since things aren't her fault) and who consequently abdicates all responsibility. This adult adolescent may be fearful of tackling life without Mom or Dad, and will probably experience some type of crisis when Mom or Dad dies and can no longer run her life.

For the adult adolescent, an overprotective parent is an easy parent to manipulate. Such a parent accepts even the most illogical of excuses about why "it's not my fault." The adult adolescent puts together a scenario of "poor, poor pitiful me," and the loving but overprotective parent feels compelled to help. For the parent, this behavior continues the nurturing role, the feeling of being needed. If the parent has not developed other interests as the offspring reaches physical maturity, the satisfaction of still being Mom or Dad can be addictive—in spite of the financial or emotional costs it can inflict on all parties.

There is a little of the overprotective parent in all of us. But if we're healthy and striving to be egalitarian, we can gradually drive those behaviors out of our relationships with our adult offspring.

### The Permissive/Insecure Behavior Trap

Most of us do not like confrontations—especially at the end of a tiring day. Bill Cosby said in his show "Bill Cosby: Himself" that parents are not interested in justice—they're interested in quiet. He was poking fun at his own solution to a screaming two-year-old: give her whatever she wants, just shut her up. Most parents, at some point, find themselves too tired to argue with a child. It's easier to give in, to say, "Do whatever you want."

The permissive/insecure parent, however, is not just motivated by exhaustion. Some parents are permissive because they don't care about their children, but anyone reading this book is unlikely to fall into that category. Most permissive/insecure parents are either following some "expert" advice or are fearful of losing the child's love. Let's look at the expert advice first.

As mentioned in Chapter 2, permissive parenting and educating came into vogue in the late sixties and early seventies. The idea was that too structured an environment resulted in neurotic children. If we gave our children more freedom, they would choose wisely, develop their imaginations, and discipline themselves as appropriate.

Anyone who's raised children knows that letting kids discipline themselves is a little like turning a dog loose in a yard full of cats and expecting the dog to exercise self-restraint. To a child, the world is a fascinating place. But he has little awareness of the dangers or consequences of decisions. It is unrealistic to expect wise choices from a child with a limited understanding of the consequences.

What motivated these experts was a real problem—the need for more balance in parenting. Less authoritarian behavior and more flexible (or egalitarian) parenting was needed. But the pendulum swung too far the other way, and we found permissiveness.

By the time their child became a teenager, the parents for whom permissive parenting was a conscious choice probably realized that it wasn't working. Yet, because we hate to challenge "experts," these parents frequently tried harder to get their permissive parenting "right"—assuming that it was their own failure that was creating the problem. And so things continued, in most cases, to get worse.

Johnny became convinced that the world revolved around his wishes. He learned to make impulsive decisions—whatever gratified him at that moment—because that was what he was allowed, even encouraged, to do. He did not perceive a need for self-discipline. That was for the "geeks" and the "nerds."

Other parents become permissive out of insecurity. Most predominant is their fear of losing the child's love. If they are too strict or hold the child accountable for his or her misdeeds, the child won't "like" the parent anymore. This stems from the parents' own sense of being unlovable and not worthy. It is a lack of self-love in the parents. Mom or Dad constantly tries to *earn* Johnny or Mary's affection. "If I give him what he wants," this logic goes, "maybe he'll love me back."

This is an addiction. Each time the adult adolescent wants something, a fearful permissive parent will feel *compelled* to give it. This is the essence of codependency: "I need you to like me to feel good about myself. I'm not OK without you."

An insecure parent has a low threshold for conflict. Arguments are a sign that the adult adolescent "doesn't like me." So, rather than have a healthy disagreement, an insecure permissive parent will do whatever he can to make the argument go away. This only buries the problem, allowing it to resurface again and again, continually unresolved.

Whatever the motivation for the permissive parenting— exhaustion, conscious choice, or insecurity—it is a seemingly wonderful situation for an adult adolescent. Usually he needs only the threat of confrontation—the raising of a voice or the slamming around of doors and furniture—to get his way. The parent may make threatening sounds, too, but the threats are seldom carried through. The adult adolescent sees little chance of punishment for bad behavior. It may take making a scene, but the adult adolescent will eventually get his way.

The parents in this trap only see that they are doing their best to love their child. They bemoan the selfish nature of their adult adolescent and anguish over their offspring's behavior. But they feel completely helpless, with no notion of how to cope differently with the situation. They keep waiting, passive and permissive, for Johnny or Mary to "grow out of it."

### Which Trap Do I Fall Into?

Chances are that you recognized yourself, to some degree, in one or more of these descriptions. Remember, most of us slide between being egalitarian and being in one (or more) of the traps. The question is which behavior pattern you are displaying *most of the time*. If you have more than one child, you may be playing a different role with the adult adolescent than you do with his siblings. Some children take charge of their own lives very early and make it easy for a parent to be egalitarian most of the time. The adult adolescent, for whatever reason, is avoiding growing up. As a result, he is probably encouraging you to fall into one of the behavior traps, at least in your relationship with him.

Where two or more parents or stepparents are involved in raising a child, it is frequent that one will fall into an authoritarian trap (the disciplinarian of the family) and another into a permissive or overprotective mode. This creates a "good guy/bad guy" duality, which is ideal for manipulations by the adult adolescent.

If you were reading the behavior traps and saying, "That's my spouse," you're probably right. What's harder is to determine what your own pattern is. At the end of this chapter is a quiz designed to help you identify your own pattern more clearly. Take the quiz sometime when you are feeling quiet and able to concentrate. Do not take it with your spouse's assistance. It is most effective if done alone, introspectively, and with complete openness. When you have completed the quiz, the answer key will help you see which parenting style(s) you are most likely to use.

Once we understand our own parenting style, and the short-comings we exhibited as our adult adolescents grew up, we are ready to begin the growth toward health. The first step in that growth is accepting our past mistakes.

## Accepting and Loving Yourself

Parents—or, for that matter, people—who care deeply about something or someone are often hard on themselves. It is diffi-cult for them to accept their strengths or to forgive themselves for their weaknesses. But coming to terms with your strengths and weaknesses as a parent is one of the most important require-ments for helping your adult adolescent become a happier, healthier adult.

Look at your list of strengths and weaknesses. Ask yourself if you were wise enough at the time you made your choices to see their long-term impact. Ask what other choices you had. Would the other choices have been guaranteed to be better? Or would they have been risky, too? Examine your motives. Most of the time you did things because you believed they were the best choice. Sometimes you did things because they were easier.

Your mistakes have served to teach you something. You have learned. You are wiser now. And your strengths can keep getting stronger, just as you can keep growing wiser. The secret is to let go of the past. You cannot change it. Love yourself for being wiser and stronger. Love yourself for trying to grow. Love yourself for always striving to learn and to be a better and better parent.

When you acknowledge that you were not perfect, and when you can let go of the exaggerated guilt and accept the real mistakes, you are ready to move on. When you can free yourself of unreasonable blame and the paralysis that it causes, you are ready to help your adult adolescent. You are ready to *truly* "make up" for the past.

Next, accept the fact that you've fallen into one or more parenting "traps." Remind yourself that you only fell into a trap because you wanted what was best for your child. You believed you were doing your best, and you were. But your best can be better now, because you're aware of what you have to change.

With that understanding, look at yourself and *accept the past*. It is part of what you *were*, not an unchangeable predestiny for your behavior today. You were human. You tried. Love yourself for trying. Love yourself for looking backward to learn where you erred. And love yourself for trying to grow and change in the present.

### "Making Up for the Past"

It is important to remember not to fall into the "guilt trap." Many parents, as they're trying to come to terms with past wrongs, become overly permissive out of guilt, even if their past parenting styles were authoritarian.

Take the case of Paula. At the age of sixteen she became pregnant. Her parents insisted on an abortion. In the years that followed, Paula developed a persistent depression, which worsened until she had to be hospitalized briefly. When she was released, she returned to her parents' home. There, at the age of twenty-five, she found nothing materially wanting. Her father gave her a credit card and told her to buy "whatever she needed." Eventually, she moved to California, where she continued to use the credit card. Her parents, overwhelmed with guilt over the abortion (which they felt had caused her depression), resented her constant heavy usage of their credit card but felt they could not ask for the card back.

The result was a continuing financial and emotional dependency. The one trauma of the abortion was now a "bat" that the parents beat themselves with. Paula also learned to use this bat anytime she needed something. At the age of thirty, Paula still had not learned to let go of the past. The pain of the past lived on every time she got even with her parents by using their money. She lived in anger, not in forgiveness and love. She also had not learned to stand on her own. She did not have the self-love that comes from the forgiveness of self and others, and from adulthood.

And did the parents' self-love improve because of their financial generosity? Was their relationship with Paula better for the money they gave? The answer to both questions is no. Only love and forgiveness can ease the pain of the past. Giving money was a temporary way for Paula's parents to ease their guilt. But it was a relief they had to constantly repeat because it was so short-lived. And their relationship with Paula remained in the parent/child mode. They could not move past this to an adult/adult healthy love relationship.

Many parents who feel exaggerated guilt about the past become controlled by it. All of their decisions in the present are controlled by what happened years ago. They do not make today's decisions based on what is the best response to the problem at hand, but in response to a problem that occurred long ago. Such decision making is rarely in the adult adolescent's best interest.

The problem lies in the parents' desire to relieve their own guilt. The decisions made on this basis simply postpone dealing with the grief and guilt head-on. They help the parents in the same sense as avoiding a much-needed fight with one's spouse: It makes that one day easier to live with, but it guarantees an unhealthy relationship in the long run.

As parents, we must decide whether we are willing to suffer through a confession of our past failings, apologize for them, and put them away. If we can do that and forgive our own frailties, then we can begin to truly make up for our past failings. We can give healthy love.

Once you think you understand your past "failings" as a parent, you're ready to let go.

### "Making It Up" with Love

When you have begun forgiving yourself, you can go to the person(s) you feel you wronged, or could have treated better, and ask their forgiveness. If you were Paula's parent, you might write her a letter like this:

Dear Paula—

I love you. I have loved you from the day you were born. I have tried to be a good parent to you. But I'm not perfect. I know I made some mistakes. I will always regret that I pressured you into feeling you had no choice about the abortion. That was wrong. You were old enough to participate in that decision. If you had decided to keep the baby or give it up for adoption, I should have given you the freedom to do that. I was just so afraid for you and for your future.

You see, I knew how tough raising a baby would be. I knew that your education, your chance at a career, and your prospects for a marriage would be drastically altered. But I should have only given you my advice, not pressured you into a decision that I made for you.

I regret that mistake deeply. But I made it with the best wisdom I possessed at the time. I have looked back with hindsight, and I see it was a bad decision. But I can't *unmake* it. It happened. I will not forget it, but I won't dwell on it either. I am human, but I know I tried hard to be a good parent to you.

Paula, I hope you can let go of the past as I am choosing to. I hope you can forgive me for my mistake. But if you choose to carry anger about the past, that is your right. I hope you will not, for I believe it will make you unhappy. But it is your choice.

I strongly believe that the only way you and I can have a healthy relationship now and tomorrow is if we let go of that incident. I realize now that my need to always give you money has stemmed from my guilt. But money won't make up for anything. So I'm going to wean myself away from giving money, and I'm going to try to give you love, and more of me, instead.

I love you, and I hurt for you. I pray that you'll release the pain, and we can get back to loving each other the way we once did.

Paula's real parents never said these words to her. In spite of this, she was able, with counseling, to slowly begin to let go of the past. She is still struggling with it. Had her parents said these words to her, it would very likely have increased the speed of her recovery. Had they followed these words with actions of love (like weaning her from the credit card) and with constant affirmations of their love, her improvement could have been radically accelerated.

In the end, there is only one way to successfully make up for the past. It takes three steps:

1. Acknowledging your imperfections and errors
2. Apologizing for them to yourself and your adult adolescent

3. Letting go of them and replacing guilt with healthy love (love of self and love for the adult adolescent).

But how can we give healthy love? Healthy love occurs in an egalitarian parenting relationship. An egalitarian parent knows how to ease from a parent/child mode into adult/adult behavior with his child. Such a parent knows how to release the past and give love and forgiveness in its place. The next chapter will discuss some of the reasons adult adolescents play the role of "child." Later we'll discuss why some parents might want to keep the game in play.

## THE DIAGNOSTIC QUIZ: LEARNING ABOUT YOURSELF

It is essential, in taking this quiz, that you not take the easy way out by picking the answer that reflects how you *wish* you would respond in a given situation. If you do that, you will learn nothing about yourself. Instead, you must ask which of the four possible responses is *most like* what you really would say or do in that situation. The more honest you are with yourself, the more you can learn, and the easier it will be to identify solutions to your current problem with your adult adolescent. So, first and foremost, *be honest.*

Second, we suggest that you and your spouse take this quiz separately and make no marks in the book to indicate your answers. Write your answers on a separate piece of paper, then use the scoring system at the end to see which behavior trap you are most likely to be caught in. You may want to share the results with your spouse once you've both taken the quiz. *But* if the two of you have had a lot of arguments over whose "fault" the adult adolescent's behavior is, we suggest you either agree to some new ground rules (like not blaming each other, and using only "I" statements) or wait until after reading "Supporting Your Spouse" in Chapter 11 (you may skip ahead to read it) to discuss your answers.

You will gain nothing by accusing each other. Most likely, you both contributed to the problem. But who contributed more than whom is a counterproductive argument. If you are going to successfully help your adult adolescent to grow up, you will need to work together to support each other and to confront the adult adolescent as a united front. You will need to lovingly help each other beware of the old patterns so that you can cease being players in the parent/child game.

## Part A: What Behavior Trap Do I Fall Into?

The following questions describe some situations that may or may not be similar to what you normally encounter with your adult adolescent. Ask yourself honestly which response is *most similar* to one you would make *if* you were confronted with each situation. If you have more than one child, assume that the child in these questions is your adult adolescent—the one who is too dependent. (Please note that the terms *son* and *daughter* are used to simplify the wording of the questions. Gender is not relevant. You may substitute one for the other if it helps make the question more like your own situation.)

1.  Your twenty-year-old son calls from college and says he's out of money. He received his monthly allowance one week earlier and had taken his summer earnings with him to college for extra spending money. This is the third month of the fall semester and the fifth time he's asked for more money. What do you do?

    A.  Explain that he needs to learn to budget his spending better. Son explains that he's trying to, but it's really hard. You worry that if you don't send it, he'll look like the "poor kid" to his dormmates. Ask him to work on his budget, and send him the money.

    B.  Lecture him about the value of money. Remind him about the number of times you've already sent him extra money. Tell him he can have the extra this time, but that he can't take the car back to school next semester—or ever again unless he straightens up.

    C.  Tell him no. He calls back later full of apologies and promises not to do it again. You make him swear to straighten up, and send the money.

    D.  Explain to him that the two of you made an agreement when he left for school. You would furnish a monthly allowance that was sufficient to meet his needs. He would budget that allowance responsibly. Tell him you know it's tough learning to live within a budget, but that you don't believe it's appropriate to send him more money at this time.

2.  Your daughter calls and says she's in jail for shoplifting. This is not her first incident, but it is the first time the store has had her arrested and is pressing charges. What do you do?

    A.  Get furious. Make statements such as, "I can't believe how thoughtless you are. You swore you'd never do this again." Agree to pay the bond money, and send the family lawyer over immediately, *but* make the daughter agree to pay you back for all expenses.

B.  Get angry with the store for pressing charges. Tell her not to worry, that you'll take care of everything. Swear to have the store manager's head, along with the police chief's.

C.  Ask what happened. Ask what she plans to do about it. Discuss ways of paying the bond. Does she have any savings? If she has a history of not paying you back for "loans," suggest she talk to someone at the jail about a bail bond loan. Offer love and suggestions, but don't pay the bond.

D.  Tell her not to mention this to anyone . . . you don't want something like this getting out. Tell her you don't understand how she can behave like this, with all the worry it causes you. Agree to pay for bond money and lawyer.

3.  Your twenty-eight-year-old son calls. He has lost his job and wants to move into your house, with his wife, until he can find another job. What do you do?

A.  Tell him it's really not convenient now. He counters that's it pretty inconvenient on him too, being out of a job. You let him move in, but tell him it's "for a limited time."

B.  Be sympathetic. Ask questions about what happened and what options are available for a job and living arrangements in his area. Be supportive, but do not offer any long term arrangements. If no alternative is available, offer a room for one week so he can find an alternative arrangement.

C.  Say OK, but he'll have to pay rent (nominal). Tell him you'll set up some job interviews for him through your contacts, and you're sure you can find him a new job in no time.

D.  Tell him it's really not fair that he lost his job. You understand how hard it must be on him. State that you'll move the desk and other furniture out of the spare room and set it up for the two of them.

4.  Your daughter graduated from college four months ago. She has become a "couch potato." None of the jobs available during campus interviews were "interesting" to her. She's not sure if she wants to go to graduate school, but has done

nothing to investigate school or other job opportunities. What do you do?

A.  Set up interviews and give her a schedule. She continually fails to make interviews, or else finds something "wrong" with all your suggestions. Every evening is a confrontation.

B.  Try to be encouraging and offer suggestions. She finds faults with your ideas and says she "just needs some time" to figure out her life. You get more and more frustrated, but when you press her, she explodes, telling you that you don't understand. You back off.

C.  Be supportive. Ask a lot of questions ("What are your interests?"). Help her find solutions if she wants help. Make an agreement with her about how long she can live at home. Include your expectations about household chores and paying for her own nonfood expenses.

D.  Comfort her, agreeing that times are tough and good jobs are hard to find. Encourage her to take all the time she needs to decide. Rearrange or redecorate her old room to make her more comfortable.

5.  Your twenty-five-year-old daughter calls home for the third time that day to ask whether she should make chicken or steak for dinner that night for her best friend from college. She'd already called to get help deciding on what to wear and what type of dessert to make. What do you do?

A.  Tell her not to worry, that you've entertained at least a hundred dinner guests and wouldn't expect her to feel comfortable making this choice at her age. Tell her that in your experience, women generally prefer lighter foods, so serve the chicken. Besides, you point out, she isn't as good at making steak.

B.  Ask what the friend liked to eat in college. Ask what your daughter prefers to cook. Suggest that if the friend is truly a friend, she won't care which meat is served. Suggest the daughter use her best judgment.

C.  Simply tell her what to do.

D.  Worry it with her, discussing the pros and cons of each. Try to guess what the friend likes. Finally agree that, while you never know for sure what is best, chicken is the safer bet.

6.  Your son calls to say he is going to be thrown out of his apartment tomorrow for nonpayment of rent. It's only been four

weeks since your last major problem with him. You're exhausted and feel as if you're on a never-ending treadmill. What do you do?

A. Get angry. Lecture him about all the trouble he is causing everyone. Insist that he promise to straighten up and to pay back this loan. Give the money to pay the back rent.

B. Fuss at him, trying to explain how much financial strain he has caused you. He may apologize or just get angry. You state that the money will have to be paid back "sometime," but you pay the back rent.

C. Get the name of the landlord, and call and threaten to sue. Offer your son the opportunity to move back home. If he insists on staying in the apartment, pay the back rent.

D. Ask if he has tried to work it out with the landlord. Ask how many months' rent he owes. Talk through the options. Suggest moving in with friends until another living arrangement can be found. Do not pay the back rent.

7. Your son calls you to complain about how unreasonable his other parent is being. What do you do?

A. Sympathize. Acknowledge that the other parent can be unreasonable. Give your son whatever he was asking for, but make him promise to keep it "our little secret."

B. Get angry with the other parent. "No one treats my son like that." State that you'll handle the problem.

C. Ask questions about what happened. State that you're not getting in the middle, that your son needs to confront the other parent with his complaints. Help your son figure out a constructive way to do that.

D. Tell your son how to handle the other parent in the future. Override the other parent, and give your son the "final answer."

8. Your son calls with the fourth request for money this month. The requests have increased in size, frequency, and urgency. The stories are beginning to sound artificial, but the desperate tone is real. What do you do?

A. Suggest that it is time for him to come home. Obviously, he's not ready to cope with all his responsibilities yet. Give the money for past-due bills on the contingency that he agree to move home.

B. Get upset: "Why are you doing this? Don't you know how

hard it is for us to make ends meet?" He gets angry. You give in, "for the last time."

  C.  Point out that he has asked for a lot of money in a very short time. Ask if there is something else going on. Ask him to come over and discuss this with you face to face. When he does, you don't give any money, but offer to help with finding a money management counselor, or drug/alcohol counselor, or other group to help him.

  D.  Get mad and confront him: "You're not using drugs, are you?" He is indignant: "How could you even ask such a question? Don't you trust me?" You either give the money but demand repayment, or say no with a lecture on straightening up.

9.  Your daughter calls. She is really worn out from all the overtime she's been working, and she and a friend have decided they need a vacation. She's seen an ad for a really good deal on a two-week vacation to Mexico, and she wants a loan. What do you do?

  A.  Say, "I'm not your banker. If you need a vacation to Mexico, you'll have to save for it."

  B.  Sympathize, agreeing that she needs the rest. Offer to pay for the trip, and give her a little extra for "spending money."

  C.  Say, "We can't take a trip to Mexico ourselves. Why are you asking us for the money?" Daughter whines and fusses. Eventually you say, "Well, if it's really that important to you, we'll find a way to help."

  D.  Ask what's been going on at work to make her so tired. State that you can't loan her the money, but help her come up with other ideas for a fun, inexpensive vacation.

10.  Your son's godparents are visiting from out of town. They have made reservations for five people at an expensive local restaurant. Your son likes his godparents and agreed to meet you, your spouse, and the godparents at your house at 7 P.M. At 7:30 P.M. he shows up, dressed in torn jeans and a sweatshirt and accompanied by two friends similarly dressed. The friends make no indication that they are leaving. All three of them are behaving in a manner you consider impolite. What do you do?

  A.  Take your son into the kitchen. Tell him he has absolutely no sense of respect for anyone else. Tell him to go apologize to his godparents, and give his regrets for not being able to join them for dinner tonight. Tell him to then leave with his friends immediately.

B. Take your son aside, and tell him you are disappointed that he is late and poorly dressed. Explain that the godparents are paying for dinner, and his friends cannot join you. Ask your son if he feels he can explain this to his friends, get appropriately dressed, and meet you at the restaurant in forty-five minutes.

C. Take your son aside, and tell him you can't believe he has done such a thing. Explain that your spouse is livid and will be upset for weeks. State that you have a mind to tell the godparents to go back to their hotel. Then tell son to get changed, and get his friends changed if they're coming along, and to return to the house within thirty minutes.

D. Pull the son into another room, and tell him you're shocked by his appearance and his late arrival. Doesn't he know how much this means to his godparents? Tell him you'll make some excuses for him, but he is to go change and meet you at the restaurant. Tell him to wear the brown jacket you gave him for Christmas. Tell him you'll pay for the friends' dinners if they get changed also.

## Part B: What Does My Adult Adolescent Expect?

The next few questions ask you to anticipate your son's or daughter's reaction to various problems he might encounter in life. His reaction can be revealing in terms of how he expects *you* to behave. Each parental behavior trap has a corresponding behavior pattern in the adult adolescent. Try to determine, as honestly as possible, how your son or daughter would react in each of these situations.

1. Your twenty-six-year-old son is arrested for the second time for writing bad checks. The first time, you had helped him through the legal process, and the outcome was probation. He has no money for bail bond. What would he do?

A. Call home, apologize, and ask you to raise bond money and find a lawyer.

B. Call home angry, swearing it's not his fault. The bank made a mistake. Expect you to help.

C. Call home, complaining about how the bank messed up and how mean the police have been. Generally feel very sorry for himself.

D. Talk to the court-appointed attorney first. Then call you and explain what's happened and what he's decided to do. Ask you to call his girlfriend and tell her what has happened.

2. Your twenty-five-year-old daughter gets suspended at work for thirty days without pay for a policy violation. What would she do?

   A. Not tell you about it until you've called the office and found out she's not there.
   B. Call, angry, and ask for money to sue the company.
   C. Call, upset and asking to move back in. She's quit her job rather than accept the suspension.
   D. Call, state what happened and say she's got a temporary job to help make ends meet.

3. Your son is driving home to his apartment at 11 P.M. when his car breaks down. What would he do?

   A. Take a taxi to your house, then ask for the money to pay the fare. Ask what he should do next.
   B. Call a tow truck. When they show up, they will only take cash. Call you, and ask you to talk to the driver.
   C. Handle the situation. Tell you about it the next day.
   D. Walk to the nearest phone and call, asking what he should do.

4. Your son's fiancee has called off their engagement. Her family had planned a large engagement party for only three days from now. A lot of your family and friends were invited. What would he do?

   A. Call home stating, "I'm worthless. She doesn't love me. Nothing ever turns out right for me." Ask if he can move home for a while.
   B. Call you saying, "Look at what she's done to me. I can't believe her family would allow her to do this to me." Ask if you can call everyone on your side of the family, and your friends, and tell them the party is off.
   C. Call home and say, "I've got some bad news. The engagement and the party are off. I'm sorry about the short notice. We'll handle all the phone calls. I'll let you know if anything else comes up."
   D. Call you distraught, asking what he should do. Might ask you to talk to her or her family to try to get the engagement back on.

## Answer Key
### Part A:
a = authoritarian,
p = permissive,
o = overprotective,
e = egalitarian.

1. A = o; B = a; C = p; D = e.
2. A = a; B = o; C = e; D = p.
3. A = p; B = e; C = a; D = o.
4. A = a; B = p; C = e; D = o.
5. A = o; B = e; C = a; D = p.
6. A = a; B = p; C = o; D = e.
7. A = p; B = o; C = e; D = a.
8. A = o; B = p; C = e; D = a.
9. A = a; B = o; C = p; D = e.
10. A = a; B = e; C = p; D = o.

### Total your answers by behavior type:
You should see a pattern emerge, with the majority of your answers falling into one behavior type. If you have an adult adolescent problem, you probably tend toward one of the three traps: authoritarian, permissive, or overprotective.

**Part B:** Your answers suggest the way your adult adolescent probably *expects* you to react:
a = authoritarian,
p = permissive,
o = overprotective,
e = egalitarian.

1. A = a; B = p; C = o; D = e.
2. A = a; B = o; C = p; D = e.
3. A = o; B = p; C = e; D = a.
4. A = p; B = o; C = e; D = a.

How does your adult adolescent expect you to behave? Also, does your adult adolescent always ask to speak to one parent? If so, that's probably the parent he finds easiest to manipulate, and the one whose behavior this quiz probably identifies.

# 5

# What's in It for
# Johnny or Mary?

Our adult adolescents have reasons, many of which are not conscious, that keep them playing the role of child. As parents, the better we understand what is motivating the adult adolescent to remain dependent, the easier it is for us to be careful not to encourage him. If we know that our adult adolescent is fearful of responsibility, we can be careful not to do or say anything to reinforce his fear. Even better, we can take steps to encourage his belief in his ability to handle life.

This chapter explains nine motivations in addition to sociological motivations (like the entitlement syndrome or downward mobility) for playing the role of child. These motivations are those most frequently seen in Dr. Stockman's practice. Others exist, but they are usually subsets of one of the major motivations outlined here. They differ from sociological pressures in that they are timeless. Whether the economy is in a boom or bust, these motivations remain. Whether it's in fashion to be a dependent child or not, these motives continue. What sociological or external factors do is to enhance or even encourage the expressions of dependency driven by these motivations.

An adult adolescent may not feel *all* of these motivations, but he will most likely feel more than one. As you read through these items, keep your own adult adolescent in mind. As you gain greater understanding of his fears and needs, you will have a better grasp of how to encourage him to enter adulthood.

## LAZINESS
One of the biggest hurdles all of us have to overcome is our own laziness. There is a slothful side to us all, a side that would like to be treated like a king or queen, with servants on all sides and all material needs met by our subjects. This is physical laziness.

As parents we try to model for our children the value of hard work and self-discipline. We may teach our kids to clean their rooms, even though they don't want to. We explain that getting to school on time is more important than staying in bed. In a hundred little ways, we try to overcome the natural preference to loaf around.

In the eighties, the term *couch potato* came to signify the physically lazy person. Between naps, the couch potato is visualized as eating junk food, drinking beer or soda, and changing the TV programs with a remote control. Some other person is keeping the house or apartment clean, cooking the meals, and paying the bills. We laugh about it, but it's no joke for a lot of parents.

Frequently an adult adolescent leaves or graduates from high school or college and, being "unable" to find a job, takes over the living room couch. One excuse follows another about why he remains unemployed. There are usually fights about whether or not the adult adolescent is "trying hard enough" to find a job. But the couch potato remains firmly planted on the sofa, allowing Mom or Dad to support him.

Other motives are frequently involved, including a fear of responsibility and a fear of independence (discussed later). And depression can exaggerate the laziness in a person who generally has overcome his or her own lazy tendencies. But we must not overlook the very simple fact that, given a chance to be lazy, most of us will be tempted to take it. We revert to our tendency to instantly gratify ourselves, to watch a movie rather than mow the lawn. As long as the parents allow the adult child to play "king of the couch," he will have a natural desire to do so. Parents, when they recognize what is going on, can learn to take the couch option away.

Another type of laziness to which we are all prone is spiritual laziness. This is different from physical laziness in that it has nothing to do with how hard a person works. A workaholic can be spiritually lazy. Spiritual laziness has to do with the unwillingness to exert energy for our own growth.

Growth means change. We cannot grow and stay the same— it's impossible. But change takes energy, and it takes courage. Because all change is scary and new, we resist it. This tends to keep us in our old ruts, which may be very unhealthy but at least are familiar. Thus we may stay in a bad marriage or any other bad situation just because we are *unwilling* to tackle the challenge of change. This is spiritual laziness.

Such laziness in adult adolescents manifests itself in a denial of the need to grow up. They will tell you they are already adults, and they will give you a long list of evidence to prove their point. Their very determination to prove they have "arrived" shows how far they have to go. Anyone who is truly growing will tell you he still has a lot of growing to do—even if he is eighty-two years old. Adult adolescents do not acknowledge their own immaturity. A problem denied, they may subconsciously tell themselves, is one that doesn't really exist.

Spiritual laziness also is demonstrated in the refusal of an adult adolescent to question his own motives, to be introspective for even a moment. Being introspective might lead to recognition of a deficiency or an area for growth. And since growth takes hard work, such introspection must be avoided. Thus, an adult adolescent rarely engages in solitary, thought-provoking experiences like taking long walks, reading philosophical books, or attending church services. He usually either bombards his senses with television, movies, parties, constant chatter, or other stimuli, or dulls his senses with excessive sleep, or alcohol or drugs, so as to avoid any little unwanted messages from inside that say, "It's time to change . . . it's time to grow . . . it's time to face yourself."

Spiritual laziness is easily encouraged by a parent who, with all good intentions, may say things like, "I know it's tougher today than it was when I grew up," or, "Don't worry about it, dear. Things will get better." Any message that places responsibility *outside* of the adult adolescent is a reinforcement of his decision to be spiritually lazy. The parent who keeps giving the responsibility back to the adult adolescent says things like, "It's tough out there. But you have to learn to cope with the world as it is, Mary. You have the ability to handle it. You only need to make up your mind to do it." This parent is like Teflon . . . excuses don't stick.

## FEAR OF RESPONSIBILITY

Laziness and fear go hand in hand. They encourage and magnify each other. One fear that is exaggerated among many adult adolescents is the fear of responsibility. The idea that they will be held accountable for their choices is terrifying. It is so scary because they are insecure in their ability to make the "right" decision, and in their ability to cope with the outcome if they make the "wrong" one.

One way to avoid responsibility is to try to avoid making choices. If you can get someone, usually a parent (but sometimes a spouse), to make your decisions for you, then the consequences will be that person's fault. And that person will be expected to fix any problems. But not making a decision *is* making a decision. When an adult adolescent abdicates his choice, he is *choosing* to abdicate. There's no escaping it. He is responsible for the outcome, because he gave away control. He could have chosen to retain it.

Let's look at an example of decision making. Think of the president of a company. He can make all the decisions himself (which would be all-consuming), or he can selectively delegate some and retain some. Ideally, he exercises good judgment in deciding which decisions to retain and which to delegate. He also, we hope, is careful about choosing the people to whom he delegates. He does not give his decision making over to just anyone, but to people he believes have good judgment. Thus, many decisions are being made . . . all the way down to what type of paper clips to purchase for the XYZ Department, and the president may not be aware of each one. Yet he is *responsible for every single one*. This is because he could have chosen to retain all decisions, or he could have chosen different people to delegate to. Each consequence results from a choice he made.

We are all presidents of our own "companies"—our lives. We can control how we react to the world around us. We can decide how we will tackle each day ... from what type of tea or coffee to have at breakfast to how well we perform our jobs. Everything that we *can* control (things other than the weather or how other people run their lives), but that we *choose* not to control, is still our responsibility. We can turn our choice over to society at large, or to our neighbors, or relatives, or "fate." But we are still responsible for the outcome. This is a terrifying realization.

It is precisely because this responsibility for ourselves is so frightening that most of us resist it to a greater or lesser degree. For the adult adolescent, resisting this realization can become an art form. He can be masterful in his ability to make excuses and rationalizations that continue his illusion about life not being his fault. Any excuse or tactic is fair, so long as it continues his illusion of not being responsible.

Usually this fear stems from a deep-seated belief that he's not up to coping with the challenge, that he is incapable of dealing with his own life's decisions and consequences. A parent can help such an adult adolescent by not accepting or reinforcing his excuses, by role-modeling self-confidence, and by encouraging the adult adolescent to believe in his own abilities. A parent can also help by helping an adult adolescent to see that mistakes are not disasters, and that failing *at* something and *being a failure* are two different things.

## FEAR OF FAILURE

No one *enjoys* making a mistake. But as we mature, we come to understand that mistakes are both inevitable and good learning opportunities. In fact, it is human nature that we need to hit our head against a wall before we *really believe* that the wall is there. We have to figure out that the easy way doesn't make us happy, before we're willing to try the way that at first looked more difficult.

Feeling judgmental toward an adult adolescent who fears

failure only means we've forgotten how much we have also feared it ourselves (and may still fear it). Look back, and you'll see times when someone criticized your work but you felt they were criticizing *you*. We all occasionally confuse the mistakes we make with being a mistake ourselves.

When such a confusion becomes more than occasional, we may do anything to earn the praise of another person. When we do this, we give other people the control over our own self-worth. ("*You* have to tell me I'm not a failure—that I'm OK.") We are giving up the presidency of our own "company" by failing to take full responsibility for ourselves. We are choosing to abdicate the most important power we have—the power over our own feelings of self-worth.

Constantly seeking praise is one manifestation of the fear of failure. It is a form of extended dependency. An adult adolescent in this mode may appear to be "such a good child." All your friends may tell you that they only wish their kids were so thoughtful and attentive. But the attentiveness of an adult adolescent who is a praise seeker is not stemming purely from genuine love of the parent. Its source is a lack of self-love. He or she is literally starving for a sense of self-worth.

Parents can help the praise seeker by *not* reinforcing behaviors that are performed only to earn praise. Such a motive for actions is a way of keeping decision power with the parent. ("I have to do this, because then Mommy/Daddy will like me.") Pushing responsibility for behavior back on the adult adolescent ("What do *you* think you should do?"), along with lots of healthy love and reinforcement of your faith in the adult adolescent's ability to overcome the inevitable mistakes, will help such an adult adolescent grow past this. Just the acknowledgment that mistakes are OK can be an enormous relief to a praise-seeking adult adolescent.

A second manifestation of the fear of failure is what we call the hermit. Hermits stay in their caves. They avoid as much contact with the real world as possible. The less contact they have, the less chance there is for them to have failed at anything. Hermits are the ultimate risk avoiders. No one can turn you down for a job if you never fill out an application. No one can fire you if you're not employed. The couch potato adult adolescent may well be hiding in the "cave" his parents are providing.

As with the praise seeker, the parents of a hermit need to reassure their adult adolescent that they believe in his ability to handle life. That they *expect* mistakes, because we all make them, but that he'll learn and grow from them. Above all, the parents of a hermit need to give healthy love—even when this means a pretty strong nudge out of the cave and into the daylight.

## FEAR OF INDEPENDENCE

To many people, being independent or self-sufficient means "not needing anyone else." This can be carried to the extreme of not wanting a commitment to a marriage, a community, or a job. This is not the kind of independence that most counselors believe is essential to mental health and to happiness.

As we stated earlier, to be happy we must meet our physical needs, be able to receive love, love ourselves, and give love to others. To that extent, we need to be around other people so that we may give our love to them and receive their love (if they choose to give it). Being independent does not mean being alone or isolated. If it did, it would be synonymous with unhealth.

So what does it mean? It means not being *dependent* on others to *give* us happiness. This may sound like circular reasoning, but it is not.

If happiness is composed of first meeting our physical needs and second meeting our emotional needs, we are independent if we *give* these both to ourselves. We "fish" and "cook" for ourselves (as we discussed in Chapter 3). We learn to give self-love whenever we feel down-hearted. We freely and joyfully accept love *when it is given*. And we give healthy love to others.

Being *dependent* on others means either we choose not to find a way to provide for our physical needs, or we choose not to meet our own emotional needs. The most common way we choose not to meet our own emotional needs is by believing that we not only want but *need* other people to love us—that our self-love is not good enough.

An independent person may rejoice in the love he receives

from others. He or she may *want* it. But he doesn't *need* it to feel OK about himself.

So why would we fear independence? Because it's different, and different is scary. It's full of all kinds of grown-up scary expectations, like being self-sufficient, making commitments, and accepting responsibility.

When we are children, we are all dependent on our parents for our physical needs. And, until we develop a sense of ourselves, we are dependent upon them for our sense of self-worth. We do in fact *need* them both emotionally and physically. Stepping into the role of adult means leaving this dependency behind. This is uncharted territory. Combine our fear of the unknown with our fear of responsibility and our fear of failure, and it's not surprising that most of us don't leap forward into independence without hesitation.

But the key to growth, to overcoming spiritual laziness, is courage. Overcoming the fear of independence takes spiritual courage—a willingness to try on a new role and find a way to make it work. None of us do this smoothly. We need reassurance and cuddling—followed by a gentle push back into the struggle. Eventually, if we are healthy, we come to see ourselves in our new roles. We perceive ourselves as adults and like it. We no longer want to be children.

Parents of adult adolescents must see their adult adolescent in his new role as an "adult." Talk to him that way. Interact with him that way. As you continually expect adult responsibility and behavior from him, and do not encourage childish behavior or accept excuses, you can hope that his self-concept will change. He will see himself as an adult. And eventually he may like his new role.

## THE ETERNAL CARETAKER

Besides having difficulty truly seeing themselves in the role of adults (with adult responsibilities), adult adolescents generally have trouble seeing their parents in any role other than caretaker. To an adult adolescent, parents don't have lives of their own or any concerns more important than taking care of their children—even if those children are over thirty.

Adult adolescents are unwilling to see a parent pull away from the caretaker role because once the parent ceases playing parent, the adult adolescent will have to stop playing child. Thus, adult adolescents will use all manner of manipulations to try to force a reluctant parent to continue the old worn-out modes of relating. Such an adult adolescent may do anything from wrecking a car to running away and otherwise cutting off communication. He may even threaten suicide to keep the parents involved.

From the financial side, adult adolescents feel that a parent's wallet should be open for life. As long as the adult adolescent feels a need for a "loan" or a little extra to help him through "the rough spots," he believes his parents should provide the money. That's their role in life. He is not out of bounds for asking; they are if they refuse him.

The reluctance of an adult adolescent to allow a parent's role to change leads to a lot of psychological games. Chapter 10 will discuss how to cope with them. For now, recognize that, just as the old and familiar role of child is hard for your adult adolescent to relinquish, it is equally hard for him not to think of you as caretaker.

## THE NEED FOR LOVE AND ATTENTION
We mentioned that *wanting* love is not at odds with being independent. But *needing* love in order to feel good about ourselves is. Wanting is healthy. Needing is not. Adult adolescents, because they have not yet learned self-love, feel a need for the love of others.

We all have the desire to be loved by our parents. Parents have an enormous impact on our sense of who we are. But for most of us, somewhere in our twenties, we disassociate ourselves a little. If mom or dad doesn't show affection when we visit, that makes us sad, but it doesn't make us feel worthless. The difference is key. There is nothing wrong with sadness—it is a want unsatisfied. We can acknowledge it, and go on with our lives. But a need unsatisfied can create desperation.

The desperate need of an adult adolescent can lead to myriad problems. Consciously or subconsciously, he feels a need for validation of his self-worth from his parents. He may seek "proof" of their love for him in all sorts of ways. If he can make them furious with him, then they must care. If he can make them pity him, take him in, or rescue him from a crisis, then they must love him. In this manner, he can confuse attention for love. Anything that makes him the focus of attention is a temporary pacifier. It relieves him of his internal vacuum. But the good feeling doesn't last, and he must continually find ways to seek the spotlight.

Another adult adolescent may do the opposite. His need may be just as desperate, but his fear of not being lovable may turn him into a recluse. He may believe he is unlovable, so he will not put himself in a position to have that belief reinforced—it would be too painful. This adult adolescent may go through all the routines of adulthood—get a good job, pay the bills, and all the rest. But there will probably be no spouse and no fun in his life. He'll go home to his apartment and lock the door. Or he may find a spouse, only to drive her away with his desperate clinging.

This is the sad child described in Chapter 1. His or her silent depression may be the only cry for help.

An adult adolescent can't verbalize this problem. He can't say, "Mom, do you love me? Do you think I'm OK?" If he could bring it out into the open like this, it would be easier to cope with. He can't bring it out because it is also his darkest fear. What if his parents say, "No, we don't love you"? The pain would be too much to bear. Better not to ask the question.

## ANGER AND REVENGE

Along with a desire for our parents' love can come a problem. If a desire is not fulfilled, we may be hurt. We may also become angry. Some adult adolescents believe their parents wronged them somewhere in the past. This belief may be based on fact or fantasy. The anger is equally real.

Incidents like "making me move just after Tommy and I started dating" or "never once coming to see me play baseball" can fester in an adult adolescent's memory. A parent may be blamed for the pain of a divorce, or for working instead of staying at home during a child's early years. There may have been verbal abuse, or that one time the parent made the child give up scout camp to go on the family vacation.

If the anger stems from a real incident, the healthy way most of us learn to cope is to acknowledge that our parent was not perfect (a hard thing for us to learn and accept), but that he or she tried. If we believe we were loved, we can let the anger go and, we hope, forge a healthy adult/adult relationship with our parent.

The adult adolescent probably is not sure he was or is loved. So he does not allow real incidents to be released into the past. They live on in the present, and anger grows. The adult adolescent may have no idea he's mad at his parent. But phrases like, "He owes it to me," or, "I deserve this," are usually a tip-off that anger is hiding below.

The anger can be released in numerous ways. It may take the form of little "hidden" revenges—like taking $5 or $10 from Dad's wallet when he's not around (excuses include "he won't notice" or "he owes me this for picking up his shirts") or accidentally stepping on Mom's flower bed. Or it may be a bigger revenge, like trying to embarrass the parent at a social function. Or moving in with a lover, not out of love, but out of desire to upset the parent ("I'll show him!").

Anger can also be shown more subtly. A daughter with outstanding intellectual skills may refuse to find any "meaningful" employment because she wants her parents to see what a failure they were as parents. She is projecting her decisions back on them: It's their fault—they are bad parents. If they participate in this game, by believing they were bad parents because she has made these choices, they accept all responsibility. She is abdicating her power to control her life, and the parents are encouraging the abdication.

Parents of an angry adult adolescent should not turn away and pretend not to notice the little revenges. They should confront the adult adolescent. If he cannot behave in an adult/adult manner, treat him like any other adult. You do not have to take disrespectful treatment. Remember, your acceptance of guilt deprives him of ownership of his behavior. As for the more subtle ways of expressing anger, the best defense is to love yourself. If you believe you tried to be a good parent, and if you have apologized for and released any mistakes you made, then you can return the decisions to the adult adolescent.

## FAMILY EXPECTATIONS

Almost all families develop roles. Susie may be "the brains," Tommy "the jock," and Jeff "the klutz." Mom may be nurse, cook, housekeeper, and disciplinarian. Dad may be the soft-touch, yard worker, great barbecue chef, and "deep pockets." Whatever the roles, all families develop them. The problem is that sometimes people change and don't want their old roles.

In adult adolescent situations, the adult adolescent may not want to give up the role of child. He may not want the parents to give up the role of mommy and daddy. Or the family may not want the adult adolescent to grow up.

How does this express itself? Think of holiday gatherings. Generally this is a time when we, as adult offspring, come back to the parents' house. There, in the presence of so many expectations about how we are "supposed to act" to fit our role, we may resume childish behaviors. This is the phenomenon of projection. Someone else is handing us a script full of instructions: say this, do that. And we are accepting the script and acting it out.

This can happen anytime we meet with people who are perceiving us in an outdated mode. High school and college reunions are notorious for people trying to pigeonhole us into their old notions of us. But we may not have acne anymore, or be interested in chugging beers. Teaching people from our past about the *new* us can be tough.

If Johnny is "the problem child" and everyone is always expecting him to do something wrong, he will probably fulfill that expectation. So an adult adolescent may be motivated (without being aware of it) by the script he is handed. "This is how I'm supposed to act. I guess that's what I'll do."

As the parents or other relatives of an adult child, we need to

watch ourselves. We need to stop projecting unhealthy expectations onto Johnny or Mary. Instead we need to project an
expectation that Johnny *can* act out the script of a responsible,
thoughtful adult.

## DRUG OR ALCOHOL USE

A final factor that may affect an adult adolescent's desire to
continue the dependency on the parents may have to do with
the use or abuse of drugs or alcohol. People with dependent
personalities generally are prone to multiple dependencies.
They may be unhealthy in their dependency on their parents,
mates, employers, or friends—or on chemicals.

It is beyond the scope of this book to address in depth the
problem of drug or alcohol abuse. Several good books on the
subject are available through your library or bookstore. At this
point, parents should be conscious that drug use (even occasional) can be a significant financial drain. It can create or
encourage financial dependency on the parent. In addition,
most drugs (including alcohol) alter the adult adolescent's
perception of himself and his life (that's what people take them
for). Continuing use of perception-altering chemicals can magnify fears, give power to rationalizations, and generally worsen
an adult adolescent's emotional dependency.

If you suspect drug use or abuse or alcoholism, read some of
the books listed in the Bibliography and contact community
resources (like Alcoholics Anonymous, Cocaine Anonymous, or
a mental health or social service agency) for assistance. They
can help you determine whether your adult child is addicted
and what to do.

But even if your adult adolescent is an abuser and "dries out,"
the dependency problems will most likely remain. Drug or
alcohol abuse is usually a symptom of a deeper problem of self-
worth and self-image. Usually the fears of responsibility, failure,
and independence; the need for attention and love; and possibly
anger over the past lie behind the manifestation of addiction or
abuse.

An adult adolescent with a drug or alcohol problem needs
help first to cope with the addiction. Once the chemical prob-

lem is solved, parents can use this book to deal with the underlying emotional dependency and encourage their adult adolescent to become an adult.

## THE BIG PICTURE

Clearly, the problem of extended dependency is a *family* problem. No one is completely to blame, but no one is blameless either. The next chapter will look at families caught in unhealthy behavior traps. You may recognize your family in one of them.

# 6

# Extended Dependency

## HEALTHY AND UNHEALTHY DEPENDENCY

Healthy dependency could be simply defined as a need for another person that is outgrown at the earliest reasonable time. Why is it important that we outgrow our needs at the earliest reasonable time? Because needs are confining to two people: the dependent person and the person depended upon. Few of us can feel anger at the five-year-old asking us to make him a peanut butter sandwich. But most of us would get annoyed with a thirty-year-old asking the same question. We have an instinctive understanding of legitimacy. One request is reasonable; the other is an imposition.

But the dependency of an adult adolescent is more than just an imposition and a burden on his parent. It is an enormous roadblock in the path of his spiritual and emotional growth. For the parent cannot always fulfill the adult adolescent's needs, and that reality can lead to tragic results.

### The Story of Flo and Flint

Jane Goodall, in her multigenerational observations of a tribe of chimpanzees in Africa, observed one dysfunctional family unit that surprised all animal behaviorists. Begun in her book, *In the Shadow of Man* and completed later in a *National Geographic* article,\* the story is of Flo, an elderly female, and her second to last child, a son named Flint. In this illuminating case study of extended dependency, Goodall writes:

> Occasionally, . . . we see what happens when a mother does fail her child. It happened with Flo and Flint. In 1964, when her daughter, Fifi, was about 6 years old, Flo gave birth to Flint. Flo was an excellent mother, affectionate, tolerant, and playful—and also a high-ranking and aggressive female. When Flint was about 4, Flo suddenly began to show her years. . . . Flint, living amid a large supportive family, had become like a spoiled human child. When Flo, in an effort to wean him, tried to prevent him from suckling or riding on her back, he would throw violent tantrums. He would even hit and bite his mother, behavior rare in youngsters. Flo, often seeming to lack the energy to cope with Flint's aggression, would give in.

When her last child was born, Flo was too weak to force Flint from the nest they had shared for his first four years of life. He was stubborn and strong, and remained dependent until her death four years later.

Following Flo's death, Flint refused to eat or to interact with the other chimps. Eventually he passed away, unwilling to take care of himself.

This story of extended dependency in chimpanzees has direct parallels in human behavior—although the line between healthy and unhealthy dependency may be less clear and the result may be an emotionally crippled person, rather than a dead one.

## Healthy Development in Young Adults

In Chapter 3's review of the five stages of development from a

---

\**In the Shadow of Man* (Boston: Houghton Mifflin Company, 1983); "Life and Death at Gombi," *National Geographic*, Vol. 155, No. 5 (May 1979). The quotation is taken from "Life and Death at Gombi," pp. 609, 614.

child to an adult, we mentioned that it is in Stages 2 and 3 that healthy development normally breaks down. Stage 2 is where the adolescent begins to rebel against the parents in order to establish a separate identity and the parents being the process of letting go. Stage 3 is when the young adult moves on, either to college, into military service, or otherwise out on his or her own.

In the case of Flo and Flint, Flint did not demonstrate the normal desire to move away from his mother. And while Flo wanted him out of the nest, she was too weak to fight him. Her ill health made her a permissive parent. She let Flint have his way, with the result that he preferred death to trying to live without her after she died. Thus, as usually is the case, there was dysfunction on both sides: an overly dependent adolescent and a parent who fell into one of the behavior traps we have already outlined (permissive).

What follows are some actual cases from Dr. Stockman's practice. In each case, an adult adolescent behavior was manifested in one or more of the children. As you read through these, look for places where extended dependency began to manifest itself.

These three cases are classified according to the parental behavior trap that dominated the case. In some families, both parents are authoritarian, or overprotective, or permissive. More often, the parents operate out of two different behavior traps. Knowing which parent was dominant in influencing the adult adolescent is not merely a question of who was home the most or who spoke the loudest. It is really defined by the child.

The parent who had the most impact on the child depends on whom the child *felt* most affected by. With two children in a family, sometimes the dominant parent is the mother for one child, and the father for the other. Determining which parent dominated and which behavior trap was the crucial influence takes time spent examining the family dynamic and the dependency mode of the adult adolescent.

Once they have determined the dominant behavior trap in the relationship with Johnny or Mary, both parents can work *together* to change the way they play unhealthy parental roles (actor, enabler, passive observer, etc.) They can then break free of them. This chapter is intended to make you more familiar with the dynamics of each behavior trap and able to recognize crucial points in its development. Full awareness of the problem is the first step toward a solution. Chapters 9 through 12 will go into detail regarding how to work out of these traps.

## THE AUTHORITARIAN PARENT

John and his wife, Anne Marie, had four children. Three of them manifested adult adolescent behavior. John was a rigid authoritarian prone to explosive anger. His anger was far out of proportion to the events that triggered it. He was frequently verbally abusive. Anne Marie was an enabler. Tending to be overprotective, she helped to create an environment where no one ever dealt with his own feelings. How did it begin?

John was raised in the country and loved it. But from his youngest years, his parents told him he would have to go to college and get a job in the city. One of his older sisters described him as "the most perfect little boy that ever was." John was totally obedient. He never expressed his feelings of hurt, anger, or confusion to his parents. He never told them, "Mom and Dad, I love you, but I'm gonna stay out here in the country and be a veterinarian." Rather, he stifled his feelings and went along with his marching orders.

When he met Anne Marie, she was also a stifler of emotions. She later explained, "My father wanted a son. I even know what my name would have been if I had been a boy. I didn't realize until recently that I have still been trying to prove to my daddy that I deserve to be on this earth. He's been dead twenty-six years, and I'm still trying to prove something."

Anne Marie found John "kind of docile, sweet and nice" when she first met him: "I didn't realize how strong-willed he was until after we were married." Within a few years, John began to demonstrate a strong, controlling influence within the family. "If he made a decision," she said, "and I didn't agree with it, the decision stuck. Then the kids came along. I was the caretaker, and he made the decisions."

Anne Marie had no experiences in her life that had taught her how to stand up to someone who verbally attacked her. With weak self-esteem, her easier route was, as she said, "to cringe and withdraw." With her husband, as with her father, she said nothing about her feelings.

As the four children grew, John increasingly lost control of his anger. The rage he had suppressed for all his childhood years was a boiling volcano within him, erupting with increasing verbal violence. The oldest child was able to go to college and move on with her life before John's dictatorial behavior became severe. The three younger children were less fortunate.

The fondest memory that two of them had was a joint birthday party when they were both in elementary school. One of them later recalled, "Dad was roasting hot dogs. Half the school was there. Everybody was having a great time. That's the only time I can really remember him seeming happy."

The youngest son, Tim, perhaps suffered the most. He said, "I was taught to perform, but then I saw no reward. In junior high I was in the science fair, and I made it to the state competition. Mom went with me to all the competitions, but Dad never went to one. The thing that really bothered me was the day after the state science fair, when I had lost, and I just wanted to go out and have some fun with my friends. I asked my dad for ten dollars to go to the movies. And he said, 'No. What have you done lately?' He had no earthly idea that I had just gone to state in the science fair. That really hurt my feelings bad."

The children had grown up in a household where rules were arbitrary and changed at whim. No one stood up to John, because he was a large, loud, intimidating man. So everyone withdrew into the silence of his own thoughts. It may appear surprising, but the result was that the three younger children had a very tough time leaving home. To Dr. Stockman, however, it was an expected result of their dependency.

All in their twenties, they did not go to college because John refused to pay for it. (They were all "losers, users, and abusers" and not worthy of the expenditure, in his eyes.) Yet none of them tried to find another means to break free. Tim went into the military briefly, got married, had a child, got divorced, and came home again. Feeling like the failure he believed himself to be, he holed up in his room, smoked marijuana when he could afford it, and played his guitar.

Every day was a shouting match from the time John got home from work until he fell asleep—usually in front of the television. Yet no one knew how to break the deadlock.

This case is a severe example of authoritarianism out of control. It is a good case to begin with, because it is so obvious. Although Anne Marie is an overprotective mother, the three sons clearly show that it was their father who was the focus of their attention. One son, when asked if his parents ever came to see him play in sports, said, "No." Then later he added, "Well, Mom always came."

Tim similarly showed his focus. Several years earlier, he did not explicitly invite his mother to his graduation from a military program, although he did invite his father. Anne Marie assumed she wasn't invited and didn't go. Tim was appalled: "I just assumed she knew she was invited." All four children said, "She was always there for us."

Anne Marie was an enabler. She tried to smooth over the conflict, to hide from it. She never dealt with the issues and problems head-on. The result was that she gave John total control over her life. She was a puppet suspended in air, waiting to react to his next tantrum or mood swing. And she taught her children that the way to "deal with Daddy" was not to deal with him. Thus, they too became trapped in suspended animation, waiting anxiously for John to pull their strings.

The adult adolescent manifestations include, in addition to all three being reluctant to leave home (or stay away), an inability to form trusting relationships with others; severe reluctance to make decisions or to take responsibility for those made; a tendency to abuse chemicals; a tendency to get into trouble with schools, employers, and the law; stifling all feelings so that they later explode irrationally; and an apparent inability to be financially responsible.

Where did these troubles begin? Did they begin in high school when they began appearing regularly? Or did they start earlier? The answer is they started when John was a child. John's "rageaholism" is related to his need to be the perfect child. His authoritarian parents taught him to stifle his feelings. They also showed him the only model for parenting he knew—dictating to others.

From their earliest years, John's children learned dysfunctional decision making: Daddy tells us what to do. They also learned dysfunctional emotions: my emotions get me into trouble; they are bad; I must suffocate them. And, of course, they developed little belief in themselves.

Does this mean that if we had authoritarian parents, we are doomed, like John, to raise unhealthy young adults and to be forever unhealthy ourselves? No, of course not. Each of us can break free of our own dysfunction. And in being healthier in ourselves, we can stop participating in the extended, worn-out parent/child game. We can be healthier with our adult adolescents. This makes it easier for them to be healthy, too.

## THE PERMISSIVE PARENT

Bill and Joyce had married while they were still in college. Money was tight, and—before the marriage—Bill's parents agreed to contribute a fixed monthly amount to help the young family while Bill finished school. Joyce graduated one year ahead of Bill and had their first child while Bill was a senior. One month, the money ran out a week before the next check was due. Needing to feed his family, Bill called his Mom and asked her to send the same amount—just one week early. Without asking what had happened, Bill's mother assaulted him with amazing verbal violence. Joyce later said, "Bill was in tears, she was so ugly to him on the phone."

Bill recalled that she had accused him of only calling when he needed money. "That just wasn't true. This was the only time I had ever called and asked for a favor. The only time. Well, I went to the bank and took a loan out against our car, and we made it through to the end of the month. And when she sent the check, I tore it into a hundred pieces. And I did the same with every other check she sent." When asked if he had ever said anything else to his mother about it, Bill replied with a curt, "Nope. But she knew I was tearing up the checks, because she kept the books."

Bill's mother never mentioned the incident, nor did Bill or Joyce. It was one of many undiscussed angers that Bill had stifled over the years. Joyce described Bill's mother as a "pretty tough old gal." No one was allowed to cross her. Even in Bill and

Joyce's home she made it clear how everything should be done—right down to the thermostat setting. It was a family rule: no conflict allowed; whatever Mother says goes.

Joyce's family background was different. Her father took the role of dictator: "There was his way, and that was it." Her mother was less severe: "She'd give you her opinions, but you could disagree," even though "you might get chopped up for it."

Bill described Joyce's family as one that liked arguing: "I was actually not accepted in that family for a number of years because I would just sit there and be amazed that people who obviously liked each other, and liked to be around each other, and went on vacations together, spent all of their time arguing about stuff that didn't make any difference."

The key point is that what was argued about in Joyce's family was trivial, "stuff that didn't make any difference." Deep feelings, of love, hurt, resentment—the stuff of true conflict and growth, were never surfaced.

So Bill and Joyce entered adulthood and marriage used to being told what to do, and used to not acknowledging, even to themselves, their deepest feelings. Bill went to work for the same company his dad worked for. That was part of the family's expectation of him, and Bill was very good at meeting his family's expectations. Fortunately, he loved his work, and it became the sole outlet for his emotions: "I am really pretty emotional in a company environment. I get mad and scream and holler and shout. I'm really passionate about company stuff."

Joyce, for her part, performed up to the expectations of society and her parents. She became the dutiful wife and moved fourteen times, towing three children, to help further Bill's career. She immersed herself in her roles: mother, wife, housekeeper, community volunteer, and corporate spouse. She lost track of herself as a separate person, and she was continually exhausted.

The result was two permissive parents. Bill was permissive because he could not stand conflict, or the expression (or even the acknowledgment) of important emotions. He also wanted to avoid, at all cost, becoming like his mother. Hating conflict and unsure of his role, he would give in just to avoid the fight. To the child wanting to wrestle through a crisis or a tough decision, this avoidance can be seen as not caring. Especially when Bill could never say, "I love you."

Joyce, on the other hand, began parenting trying to imitate her father. "I started out authoritarian with Ellen," their first child, "but I got worn down fast. By the time Mike arrived, I was definitely permissive." Dealing with the constant moves on top of all the normal wear and tear of parenting was too much. Trying to do everything perfectly, she was chronically overtired. Joyce would set rules but then let the kids "get by" with not living up to them.

Ellen was twenty-six, Mike was twenty-five, and Matt was twenty-two. All three had finished college and to the outside world would appear to be doing well. But all three carried evidence of their permissive upbringing—especially Mike.

Mike had been an introverted child by nature. He preferred playing alone in the yard, watching ants come and go from their mounds, to playing with other kids. He would have had a difficult time expressing his feelings just given his personality. But in a home where the only conflict allowed was arguing about stuff that didn't matter, and the important feelings were tightly suppressed, Mike became severely disassociated from his own emotions.

In his early childhood, Mike channeled his aggressions into sports. Bill recalls with enormous pride how Mike was "the littlest kid" on his Little League baseball team and how fiercely he played: "He would absolutely sacrifice body and everything else. He would dive into the base, no matter who was in his way. He was an absolute overachiever." But in those crucial years, Mike didn't begin developing the self-confidence his achievements could have fostered. For, although his parents were very proud of him and loved him deeply, those feelings were rarely expressed.

Asked if he had ever told the kids that he loved them, Bill replied, "I have . . . over the past year. But I'm not sure that I've done that very much in my life. We just were not a very touchy-feely, emotional family, other than arguing and fighting."

Mike's internalized anger began showing up as silent rebellion in his teen years. He underachieved in high school and began drinking excessively. He was arrested and convicted of public drunkenness. He also "invented the game that the kid with the neatest toy wins," according to Bill.

After college he became intensely jealous of his brother's sports car. He bought it from him even though he had to sell his own paid-for car and take out a loan to do it. The sports car fell apart—needing $2,000 worth of repairs almost immediately. Mike had barely driven it and was forced to sell it at a loss. Other similarly poor financial decisions followed.

While in medical school, he was convicted of driving while intoxicated, fined, and given two year's probation. Bill explained, "It cost me about $5,000, for which he has never said thank you or anything else. And if he gets caught again, it's an automatic ninety days in jail and a good possibility of getting his medical license pulled. Yet he keeps going out and drinking and driving—just setting himself up, to justify the fact that the world has been ugly to him."

Mike could not express his emotions without chemical assistance. So he would drink or smoke marijuana, and then get into fights with people he'd never seen before. He coupled this problem with consistently bad decisions in the area of his personal finances. Although he made a good living as a doctor, he had come home again for a while, to "get on his feet."

Mike felt that he had tried to conform all those years and hated it. He felt no ownership of the decisions he'd made— feeling they were pushed on him by others. Thus, he felt no ownership of the results of those decisions. Asked if he felt any need to change the way he dealt with the world, he replied, "No. I'm getting along OK the way I am."

Mike was exhibiting the most fundamental aspect of adult adolescent behavior: denial. In the face of his own depression and failure to cope, he denied that any problem existed. He also showed his resentment toward all forms of authority who tried to hold him accountable for his actions by continuing to flaunt his drinking and driving while on probation. He began and ended every day with a marijuana cigarette, and his drinking was out of control. There was no question that he was headed for greater and greater problems. Yet his parents felt helpless.

What had happened was that insecure parents, afraid to express their important feelings, had created a pattern of denial, which Mike adopted as his own and took to new heights. Mike's parents were only beginning to realize how they continued to participate in Mike's denial—thereby enabling his dependencies on them and on the alcohol and marijuana. They were trying to become healthier in their relationships with him, and to express the love they felt as well as the disappointment, anger, and hurt. But it would be a long road, because neither one was comfortable with looking inside and even acknowledging his deepest feelings, much less *speaking* them to another person. But the signs of change were present.

## THE OVERPROTECTIVE PARENT

Nora had divorced her first husband when her daughter, Laura, was ten and her son, Nathan, was twelve. Before the divorce, their father had rarely been home, and when he had been, he was frequently drunk. In either event, he was emotionally uninvolved. Occasionally he was physically present, but he was rarely emotionally present. After the divorce, their father moved to another state, and the children were primarily parented by their mother.

Nora diagnosed herself as overprotective: "I guess I want to save them from having that pain and that hurt." The result of excessive protectiveness is what can be called meddling—refusing to allow the children to make decisions on their own. Since Nora believed she knew the "right" way to do things, she believed it was her responsibility as a loving mother to make sure her kids did things the right way.

What was different from an authoritarian parent was that she didn't give orders like a drill sergeant. Rather, she would get intensely involved in their day-to-day lives, offering advice on everything from what to wear to where to get a job.

Nora offered the example of her daughter, then nineteen and recently returned home, who got a job in a bar: "I told her then, I said, 'Laura, if you think the day will ever come that I'm proud of you because you made your way up to head waitress in a bar, that day's never gonna come. If you go to the grocery store, and you start out on the bottom, and you become head checker or you work your way into produce manager or something, then I'm gonna be proud of you. Because you worked your way up from the bottom. But I don't approve of you working in a bar.' ''

Laura, like her brother, had a very difficult time taking responsibility for herself and making decisions. When Laura did make one, like getting a job, Nora was quick to point out why it was not the "right" decision. Nora admitted that she had done the same kind of thing with Nathan, who was married for the second time although he was only twenty-two.

Because of the problems with her first husband, Nora believed she had to "protect" the children from the pain she had felt and that the world might inflict on them. The kids had had no idea there were any marital problems until their mother packed up a U-Haul trailer one day and moved them all to their grandmother's house. She was a dedicated parent, easily moved to feel guilt about the fact that she had to work while the children were going through adolescence. And she felt guilt about not sticking it out with her first husband.

"Parents," she said, "have the power, and it's frightening, to create any kind of human being they want. And if you're not there to point them in the right direction, and I didn't have that option since I was a single parent, well . . . I'd give anything if I could go back. I think if I had it to do over again, I had those kids, that gave me a responsibility. And as long as the conditions were livable with my ex-husband, I honest-to-God believe that I should have stayed. I think leaving had a traumatic influence on their lives. Had I stayed, I would have still been there when they got home from school. I chose to have those kids, and therefore I could, I *should* have made that difference."

Nora subscribed to the *tabula rasa*, or blank page, theory of childhood development. She could "create any kind of human being" by being home when the kids got home from school. Her failing, she believed, lay in not sufficiently protecting her children from life's traumas (divorce, adolescence, whatever). The children believed this too. Neither one assumed responsibility for his own choices, and both frequently made bad decisions.

Nathan's second marriage seemed just as ill-fated as his first. And he had not learned to control his impulse buying. He sold a car he needed to commute to work in to buy a dune buggy. He couldn't keep it repaired and gave it up. He then bought a very expensive motorcycle, couldn't meet the payments, and let it be repossessed. He owned a race car, even though he knew he couldn't afford to keep it up or race it. Nora said, "He knows he can't afford to race it, but it's just another of his little toys."

Nora's second husband, Dan, saw Nora as unwilling to allow the kids to suffer the consequences of their decisions. He said, "A lot of Laura's problems are due to Nora's permissiveness toward her. She always lets her off, no matter what it is. Laura flashes those big eyes, lets a few tears out, and says, 'I'm sorry. It won't happen again.' And everything's cool until the next week, when something else happens." Asked why Nora kept believing Laura's apologies and promises, he replied, "I don't know. I mean, how many times can a person be burned before they realize, 'Hey there's something wrong'?"

Dan felt that Laura did not believe that rules applied to her, whether it was skipping class in high school or breaking house rules: "She realizes that Nora is not going to stay mad for more than twenty-four hours. And after that, everything's OK. Or if new rules have been put down during that period, they're not going to last more than two or three days. Nora's permissive enough to bend the rules. Laura knows how to make Nora feel guilty. And boy, you make Nora feel guilty, and you've got her eating out of your hand."

When Dr. Stockman asked Nora why she wouldn't set a deadline for Laura to get out of the house, she stated adamantly, "I just won't do that. I'm not turning any child of mine out into the street."

The overprotective parent is difficult to pigeonhole. Even Dan, Nora's second husband, tended to call her behavior permissive. But a permissive parent rarely interferes with a child's decision making. Rather, he or she may moan about the results but will let the adult adolescent do as he sees fit. At all costs, a permissive parent avoids confrontation.

Nora constantly interfered with decisions, but she did so from the inside out. She didn't give orders. She got into the thought process and tried to convince Laura or Nathan why there was only one right answer—her answer, whether it was not working at a bar, or getting a certain type of education. This is meddling, or overprotecting.

In addition, the overprotective parent constantly "rescues." Although Laura might violate one rule after another, Nora made excuses for her and continued to house, clothe, and provide spending money for her. It was done with great love and a deep sense of responsibility, but it was also unhealthy. It kept Laura (and Nathan) insecure in their own ability to make decisions and cope with the outcomes. It kept them adolescent forever— dependent on their mother.

Nora's fundamental belief that without her the children *could not* make good decisions was her primary reason for meddling. What kept Laura and Nathan in their unhealthy dependency was more complex.

## IT'S NEVER TOO LATE
All three of these families had severely dysfunctional parent/ child relations. Yet none was hopeless.

No matter how long you have been in your particular behavior trap, it's never too late to break those habits. You can stop participating in the unhealthy patterns that are encouraging your adult adolescent to remain dependent. The next chapter will show you how to stop playing parent.

# 7

# Stop "Playing Parent"

We've seen the various motives that can keep an adult adolescent playing child. But what motives or patterns do we as parents have that encourage us to play parent beyond the age when it is appropriate?

We may find the behavior of our adult adolescent somewhat (or even highly) objectionable. Yet things don't seem to change. Somehow, we keep behaving in a manner that either encourages, or fails to *discourage*, the dependent behavior of our offspring.

The parent/child game takes two players. If we want to stop playing our part, it's helpful to understand our own stumbling blocks. Once we understand, we can consciously "reprogram" our behaviors and motivations. We can break free of those we no longer like. We can make egalitarian parenting more like second nature than a constant struggle. It can become a habit.

## WHY IT'S IMPORTANT TO STOP PLAYING PARENT

Can you imagine playing poker by yourself? It would be hard to act out the two roles, one player bluffing, another raising the bid, and finally the first calling the hand. It would be a very boring and *ineffective* game if played alone.

The parent/child game is similar. What good is having a tantrum if there's no parent to either surrender the game or call the bluff? How can a parent feel nobly put-upon or like a valiant rescuer if there's no child "requiring" that response?

It's like trying to have an argument with someone who won't fight back. Imagine this conversation:

JOHN: You're a lousy good-for-nothing loafer.
BILL: You may be right. [*said without sarcasm—adding a smile*]
JOHN: What's the matter with you? Can't you stand up for yourself?
BILL: You're entitled to your opinion. [*smiling again*]

This is guaranteed to drive John nuts. He will probably call Bill a wimp or a sissy, or generally try to escalate the insults until he finally gets the desired response (anger or hurt) from Bill. If Bill steadfastly refuses to be insulted, John will eventually give up.

It is the same between a parent and an adult adolescent. If you refuse to play parent, the adult adolescent will either have to find someone else to "play" with or give up the game. If your adult adolescent is causing trouble, you are probably still playing parent.

## WHY WE PLAY PARENT
When an adult adolescent is old enough to be independent, playing parent means falling into one of the three behavior traps. If we hate the unhappiness of our adult adolescent, or his unacceptable behavior, why do we continue in our trap? Several factors tend to keep us where we are.

### Reluctance to Change
We all share a desire for predictability and consistency in our lives. We're creatures of habit—some of us far more so than others. We'll park in the same spot at the office every day. We

probably drive the same route to work or to the train or bus station. We sit in the same chair at the dinner table and have the same thing to drink with our dinner each night.

How much a creature of habit are you? Do you eat the same thing for breakfast seven days a week? Do you get irritable when you're on vacations and your routine is disturbed? The more a creature of habit you are, the more difficult it probably has been for you to try to change the way you relate to anything— including your adult adolescent.

Yet, even if we are relatively flexible people, loving another person tends to bring out the clinging vine in all of us. We have let down our defenses in order to love another; that makes us vulnerable, scared, and quick to feel threatened. We don't want the other person to reject our love or to desert us. We want to keep that person in a role of relating to us that *we* are comfortable with—even if that role is old, outdated, and in desperate need of change.

But change is scary. It is synonymous with the unknown. Many of us would rather put up with a relatively unhappy marriage than risk a major change—either through changing our own behavior, entering counseling, or going through separation or divorce. It is the same with our children. It is less frightening to deal with the unhappy known entity of our current relationship than it is to risk changing it. After all, what if we make it worse? What if the child never speaks to us again?

Change is also tiring. It takes a lot of energy and effort to modify behavior. Could you imagine, if you had no habits, making a completely fresh decision every day about what brand of toothpaste to use, what type of soap to shower with, where to eat lunch, and what grocery store to shop at? Could you imagine going to a different doctor each time you got sick? Or never sleeping in the same house twice?

Making choices is a tiring business. Making choices that go against our habits is even more taxing. Each of us has only so much energy, and there are so many demands on us for that energy: jobs, house, neighbors, church, children, errands, and more. Sometimes the thought of taking on one more goal or task can be immensely depressing. So we prioritize our days and our lives, and we choose the things we "have to do" and direct our energy to those things first. Other items, like cleaning out the attic, or having a heart-to-heart talk with Johnny, or taking time out just to be alone and think, are those we plan to get to "one day."

What usually happens to those things is that we never get to them. "One of these days" becomes "none of these days." We find multitudes of more important things to do first.

So the comfortable way, regardless of how unhappy we are with it, is the way we tend to stick with. Like an ocean-going supertanker, we have a hard time changing course. So we plow ahead, instead of seeing the reef in front and steering a new course to avoid it.

This is the first pattern we *must* change if we hope to find a new way of relating to our adult adolescents. Instead of fearing change, we must look forward to it. Without it, life is a stagnant, algae-covered pond, choking on itself. Without growth and change, we die inside, little by little. So just as we must value hardships as a healthy part of life, we need to value change as healthy and essential for our own happiness.

This is not to say that undirected change is healthy. Trying to use a different brand of toothpaste each week and spending hours figuring out new places to park at the office are clearly going to yield little emotional health for the energy invested. We also need to *choose* changes for ourselves—ones that we alone control and ones that move us further along the road of emotional health and growth.

Reacting only to changes from the outside makes us feel out of control. It is the same as the extended dependency of the adult adolescent—we are being controlled by others; we accept no responsibility for our own destiny. Choosing change and growth is accepting responsibility for our own emotional health. So we must not only *not fear* change, we must seek it out and cause it to happen.

Avoiding change actually creates a situation where we are not in control of ourselves. It is something we all fall into—this hidden loss of power over our own lives. Yet the irony is that we may perceive our ability to withstand the need for change as proof of our strength, our determination to keep things the same, our being *in control* of the situation. Yet in reality, the situation is controlling us.

## Desire to Control Others

While we rationalize our way into believing we are in control of our lives, in spite of our avoidance of changes in ourselves that are essential for growth and health, we at the same time can be very busy trying to reform or correct the behavior of other people.

It's humorous, really, if we can look at ourselves with a little distance. There we stand, long-suffering oak trees, unwilling to bend with the breezes, unwilling to pick up our roots and move to healthier soil. Yet we can preach to all other types of people: the flexible-reed types (who are "too flighty") or the tumble-weed (who can't seem to settle down.) On and on we can go, listing the faults of others and how *they need to change* in order to be more in keeping with our views of what is right, healthy, or normal. Somewhat like the parable about the man who was quick to point out the splinter in another man's eyes but completely unable to see the plank in his own, we all tend to ignore our own faults but to see with great magnification the faults of others.

And, while we may resist change in our own lives, we some-how feel that if we could just get everyone else around us to do things "our way," then we'd be happier. The extension of this? "I'm not responsible for my own unhappiness—*you are!*"

When we have this belief hidden somewhere deep down inside, we will also have an enormous desire to change others. This is a desire to control another person—and it's the surest way possible to an unhealthy relationship.

Think of how you feel when your spouse, or friend, or other person in your life comes up to you and says, "Mary, you really need to lose some weight." Or, "Jack, when are you going to stop smoking (or drinking or eating junk food)? You *know* how bad they are for you!" Or, "Alice, you wouldn't have all these problems if you'd just do such-and-such."

For most of us, this is angering, hurtful, or depressing. It's certainly not going to make us feel good. This is because underlying such statements is an implied judgment, such as:

"You're not much of a person because of your weight," or, "I can't like you until you quit eating junk food," or, "You can't run your own life—you need me to tell you what to do."

When others try to control us, we feel anger, resentment, and a host of other negative emotions. Yet, somehow, it's so easy to forget that and to say those same types of things to other people—*especially our children*.

When our children were infants, we did have complete control over their lives. Mary could choose when to cry and when to sleep, but we decided when she was fed, changed, or put into her crib. As children grow, we have less and less direct control. Johnny learns to feed himself, bathe and dress alone, and cross the street without our help. We adapt to this growing independence by changing the way in which we exercise control. Mary may be too big for a crib, but we can still confine her to her room or withhold her allowance. We learn to issue commands— "Don't touch that"—and follow up with negative consequences when commands are ignored. These issues of control become the primary battleground between parents and children, and the area where children either learn or do not learn healthy decision making and a sense of responsibility.

It might be helpful at this point to differentiate between parental authority and control. Parental authority can be thought of as the setting of reasonable limits with the child's best interests in mind. Control, on the other hand, is more helpful to the parent than to the child. It gives the parent a sense of power and, as a result, gives the child a sense of powerlessness. Control is not necessarily rational or reasonable. It is a win/lose game, and its purpose, stated or unstated, is to keep Johnny "in his place."

The result is invariably a lot of anger between parent and child. It also usually results in deep feelings of insecurity in the child. When you always lose, you begin to believe you are a loser. Thus, for every battle the parent "wins," parent and child actually both lose. The parent loses the opportunity to have an open, loving relationship with the child, and the child loses an opportunity to learn about love, decision making, and his own self-worth.

Ultimately we can control no one except ourselves. We cannot *force* our spouse to see the world as we do and therefore make every choice that we would (whether it be what to wear, or eat, or say). Nor can we force our adult adolescents to do what we want them to. Oh, we can give it a noble effort. We can whine, withhold love or money, manipulate, and otherwise exert our influence to try to control. But ultimately it is the other person's choice whether to give in to us or not. And if that person does "give in," he feels like he lost and consequently like a loser.

We cannot expect people whom we try to control to love us, because we are doing things to them that deny them the right to be responsible for themselves. We are being unhealthy in our relating to them—and they will most likely be unhealthy back to us.

But how do we know when we're crossing the line between reasonable parental limit setting (authority) and unhealthy attempts at control? Let's look at two different conversations. The first is egalitarian parenting, setting reasonable limits. In this example, Johnny is sixteen:

JOHNNY:  Mom, I'd like to take the car down to the beach on Saturday, OK?

MOM:  [*after discussing with spouse, if appropriate*] I understand your desire to go to the beach with your friends. However, I am concerned about your driving so far two weeks after getting your license. Would you settle for taking them out to the movies this weekend? When you have some more experience, and I feel you're ready, I'd be happy to let you take the car to the beach.

JOHNNY:  But, Mom, I'm ready *now*!

MOM:  I know you believe you're ready, but I have to exercise the best judgment I can. I may be wrong, but I believe you shouldn't drive to the beach just yet.

This is an ideal type of conversation. The teen's feelings were acknowledged ("I understand your desire . . ."), and a rational explanation of the decision given. Even though the teen clearly disagreed with the decision, the fact that it was not arbitrary will give him respect for his parents and keep him from feeling victimized.

On the other hand, unhealthy control is frequently communicated with anger or put-downs. The legitimacy of the child's feelings is not recognized. He does not feel heard. Usually no rationale is given for a decision (even though there may be very good reasons for it). The result is a teen who feels misunderstood and at the mercy of irrational, uncaring people. Such apparent irrationality leads the child to believe that adults make decisions in arbitrary ways—not a good model for him to follow as he enters adulthood. Here's the same scenario with a controlling parent:

JOHNNY:   Mom, I'd like to take the car down to the beach on Saturday, OK?

MOM:   No. (Or: No way. You're always asking for something, but what do I get in return?)

JOHNNY:   Why not? Don't you trust me?

MOM:   I just said no. Keep bugging me, and you'll never get to use it. (Or: Why should I trust you? What have you ever done to earn it?)

JOHNNY:   You don't understand anything. I ought to run away from home.

MOM:   Fine. I'd expect as much from a kid like you. (Or: Yeah, right. You'd never make it out there without me. You can't keep your room clean, much less hold down a job and pay for a room somewhere else.)

It's pretty easy to see that while Johnny's mother may have had perfectly understandable reasons for not wanting to give Johnny permission to take the car to the beach, she never explained them. Furthermore, she didn't acknowledge that she'd heard Johnny or that she understood why he'd want the car. Even worse, she put him down. Johnny feels controlled, unloved, and like a loser. Mom is also a loser here. Although she won the battle, she ended with angry feelings and a sense of being put-upon. You can almost hear her thinking, "That ungrateful brat. . . ."

We can also be controlling as parents without saying a word. When an adult adolescent is around, we can sigh, roll our eyes, ignore his conversation or actions, or laugh inappropriately. All these things and others can convey our disapproval of him. These actions may be more subtle than issuing commands, but they are still an effort to control.

Control can be even more difficult to spot when it hides as "love." Continually giving money or gifts can be a way to keep the other person indebted or to be sure that the other person at least keeps coming around and being attentive. Giving unasked-for motherly or fatherly advice is another way that "love" can be the mask for control: "You know, what you need to do is. . . ."

An authoritarian parent is most likely to control via commands and anger. The permissive parent fears conflict and loss of love and will try to "control" against these by refusing to exercise rational limit setting—"If I give Mary what she wants, she'll see how much I love her, and she'll love me back." The overprotective parent uses control the most skillfully. It may be in the forms of commands, gifts, or, more often, endless advice, which implies, "I know what is best for you, and you don't." And this advice is skillfully given. It is often not verbal, or it may be hard to detect when it is verbal. "Do you think that's a good idea?" with just the right inflection is another way to give advice, to say, "I think your idea is bad."

Whatever our preferred method of trying to control our adult adolescent, we *all* try to control. If trying to control only guarantees an unhealthy parent/child relationship, how can we break free of our habit of trying to run our kids' lives?

First we must see that we are doing it. We must try to hear and see ourselves through our adult adolescent's eyes. A spouse can agree to help us with this by assisting in analyzing conversations with the adult adolescent. Tape-recording a conversation can be very helpful. As we become aware of our verbal and nonverbal control messages, we can then work on changing them. This process of releasing the desire to control others is part of the most important step in the process of ending the parent/child game. It is called letting go, and we'll discuss it in detail later in this chapter.

## Desire to Protect
The desire to protect a child begins with the pregnancy. The mother tries to eat the right things, take the right vitamins, and get good prenatal care. Once the newborn arrives, we worry constantly about its safety. Electrical outlets are plugged with safety covers, safety catches are put on medicine cabinets, sharp objects are removed from reach, and so on. We agonize the day our child first walks somewhere alone. It's very hard to stop protecting.

But just as the young child has to learn to tie his own shoes or walk to school alone, the adult adolescent has to learn to earn a living and pay his bills, to make difficult choices and manage their consequences.

The challenge for the parent is to let the child do things on his own—whether it's baiting his own fishing hook or selecting a spouse. The parent who wants "only the best" for the adult adolescent, and who feels that "father/mother knows best," is likely to cling too long to the protective role. When any of us believes that there is a best answer to every question, and that we (with our additional years of wisdom and experience) define what is best for our child, we are falling into the overprotective mode.

Retraining ourselves involves understanding one key point: *we are not all-knowing.* For us to always know what is best for our adult adolescents, we would have to:

- know everything that the adult adolescent feels, thinks and needs;
- know everything about the future ramifications of each available choice; and
- know with absolute certainty the best "destiny" for the adult adolescent to follow.

None of us can claim this omniscience.

So how is it that we manage to delude ourselves into thinking we know best? Part of it is habit. When a child is very young, we feel pretty confident that we know more about what's good for him than he does. We become *comfortable* in the role of boss, satisfied that our "management" of the child has prevented untold numbers of potential disasters. As the years pass, our self-defined role becomes inflexible—we will manage the child's life, even if the "child" no longer needs help managing it.

Overprotectiveness goes hand-in-hand with the desire to control, but it goes further. It is based on a fundamental lack of faith in the adult adolescent's ability to make a "good" decision. The key word is *good*. We don't believe that the adult adolescent can come up with the decision we believe to be the correct or good one. We feel we must take the adult adolescent by the hand and guide him through life's decisions.

The end result of overprotectiveness is an adult adolescent who feels he can't make a good decision and a parent who reinforces that opinion. Here's the type of conversation that might occur between an adult adolescent and her overprotective father:

MARY: Dad, I have three job offers. I can't decide if I should keep working at XYZ, Inc., or if I should take one of these offers . . . and if I should take one, I don't know which one to take.

DAD: Yes, dear. I know this kind of decision is very difficult. Let me see the information they gave you. I'll study this and call a few friends of mine. Then I'll tell you what I think you should do.

Notice that Dad didn't ask how Mary felt about the offers or if there was a choice she preferred. He implied that the decision was too difficult for his "poor little girl" to make and took the decision away from her. He would review the material and do the research and deliver a decision. The daughter was reinforced in her belief that she can't do this sort of thing on her own. She learned nothing about the process of making decisions, since Dad was going to handle it. In the end, her father has encouraged the continuation of the extended dependency.

In such a situation, the parent's subconscious motive is: "I feel good when Johnny never makes a mistake. I believe I am doing a good job as a parent to prevent mistakes by helping him make decisions." There are two fallacies here. The first is the assumption that the parent knows best. In fact, what the parent feels to be a mistake may be the best choice for the adult adolescent. The second fallacy is that the parent is helping in decision making. Actually, the parent is not helping but is removing the decision from the adult adolescent. The parent is thereby encouraging the inability to decide.

In a society that likes to judge our "success" as parents by what college our child attends, how much money he makes, and whom he marries, it is easy for us to judge ourselves the same way. Because our neighbors, friends, relatives, or religious leaders tell us that it is our fault if Johnny or Mary turns out "wrong," we are quick to believe it ourselves. So, to prove the value of our parenting, we try desperately to prevent Johnny from making a bad choice. This is not healthy for either ourselves or our children.

What we all need to retrain ourselves to remember is that we are good parents when we teach Johnny or Mary how to make decisions. Whether we agree with the outcome of the decisions or not, and whether or not Johnny later feels he made a mistake, we must learn to be proud of him for making his own choices and facing the consequences of those choices. We need to rejoice in his growing ability to handle himself and in his expanding self-confidence.

When we hear ourselves making statements that begin with, "But what if . . ." (as in, "But what if it doesn't work out?"), we need to stop and remind ourselves of our goal. We want to be loving parents. We can love by releasing our desire to control and to protect. We can provide love, encouragement, and a sounding board. But we need to let our adult adolescents make their own choices and live with them.

## Lack of Balance

Western culture is a little like the character Mr. Spock in the original Star Trek series: determined to squelch the human side and accept only the logical, rational side. Men, in particular, are not allowed to act "soft"—the only acceptable emotion to display is anger. Corporations frown on emotional expression and promote people based on analytical/rational skills. A businessman never confesses to acting based on intuition. At best he can call it management judgment, or if he's a real radical, a hunch.

Therapists who practice rational/emotive therapy, like Dr. Stockman, believe that most family and personal problems arise from an imbalance between the use of our rational/logical faculties and a healthy understanding of our emotions. When we deny or stifle our feelings, we are denying an essential part of our humanness. Yet emotions unleashed can be just as unhealthy.

Some people seem to operate on a solely emotional plane. The rageaholic is one example. There is no logic to his explosions of rage; therefore there is no understandable way for others around him to respond. But what usually causes rageaholism is the long-term effort of the rageaholic to stifle his feelings of anger or resentment. After he has spent years doing what he believes is expected or required of him, the facade deteriorates, with rage gushing out like water through the holes in a dam. Other overly emotional people may cry over every little thing, whether it's a sad story on the evening news or Mary's tough day at work. Without a rational filter, the behavior of this kind of person can be knee-jerk reactions, "anything to make the pain go away." Frequently such parents are permissive.

Neither the Mr. Spock role nor a pattern of uncontrolled emotionalism is healthy. Being too rational prevents us telling others how we feel. Expressing our feelings without any rational screen is neither constructive nor loving.

For those of us who err on the side of too much rationalism, we need to practice feeling things. The best way to begin this is quietly, alone, listing all the things in our lives that we're happy about and all the things that we're anxious, fearful, angry, or hurt about. At the beginning this can be tough, especially when we've practiced telling everyone, "I'm fine, thanks," for so many years that we almost believe it ourselves.

But over time, we can start tapping our feelings. Maybe our

job isn't so great. Maybe we're unhappy about our sex life. Maybe we're really proud of something our spouse is doing and haven't acknowledged it before. Maybe we really love the neighborhood we're in but have been taking it for granted. As we become aware of some of our feelings, and take solitary time to get to know them, more and more will come forward. Frequently they start to become known in dreams.

Opening up to your feelings can be a period of intense personal growth and awareness. It can also be scary (as all change is). If we've denied a hurt or joy for a long time, and then finally give it a chance to resurface, it may do so with frightening strength. This is where the rational filters need to play their proper role.

This is not to say that we should filter out the feeling. Quite the contrary—we need to *feel our feelings*. But *expressing* them is something else. Saying what we think without filtration is like the five-year-old saying to the lady in the store, "Gee, you're fat!" The rational mind's rightful role is to consider the potential harm or good that expressing our feelings can yield. Often it is not whether or not we express our feelings, but *how* we express them that determines whether exchange with the other person is damaging (unhealthy) or growthful (healthy).

The growth-producing expressions of feelings are timed for reasonable moments. For example, the best time to tell your spouse that you feel your sex life needs some attention is not right after he tells you he's been fired.

Healthy expressions of feelings are also carefully phrased. Statements such as, "Your lovemaking isn't making me happy," are not productive. This is because they are "you" statements, which do not express the feelings, but place blame on another person. The feeling might be, "I am unhappy with how infrequently we have sex. I love you, and I love sharing that love physically with you. I feel hurt and lonely when we don't make love for weeks at a time." Notice how different that is to a blaming statement. The "I" phrases don't accuse the spouse of anything or assign fault. They are merely statements of the situation as felt by one person. Such phrases leave room for further discussion and for suggestions about how things can be improved.

Each one of us suffers, to some extent, from an imbalance between these thinking and feeling sides of ourselves. It is not reasonable to expect that we will be in perfect balance all the time. But if we want to be healthy and give healthy love, we must strive for a better balance. If we tend to be unfiltered in expressing our feelings, we need to filter better. If we tend not to acknowledge our feelings, even to ourselves, we need to learn to feel our own feelings—and then learn to express them.

Whichever way you tend to err, imbalance in your relationship with your adult adolescent will encourage dependency. The adult offspring of an overly rational parent may feel starved for love and create crises, or move home, or ask for help with decisions, just to get attention. The offspring of an unfiltered expresser of emotion will have trouble forming attachments to other people, since she will not have any trust in emotions—they inflict pain. Frequently the overly rational parent produces an overly emotional child, and vice versa. In either case, a healthy adult/adult relationship is unlikely to result.

There is no relationship between whether we tend to be overly rational or overly emotional and which type of parental behavior trap we fall into. There are parents of both types in each trap. All that can be said is that each of us is somewhat out of balance. Determining to which side we slip, being conscious of it, and trying to achieve greater balance will make each of us happier as individuals and improve the way we relate to those we love.

## LETTING GO
Letting go is one of the most challenging growth opportunities any of us ever faces. Its principles defy much of what our culture teaches us. But without it, we cannot be healthy in our relationship with our adult adolescents. Letting go means making ten choices:

1. Letting go is accepting and loving others as they are, not as we would like them to be.
2. Letting go is accepting that we cannot control or change another, that we can only control or change ourselves.
3. Letting go is encouraging others to make their own decisions and to learn from the results.

4.  Letting go is allowing others to feel pain or depression, and to struggle through and grow at their own pace.

5.  Letting go is suspending our judgment so that we can really hear what others say, doing our best to see the world through their eyes.

6.  Letting go is releasing our belief that what *others* say, do, or believe about us as people and parents can define our self-worth; it is not needing approval from others to believe we are valuable.

7.  Letting go is understanding and acknowledging the pains and failures of the past, and then releasing them; it is preferring to live in the only time where we can make a difference—the present.

8.  Letting go is admitting that we are powerless in certain situations, that the outcome is not in our hands.

9.  Letting go is releasing our outdated images of ourselves and others.

10. Letting go is striving to be emotionally healthier every day and fostering emotional health in those we love.

If we choose to live these ten concepts, then we cannot help but be healthier in our relationships with our adult adolescents. We will stop playing parent and thereby stop encouraging the adult adolescents to play child.

If we will learn to redirect our desire to protect into a desire to foster independence, if we overcome our desire to control others while fearing change in ourselves, if we work to balance our rational and emotional sides, and if we progress toward letting go, then we will be happier and infinitely healthier adults. What better role model could we offer our children?

It sounds like too much change to hope for. But one family after another in Dr. Stockman's practice has shown that it is a reasonable goal. The next chapter will examine three families who traveled from severe dysfunction to healthy love, and who continue to grow and develop with each passing month.

# 8

# Three Families Who Are Making It Work

Dr. Stockman has been fortunate enough to witness many happy stories of families who tackle their dysfunction head-on and grow beyond it—families who learn that good emotional health is possible but that it takes effort and a willingness to change. In each case, the effort has reaped invaluable rewards. The parents have grown as healthy individuals and have learned to express their feelings. The adult adolescents have committed themselves to walking the long path to adulthood.

Whether the family was authoritarian, permissive, or overprotective, the key to the success of each was that the parents learned to assert their rights and to respect the rights of their adult adolescents. They also looked at their own patterns—the need to control, the desire to protect, the lack of emotional/rational balance—and chose to change, to let go, and to make being healthy *themselves* their primary goal.

While the pain of long years of dysfunction doesn't go away overnight, it does go away—if we choose to let go of it and encourage it to leave. And the joy and love that replaces it are worth more than any cost the changes might extract.

The following three case histories describe actual families who have accomplished miracles of growth. They all began in a state of anger, depression, and severe unhealth. Today, all three have learned how to halt the downward spiral of adult adolescent problems and how to foster everyone's self-esteem and happiness.

## THE AUTHORITARIAN FAMILY

When Rob and Sharon first came to see Dr. Stockman, they had a daughter, Melissa, who was twenty, and a son, Rick, then twenty-four. Melissa had received poor grades in high school and was, at one point, so severely unhappy that she had attempted suicide. She was subsequently admitted to an inpatient psychiatric facility for nine months. Rick, at nineteen, had dropped out of college and come home to live. He insisted on being waited on by his mother, picked fights with his dad, and began a romantic relationship that closely paralleled his parents' dysfunctional marriage.

In spite of the thousands of dollars Sharon and Rob spent on inpatient care for Melissa, her depression improved only slightly. She dropped out of high school during her senior year. Rick continued living at home, causing daily arguments, and the stress within the family reached such a severe pitch that Rob and Sharon's marriage seemed doomed. Melissa seemed headed for permanent emotional disability, and Rick for an emotional roller coaster ride in his relationship with his girlfriend.

Sharon and Rob came to see Dr. Stockman initially because they wanted him to "fix" the kids. They were both loving, caring people. Within a reasonably short time, they both realized that there would be no easy fix, and that they were part of the problem. They began to understand the roles and behavior traps they had each become accustomed to. They understood that they would have to learn about their own patterns and change them before anything could be expected to change at home.

Looking at their own role models for parenting, Rob and Sharon admitted that they both came from unhappy, nonegalitarian homes. Rob's mother was completely dominated by his father—a military man of high moral standards.

"The earliest remembrance I have of my father," Rob said, "is as a very strict disciplinarian. I remember I wasn't allowed to have friends come over and play with the basketball net over the garage because my dad felt we'd tear the net down. I began to think I wasn't good enough to have friends over. So I began to withdraw. I withdrew into comic books and fiction. The result of that was an evolving hate for my father. I respected him, but at the same time I hated him.

"I figured that he didn't like me or something. So I tried my best to do well in school. And I did well in school, but he always wanted more. So I turned to sports. In sports I did pretty well, and my dad would recognize me in a positive way.

"He went to all my games, and I really appreciated that. But there was still always criticism: 'Why did you hold the ball that way?' or, 'You should have done so-and-so,' instead of, 'Gee, Son, you really played a good game.' And he never shared anything with me on a personal basis. We never sat down and talked about feelings.

"Mom was completely dominated. She was definitely permissive."

"What was the role you learned?" Dr. Stockman asked.

"I was definitely authoritarian."

"What did you do as a parent that confirms that role?"

"I can think of lots of examples, like trying to control everybody's life. When my kids were growing up, I really, looking back on it, expected them to act like adults early on. I deprived them of feeling like children—of being children. I judged them at every turn. I did not encourage. I did quite the opposite. I was very demanding. I felt my son ought to play sports, the way I did. And when that didn't happen, I was very disappointed. I let him see that disappointment. I'm sure it undermined his self-esteem tremendously. For a long time, I went through a lot of guilt about that, and I still have some I'm working through.

"With my daughter, I was always critical of her and her relationships with boys. I let her know it, and I'm sure that hurt her. She and her mother would get into an argument, and I would always come to her mother's defense. I would get very upset with Melissa and make her feel real bad. We'd get into shouting matches. I'd feel a lot of guilt later and apologize, but when your behavior doesn't change, apologies become hollow.

"Once in a while, I'd say to myself, 'Well, I've been mean to the kids, so I'll be nice to them for a while.' And when they didn't change *immediately*, I'd say 'Well, dammit, they're not responding. So something is wrong with *them*.' "

Sharon's parents were the opposite of Rob's. Her father was totally dominated by her mother. Her earliest recollections are of constant fights.

"My mother nagged my father," Sharon said, "mercilessly, relentlessly. She did it to us kids, too. I adored my father— absolutely worshipped him. And it really hurt me to see her do that.

"My mother was definitely authoritarian. My father was permissive. My father felt that he'd made his bed, he had to sleep in it. My mother's thinking was, 'If something is wrong, it's because people aren't doing things my way.' "

"Yet," Dr. Stockman points out, "you married a man who is authoritarian like your mother."

"I think it was a case of needing to take care of some unfinished business. I think I needed to resolve some issues with my mother. That was a lot of what I saw in Rob, although I couldn't see that at the time. All I saw in the beginning was how intelligent he was and that he seemed to be very kind."

"When did you begin to realize that he fit a different role— one that you weren't happy with?"

"That took a long time. Denial permeated my life from the time I was a little girl. My mother taught me denial. I'd say, 'Mother, I'm cold,' and she'd say, 'No, you're not.' Or I'd say, 'Mother, I'm sad,' and she'd tell me I wasn't. So all my life I went around saying, 'Everything's fine.' I thought if I told people how I really felt, they wouldn't like me and wouldn't want to be around me. And all those feelings were too scary anyway, so everything was always 'just wonderful.' Some of those feelings were so scary, I was afraid I'd just lose control. Because I had so much hurt, so much fear, that if I were to admit it, they would all start coming out. And what would I do with them?"

"So," Dr. Stockman commented, "you had feelings as a child

that you couldn't express. Melissa and Rick had feelings as young children, too. As a young mother, were you aware that they had feelings the way you had?"

"Yes. One of the deep resentments I had against my mother was that she never understood me. When I would try to tell her anything, she would deny my feelings. I've tried so hard with my children to understand them that I went too far the other way. I gave them a lot of compassion and understanding, but I didn't give them structure."

"And that threw you onto the side of being permissive and overprotective?"

"That's right. Even though I tried to understand the children, I don't know that I gave them the kind of understanding they needed, although I think I did the best I could at that time. I think the kind of understanding I gave my children was so permissive and so overprotective. I understood them when they were afraid. But instead of helping them talk through their fear, I would do something. I would hear that they were afraid and try to fix it. So my understanding wasn't on target."

"What as a young mother might have helped you?"

"Having had a better role model as a child. Having had a husband who had had a better role model. Recognizing that there was a problem and doing something about it. Some kind of counseling."

As Rob and Sharon came to understand the unhealthy role models they had adopted from their own parents, they could look at their parenting of Melissa and Rick and see where things might have been done better. Rob was the order giver, he was the general. Sharon was the enabler. Too fearful to disagree with Rob, she acquiesced and encouraged the children to do the same.

Sharon recalled one incident with tears: "Rob would get so angry and talk so sarcastically to the children. When Melissa was about three years old, we were getting in the car to go somewhere. And her little legs couldn't step up into the car. And Rob was shouting, 'Come on! Come on! Come on!' His tone was real mean. The underlying message was, "you're stupid, slow, and lazy." And I was so upset, but I didn't say anything."

Rob and Sharon came to see how they worked together to make things worse. The more orders Rob gave, the more Sharon stifled feelings of hurt and resentment. As soon as Rob wasn't around, she would try to "fix things" with the kids. She'd make excuses for his behavior, tell them that he really loved them, and then remove any punishments he had levied. Rob would come home to find things not done and be even angrier than before. So Sharon began doing the kids' chores for them. By not speaking up, and by protecting the kids and letting them get by without meeting their obligations, she contributed to the dysfunction.

The family, however, showed the dysfunction of the authoritarian role model. Everything that everyone did or thought or felt was determined by Rob's mood or Rob's orders. Everyone was reacting to or against Rob. Even in Rick's rebellion, he showed it was his father who was controlling him, because he only picked fights when Dad was around to play parent. Melissa's depression and low self-esteem resulted from not feeling she'd lived up to her dad's expectations. Mom wasn't the problem—anything was good enough for Mom—but Dad was never satisfied.

Eventually Rob and Sharon agreed that they were playing parent in unhealthy ways. Rob let go of his intense need to always be in charge. He let Sharon become an equal partner in decisions that affected them both, and the sole decision maker when things affected only her (like choosing to do Rick's laundry for him). Rob quit trying to control Sharon, and she no longer had Rob to blame for the decisions that were made.

Together with Dr. Stockman, they decided that things at home were going to change radically. Rick was given a deadline for moving out. Before that deadline, he'd have to live by some new rules if he was going to stay with Rob and Sharon. These included doing his own laundry, doing a set list of household and yard chores, paying his own phone bill and car expenses, and letting his parents know by 10 P.M. if he wasn't coming home that night.

As is usually the case, Rick rebelled. He declared that they didn't love him, that they were just trying to control him, that none of his friends' parents were so unfeeling, that life was tougher than when Rob and Sharon were growing up, and, of course, the "I know you can afford it" argument. There were slammed doors and a lot of arguing for a few days. But when Rick figured out that his parents weren't going to back down and that his mother—usually his guaranteed rescuer—was an equal participant in this decision, he finally resigned himself to the new roles his parents were playing.

In return for him abiding by their rules, Rob and Sharon agreed *not* to tell him what to wear or say anything negative about his friends. They agreed that he could stay anywhere he wanted overnight, as long as they were told by 10 P.M. that he wasn't coming home. By backing off from participating in (or meddling in) his decisions, they gave him back total responsibility for his choices.

They made all these changes while repeatedly telling Rick that they loved him and they wanted to help him get on with his life. To Rob and Sharon's surprise, after the initial rough few days, things improved dramatically. Rick seemed to adjust to the new rules, while keeping a sharp eye on his parents for any weakening. When there was none, he got on with the business of finding an apartment. A week before his deadline was up, he moved out. Since then he has held the same job, paid all his bills, and blossomed in self-esteem. In fact, his self-esteem has grown so much that he broke off his codependent relationship with his girlfriend. The reason he gave was, "She's too dependent on her parents."

Melissa has also blossomed, although it was a tougher road for her than for her brother. She began to withdraw less and to believe in her father's love for her. Rob concentrated on building up her trust.

"I've learned," he said, "that these things don't happen overnight. You've gotta build an emotional bank account, and that doesn't happen quickly. You need to build a trust relationship. And I was starting with an empty account.

"Melissa is still very dependent on us, but it's much better than it used to be. She's gotten her high school equivalency degree and is holding a part-time job. She feels better about herself. We both listen to one another more than we used to. Now and then I'll regress a bit, or she'll regress a bit. But I tell you, it's such a good feeling when she says, 'Dad, what do you think about so-and-so?' The fact that she wants my opinion on something makes me feel so good. It makes me feel like I've made a little progress.

"Sometimes she starts telling me about everything she's worried about. And I have this inclination to say, 'I told you so.' But I don't. She's still scared about going for some sort of technical training. I think that's why she works part-time at night—so she doesn't have to deal with too many people. But she's been accepted to a trade school this fall, and she's starting to get excited about it. She's even figured out how many hours she'll have to work part-time to have enough spending money. I can't tell you how proud that makes me."

Sharon agreed. She acknowledged that she still had a tendency to overprotect Melissa. And she knew that once Melissa completed her six months of training, she would need to work with Rob to set a deadline for Melissa to move out on her own.

"The most important thing you ever said," she said to Dr. Stockman, "is, 'If Rick doesn't move out, how will he ever believe in himself?' Well, we've seen the answer with him. He's on his own, and he's growing up so fast. In fact, I told him I'm so proud of him that I hope I can be like him some day. That's what I want for Melissa, too. She's had such a tough time, it's harder for me to nudge her out. But I know how important it is, and I know now that it's the most loving thing we can do."

Rob became philosophical about parenting. His advice to all parents: "The first thing is be a good listener. Be willing to step back and try to watch what's going on in the family. And don't get caught up in every single little thing. Don't be too quick to try to judge and rush in and take control of the situation. Step back, and make an objective assessment if you possibly can. And then get the family together and talk about your observations, and ask others if they're accurate. And maybe you can have a better understanding of where people are coming from. I certainly didn't do that before. I wanted to control everybody.

"Also, be willing to change. Change is awfully difficult. By talking to people in 'I' messages instead of 'you' messages, you can be much more effective. Acknowledging the feelings of other people is critical. Listen to other people.

"And most importantly, catch people doing things well. Don't always look for the errors. Encourage good behavior. Compliment it. Tell people all the things you love about them."

Rob and Sharon's marriage had become healthy for the first time. They gained new respect for each other. They also became happier as individuals than ever before. And their two adult adolescents were growing toward adulthood so quickly that Sharon and Rob's efforts were being abundantly rewarded. Rob learned what being an egalitarian parent means, and he continued working to eliminate his authoritarian behavior. Sharon continued learning to stop withdrawing and denying her feelings. She started participating in decision making, and refusing to enable Rob when he slipped into an authoritarian mode.

Both say it was a tough few years, but not nearly as painful as doing nothing would have been. "Even for a die-hard authoritarian like me," Rob said, "there's hope."

## THE PERMISSIVE PARENT
Paul and Edith were raised in a small town within a strict fundamentalist church community. Edith felt strongly affected by her upbringing; she truly believed that she was destined to go to hell. When she had begun dating Paul, and they began to "pet," she was sure the only hope for her soul was to get married. So they married, in spite of being essentially incompatible, and had three children: Philip, Barbara, and Keith.

When Keith was only a few months old, the marriage had deteriorated to the point where Edith moved to a small cottage her parents owned and eventually filed for divorce. Edith struggled to make ends meet, working full-time and raising three young children. Finally she realized that she needed further education if she was ever going to increase her income. She and Paul agreed that the older children would attend the same religious boarding school that Paul had attended and that Paul would keep Keith for a few years. So Keith, at age eleven, moved in with his father and stepmother.

All went reasonably well until Keith's junior year of high school. He had been maintaining an A average at a school that the family acknowledged was substandard. Keith described the classes there as "almost remedial, they were so easy." With an IQ over 150, he could get As with almost no effort. But for some reason, during his junior year he rebelled. His average fell to a C.

Paul had been the "in charge" parent at the time. And while Edith was clearly authoritarian, Paul described himself as permissive.

"I have a very hard time opposing people," Paul said, "I hate conflict. I'll move away from it."

Paul admitted that he never disciplined Keith unless Edith or his second wife, Karen, forced him to. While the older two children completed boarding school with near-straight As and went on to do exceptionally well in college and in their professional lives, Keith just seemed to stall out.

He also developed several patterns typical of underachievers. First, he avoided conflict whenever possible. One of the means he used to do this was denial. Keith denied that anything was ever wrong—with his parents, with the school, or with himself. The second, closely related to denial, was escapism. Keith escaped into fantasies of somehow getting beyond all his problems by some stroke of fate.

Later, at the age of twenty-one, he recalled his high school attitude: "Mom would ask me what I wanted to be when I grew up, and I would say, 'I want to be a millionaire.' How? I guess I figured I'd inherit it or something. I don't know. Of course I'm not going to inherit it, because neither of my parents have millions."

Keith then began to describe his current attitudes. The fantasy element was still present in his life, although he was conscious of it and working to overcome it. "Somehow, I think I'll find the perfect job for me. And I'd like to be able to find it easily. That's one of my problems, I want everything to come easily, because there was a time when it did. School was easy. Life was easy for a while. And I was enjoying myself terribly. And then all of a sudden it got difficult."

Keith began going through the second and third stages of

healthy development—the beginnings of separation from the parents—while he was under Paul's care. Since the only structure in his life had been placed upon him by Edith, his stepmother, or the school, he kept ignoring authority. The primary role model and parent in his life was teaching him to avoid conflict and was letting him off the hook for his misbehaviors. Keith developed a feeling that he was entitled to being let off the hook, that rules weren't for him. The result was a hostile attitude toward those who tried to tell him differently.

When Keith graduated high school, he moved back in with his mother. The angry feelings in high school didn't go away, because they were denied. They stayed inside and built up. Keith was a volcano with a locked lid. He used fantasies and denial to keep that lid locked. He also used another method of escape. Keith turned into a "couch potato," sleeping long hours and watching television endlessly.

"It all comes down to being lazy," Keith said later. "I allowed myself to get hooked into stupid television shows that weren't very entertaining. But I'd start to watch them, and I didn't stop—just because I didn't feel like changing the channel. Or if I didn't watch the television, I'd have to do something else. And I didn't want to do anything else. It was my escape."

Edith, being an early riser and a self-confessed workaholic, was furious. Her authoritarianism came to the fore and fight after fight resulted as she told Keith how lazy and sloppy he was.

Frustrated and wanting Keith to get on with his life, Edith came to see Dr. Stockman. Together with Paul, they worked out a plan to wean Keith from his dependency and encourage him to acknowledge his feelings. Edith recognized her authoritarian behaviors and agreed to let go of her need to control. She confronted Keith with her feelings: "I am hurt and sad that you forgot to pick up some bread on your way home." But she stopped telling Keith what he should do to fix the error ("Go back to the store right now, young man, and get that bread").

Paul, for his part, agreed to set rules and stick by them. He and Edith agreed that Keith could continue to live with her as long as he paid part of the electric and phone bills, earned all his own spending money, and continued going to college. Paul would give Keith money toward his school and personal expenses in direct relationship to his grades. Since Keith's outstanding intellectual skills were well documented, there was no doubt that he could maintain a grade point average of 3.0 at the local university if he chose to. Paul set up a sliding scale where he paid Keith nothing for a 2.0 and progressively more money as Keith's grade point average rose.

For Edith, letting go of her need to control was critical. With Keith so strongly affected by Paul's permissive parenting, it was natural for her to want to compensate for it and try to structure Keith's life. She also had to release her anger with Paul—whom she had blamed for Keith's failure to live up to her expectations of him.

Working part-time and going to college, Keith still tended to feel mistreated. His parents, who were refusing to give him the financial assistance he felt he deserved, "expected too much." His employer, who had a lot of rules about behavior, was "too rigid." Keith clearly expressed his anger through such criticism. Yet when asked if he was angry with his parents, he would say no.

Paul struggled with the need to deal with Keith's hostile phone calls. An adult adolescent doesn't usually accept a change in the rules of his parent/child game quietly. Paul wrote Keith a long letter outlining his sliding-scale payment plan and his thinking behind it. He also was sure to express his feelings in the letter—telling Keith he loved him and believed in his ability to succeed in school and in life. But he was firm in his rationale for setting limits.

"I told Keith that a 3.0 average was certainly within his capabilities and that I didn't want to pay for anything less than that. Keith was pretty upset. He said, 'With all the pressure I'm under, you're just applying more.' I tried to encourage him. He seemed pretty interested in the job he was doing. I told him not to close the door on a future with that company. I've known lots of people who worked for them, and they pay well and have good benefits. I suggested that he stick with them through his college years and keep the door open. If he did well in college, then he might have a good future with them.

"His reaction was to accuse his sister of putting me up to this, because he just couldn't believe it was me. But I explained that there's nothing really easy about life. There's no difference between going to university and life after. I said that I felt that his mother and I were not doing him justice by subsidizing mediocrity.

"The frustrating part for me is that we went through this whole thing with him in high school. Of course, now we have some firm rules that we're going to play by. And he knows the rules are firm.

"I think where we went wrong with Keith is that he was spoiled all his life. I think he got to the point where he knew he could get what he wanted—especially from me—without putting any effort into it. He's going to have to face life. And he's not going to face it unless we make him face it, by not supporting his mediocrity."

For Paul, this was a difficult new role to assume. Keith had some harsh things to say to Paul—in spite of Keith's normal aversion to conflict. The lid was beginning to open on the volcano. And because Edith limited her rule setting to Keith's specified obligations and didn't get drawn into any "Dad is so mean to me" discussions, Keith started expressing his anger with her more—although he was a long way from really acknowledging everything he felt. It was easier to conflict with his father over the telephone or through the mail than it was to conflict with his mother face to face.

While it was a trying period for everyone, Keith made a critical breakthrough. He came to terms with the inevitability of growing up and assuming responsibility for his own life. While he still needed to grow and learn about his feelings, and how to express them, the biggest hurdle in his life was crumbling—the fantasy that somehow, some way, he could be taken care of forever.

His tendency toward denial would continue to be a challenge for Keith. To acknowledge his anger would mean dealing with conflict—and that was something Keith had learned to fear.

Keith became aware of his fear of conflict: "I get upset, but I avoid confrontation, because I don't like confrontation. I really don't. I avoid it in most situations. Or if I'm angry at somebody, I add a little bit of humor or a joking smile to it and say, 'I'm really pissed off at you,' and I get my point across."

Keith decided that he needed to get out of his mother's home. There was some healthy defiance in his determination to move out—an "I'll show them I really can make it on my own" attitude. There was also a sincere desire to grow up and be more responsible for himself. Keith found a roommate, worked out a budget, and obtained a loan from the local college to finance his academic expenses. He threw himself with more enthusiasm and commitment than ever before into his current semester of schoolwork and into his part-time job. Although he felt angry with the sliding-scale payment system, he came to accept it.

Keith calculated how many hours a week he needed to work to supplement the income he expected to earn from Paul by accomplishing his 3.0. He began looking for an apartment to lease at the beginning of the next semester.

It may seem like a small step to someone outside the family, but to Paul and Edith, it was an occasion worth celebrating. Keith had begun taking his first strong steps in the direction of controlling his own life. Edith had released her desire to control it for him. And Paul had found the strength to stop encouraging Keith's dependency. While there would be more hurdles to overcome, the first and toughest was behind them.

## THE OVERPROTECTIVE FAMILY

Overprotective parents are usually the most difficult to describe. The Atwell family was no exception. Victor Atwell had been raised by a severely authoritarian mother and a permissive, submissive father. His mother ruled the home in all respects, and Victor resented that deeply. He adored his father and held him as a role model. Yet Victor couldn't separate himself from the rigid childhood he'd known. For every question there was a "right" answer. And in parenting, there was supposed to be, he believed, a "right" way to guide the kids. So while Victor was determined not to be a dictator like his mom, and not to be submissive like his dad, he ended up absorbing some of both their traits.

For Victor, there were certain things that parents and kids did and didn't do. One belief he held was that the women take care of the women, and the men take care of the men. For that reason, he left his wife Natalie in charge of their daughter, Pam. Natalie took Pam to her extracurricular activities, taught her how to cook, showed her how to run a home. Victor took charge of their son, Neal. He enrolled Neal in the Boy Scouts and went camping with Neal's troop.

Victor felt this was quality time spent with Neal. Neal saw it differently. "We never truly did anything together," Neal said later. "Oh, we went camping together. But that was Dad's decision. It was like it was his hobby or something. I didn't mind it, but it wasn't really time we spent together."

With all the expectations Victor held up for himself, his wife, and his two children, he was at a loss as to how to enforce them. He didn't want to be a dictator, and he didn't want to give up control. So he tried to control from within. This was the overprotectiveness in him. He'd lay down some rules, but as the kids grew older, he more and more tried to persuade them to do things his way. Victor was a persistent person, and when he knew how his son or daughter "should" do something, it was impossible to change his mind. The result was that both kids learned only two responses: do it the way Dad wants, or go to Mom.

Natalie was overprotective in a different way. Although raised in a fairly egalitarian home, Natalie showed a high need to control her children and her husband. Since Victor was determined *not* to be controlled and not to give any appearance of being controlled, Natalie was challenged to be very subtle. As their marriage progressed through the years, it was finally Natalie who truly ruled the home.

Neal described her technique: "Mom was controlling without letting anybody know she was controlling anybody. Since Mom's death, you can tell how she had everything under her own control. Dad is running around all the time, trying to figure out what to do."

Natalie was overprotective with Victor in that she "managed" his decision making from the inside out, just as he was trying to manage the kids' decision making. But she was overprotective with her children as well.

Part of her overprotectiveness with her children stemmed from a severe illness early in Neal's childhood. The sickness left him mildly disabled for years, and Natalie blamed herself for not taking him to the hospital sooner. She vowed to be more careful with Neal, and with his younger sister. She became determined to spare them both any pain.

This is another trait of an overprotective parent, being motivated by guilt. Believing she knew what was best, combined with the heavy burden of believing herself responsible for the outcome of everything affecting her children, Natalie never disengaged herself from her children's decision making, even when Neal was in his late twenties and Pam was twenty-three.

Two years before her death, Natalie and Victor had begun counseling with Dr. Stockman. The event that triggered their seeking help involved Neal.

Years earlier, Neal had graduated high school and received an acceptable score on the SAT college entrance exam. He had been accepted to a local public college and was intending to attend. Victor then stepped into the decision-making process, a step he later acknowledged was a mistake.

"He tested well enough," Victor said, "that I figured he could get into a better school. And he did. But that was a mistake. I encouraged him to go, and he went. We should have pulled him out after one semester, but I kept pushing him. He stayed three semesters and was miserable. He flunked out, and we enrolled him in a technical school. He graduated from a six-month training program we selected for him. But when he got a job in that field, he found out he didn't really like it.

"So I got him an interview with my company, and encouraged him to talk to them. They offered him a job. I talked him into taking it. He's doing OK there, but I know now that we shouldn't have made so many decisions for the kids."

At twenty-six, Neal was married, had a three-year-old child, and was working for his father's firm. He made a good salary but never seemed to be able to save anything. Victor explained the problems as follows: "Neal's the kind, the first thing he sees, he wants to buy. He would never be able to have any money. He can't control money. Neal will never have any savings. He can't keep money in his pocket."

One of Victor's expectations about sons was that you quit giving them money at a certain age. His overprotectiveness with Neal primarily involved interfering with his decisions. Natalie felt no such limitation. Things came to a head when Neal and his wife decided to buy a home. They had a lease on an apartment, which they could not get out of, when they found the house they wanted. They also had no savings to use for a down payment and insufficient credit history to get a mortgage. Neal knew where to go. He went to his mother.

"Neal initiated that through his mother," explained Victor. "He wanted the house, and his mother said, 'Oh, we really ought to help him.' She wore me down. I really believe she would have divorced me if I hadn't agreed. So we cosigned for the house. Then the tenants they subleased the apartment to moved out, and they couldn't make their payments on both commitments. So they moved back into the apartment and quit meeting the mortgage payments. Then the mortgage company came to us and asked us to make the payments."

At about the same time, Neal's wife miscarried a child and Neal quit going to work, without calling in to tell his supervisor where he was. Since Victor worked for the same company, the supervisor called him to see if he knew where Neal was. Victor found Neal at home, in a deep depression, refusing to answer the phone.

It was at this point that the Atwells came to Dr. Stockman. They finally acknowledged that they had both been too involved in their children's lives. (Pam had developed similar problems with financial dependency and poor decision making.) They decided that it was up to them to start pulling back.

This was more difficult for Natalie than for Victor, because her guilt motivations were so strong. She was beginning to make progress shortly before she discovered she was terminally ill. With Natalie's illness, Victor became an equal partner again in their marriage. He began negotiations with the mortgage company and began trying to sell the house. Due to severe overbuilding in the development Neal had chosen, however, a used home was hard to sell. Brand new ones right down the street offered builder financing. So the problem dragged on, and Natalie passed away.

Victor adopted a new expectation of himself regarding his children: stop interfering. He wanted to be an egalitarian parent and attacked his goal methodically. He found a way to extricate himself from Neal's financial situation: "We're either going to negotiate a settlement with the mortgage company, or Neal and his wife are going to file for bankruptcy. For three years they'll have to turn their disposable income over to the bankruptcy court. And this will get me out of it. It's gonna cost them some money and me some money—but not near what it would have cost me otherwise."

Victor also withdrew financial support from Pam, who had spent seven years in several different colleges and degree programs without ever attaining a degree. She, like her brother, rebelled at being weaned. But both began to learn about making decisions and living with the consequences of their choices.

Pam made the most immediate progress. She took a full-time job with the university she planned to graduate from, which provided her with a free-tuition benefit. She planned to complete a bachelor's degree part-time in the next one to two years, while completely supporting herself financially.

Neal was still stinging from the possibility of facing bankruptcy. Unlike Pam, who was quite quick to communicate her anger with Victor, Neal tended just to get depressed. But he was coping. He had not missed any more time at work, and he was trying not to dwell on his problems with the house. Neal was also learning to survive without Natalie to intercede for him.

Pam described it this way: "Mom was our communication link with Dad, especially for Neal. That's why he suffered so when she died. She was the go-between—between my father and Neal, and between my father and me. If you wanted something, you would ask Mom. Then she would pick the time to talk to Dad. So she was very important—more so for Neal. I was more the rebel."

Natalie's death was an involuntary weaning for the children.

Although Neal was twenty-nine and Pam was twenty-five at the time, they were still comfortable with being protected by her. With her gone, and with Victor's desire to help them become independent, many things changed in all their lives . . . for the better.

Victor began trying to give the children his feelings, not his money. He tried to encourage and love them, and to give them his time. He also gave them back their decisions to make for themselves. And while Neal had a tough three years ahead if the outcome of the mortgage problem was bankruptcy, he would be free of ties when it was over.

## YOU CAN MAKE IT, TOO!

These three families all began with severe manifestations of adult adolescent behavior. In addition, the parents in each case played strongly dysfunctional roles. Yet all three families showed remarkable healing. Each made a commitment to health and began to achieve it.

Chances are that your own adult adolescent is not as severely dysfunctional as some of those portrayed here. But even if he is, there is no cause for despair. While you cannot force your child to be healthy, you can choose health for yourself. And being healthy yourself can be the most important influence in starting your adult adolescent down the path toward growth.

But choosing to be a healthy parent isn't an instant switch. We can't snap our fingers and become egalitarian parents (unfortunately!). We have to unlearn our bad habits and learn some good ones. The next chapter shows you how to be more egalitarian. To break out of unhealthy patterns we usually need some support. Chapter 11 will help you set up support systems that will encourage you to continue your growth.

# 9

# The Egalitarian Parent

We have discussed at length the three behavior traps most parents fall into, but we have only briefly described the "ideal" parent that we might aspire to be. While none of us can be an ideal parent all the time, it is helpful to clearly understand the kind of parent we want to be *most* of the time.

The term *egalitarian* refers to a person who believes in human equality. An egalitarian parent, therefore, believes that the child has equal value to the parent. This means that the feelings and needs of a son or daughter deserve as much respect as the feelings and needs of a mom or dad. While the egalitarian parent may control access to the family car, or to his own money or property, he exercises authority with reasonableness and sensitivity. With respect to all things emotional, the egalitarian parent believes in total equality with his child.

What does all this mean in day-to-day living, particularly with respect to an adult adolescent? In addition to respecting and enforcing the rights of parents *and* the rights of young adults, we can think of egalitarian parenting as having five key

154

elements: reasonableness, dependability, honesty, communication, and love. These five elements interrelate, building upon
one another. But, beyond any doubt, the most important is love.

We'll take a look at these five elements first. Then we will
examine a situation of egalitarian parenting in action.

## REASONABLENESS

Chapter 7 mentioned the importance of balancing the rational
and emotional sides of our personalities. If either side dominates,
our behavior will be out of balance, or unhealthy.

Egalitarian parenting requires that we give appropriate
weight, depending on the situation, to the logical and the
emotional sides of an issue. If we are called upon to make a
decision, we need to consult both sides of ourselves: what the
analytical/rational side of us would do, and what the emo-
tional/intuitive side would do. Some people refer to this as
exercising good judgment.

We need to be rational to the extent that our decisions need to
generally make sense. While our children don't have to agree
with us, our decisions must, as much as possible, have an
understandably logical basis. Yet sometimes we can't articulate
our reasons for believing a certain answer is appropriate—we
just *feel* that it is. These may be times when our intuition is
insisting on a response that may not be easy to explain.

There is nothing wrong with giving our intuition control
sometimes, even if it flies in the face of logic. What reasonableness requires is that we be willing to explain our decisions,
whether they are logical or not. Obviously, it's easier to explain a
logical choice—you lay out the thought process in the rational
steps you followed, and anyone can understand what you did
(whether or not the other person agrees). If our decision is
intuitive, we don't need to be embarrassed by that. We just need
to be forthright about it: "I can't really explain why, Mary, I just
feel deep down inside me that this is the right thing to do. I'm
sorry I can't explain it further. That might be frustrating for you.
But I love you very much, and my instincts tell me to do this."

We need to be careful not to abuse the trust of others by
always saying, "I can't explain it. . . ." Where we can explain

ourselves, we should do so. That will make it easier for our adult adolescents to trust us when we make a decision based solely on intuition.

Of course, explaining doesn't mean that you answer every request with a twenty-minute discussion of how you choose to say yes or no. But it is a good idea to let your thought process show, and sometimes in great detail. This is a teaching opportunity, as well as a demonstration of the pains you go to to make the best choice you know how to make. Both the effort of teaching and the effort of struggling with decisions tell the adult adolescent that you value him, that you believe his feelings to be as important as your own.

Reasonableness involves compromise. The beginning of compromise occurs when we pay attention to the feelings of everyone affected by a decision we are trying to make. Rather than making a decision in isolation, we can seek information from the affected people: "How do you feel about this, Johnny?" "Tell me what you would do if you were in my shoes." "How will you feel if I say yes/no?"

When we value someone else's feelings as being as important as our own, we can't help but want to compromise. Compromise is not always possible, but it is possible more often than we realize. For example, Johnny's car has broken down, and he wants to use his mom's to go out on a date Saturday. On the surface there appear to be only two options: yes or no. Where is the compromise? It lies in expanding the options. Mom might say, "I need the car Saturday, but perhaps you and your date can go out on Friday instead," or, " I need the car until 8 P.M.; can you two go out after that?" or, "My car is tied up, but perhaps your sister will loan you hers—why don't you call and find out?"

It's a rare situation where no compromise can be created or where options cannot be expanded. There's a real joy to learning how to come up with a long list of options. It gives everyone a sense of having more control over a situation—of having more choices. And the more choices that are created, the greater the likelihood of finding one that is mutually acceptable. Expanding the options is how we can all find a way to solve problems.

It's like the saying, "Don't tell me why you can't do it, tell me how it might be done." It's looking until a positive solution is found.

Reasonableness in decisions also requires that we give our decisions time. It's hard to make good decisions in a rush.

Reasonableness also requires that we be willing to work at making our choices. Working at making decisions is essential for two reasons. First, it shows that we are taking care to think through things that affect our offspring. The fact that we are willing to wrestle with a decision and base it on the best reasoning we are capable of shows that we care—that we understand there is an impact on someone we love. It shows that we want to do the best we can where our child is concerned.

Second, reasonable decision making is important because it teaches good decision making. Adult adolescents are usually poor decision makers. If they can observe us wrestling through the process and arriving at a reasonable, explainable decision, then they will have a good role model. This requires that our reasoning process not be hidden. We need to not only make reasonable choices, but also to *explain* them as best we can.

Good decision making is a learned skill. Most of us had very poor training in that area. As parents of adult adolescents, we especially need to learn to practice what we expect our adult adolescents to do: make good decisions. If you feel a need to improve the process of your own decision making and your ability to make decisions as a team (with your spouse), you could try reading some of the books we recommend in the Bibliography. Or you might enroll in a course in logic, debate, leadership, or management skills at your local college. These skills are like any other; they can be learned.

The important thing is that we try to show our adult adolescents that we are making rational, reasonable decisions. Decisions that contain as one element a consideration of the feelings (emotions) of everyone involved. Decisions that value each person involved as an equal and as an adult.

When we make choices in this way, even if our adult adolescents disagree with us, they will feel we were not arbitrary. And, more important, they will see that we cared enough to struggle through the decision rather than give a flip response. They will know, deep inside, that we value them.

## DEPENDABILITY

Dependability means several things. It means being consistent—reacting in basically the same way to similar situations. It also means being reliable or trustworthy. We believe that dependable people will not deliberately hurt us and that they will be there for us when we truly need their support.

Being reasonable is the first step in egalitarian parenting. The second step is keeping it up. If we oscillate between being reasonable and being unreasonable, the adult adolescent will be confused. Since treating him reasonably is one way to show that we care, if we are inconsistent he will be unsure of how much we value him. Given human nature, he will tend to assume he is not valued. He may also assume that making split-second or inconsistent decisions is OK and model himself accordingly.

We all tend to feel insecure. As infants, we gained confidence that our needs would be met only by having them consistently met. Little changes when we grow up. We want to be able to trust and rely on the support of our spouse. While our tolerance for other people's off moments or periods of inconsistency enlarges as we understand the world better, we still expect that the great majority of the time the people we love will exhibit predictable, supportive behavior. We desire this dependability because we want a sense of security, of reliability. We want to be able to count on our spouse or other close family and friends to be there for us when we really need them.

Our adult adolescents expect the same. While they may not agree with our value system or our determination to encourage their independence, the very fact of our dependability is a form of security to them. If we change from being authoritarian or overprotective or permissive to being egalitarian, we may appear to be inconsistent by their view of things. We should explain, "Look, I've decided that I can improve on myself. I've changed my philosophy about a few things. I may slip up occasionally, but I'm going to try from now on to treat you like an adult."

This acknowledges that we know we're not being consistent with the past, but that we are going to be consistent from here on, as best we can, with our new philosophy. Then we need to do it. And when we slip into an old behavior pattern, we need to apologize for the inconsistency: "I'm sorry I yelled at you, I know better. You're too old for me to be telling you what to do. I apologize."

Thus, dependability doesn't mean *never* making a mistake. It means consistently doing our best to adhere to our philosophy of egalitarian parenting, and apologizing when we don't live up to our own goal. This requires some humility. But there is no better way to convince an adult adolescent that we value him as an equal than to consider him worthy of receiving an apology. He may not be gracious in how he receives it. (We'll address his reactions specifically in Chapter 10.)

The important thing is not what he says, but what *we* say and do. If we are consistently and believably doing our best to be egalitarian, he'll learn to rely on our reactions. We'll be dependable, even if he doesn't always like what we have to say. Eventually, if we are consistent, our adult adolescents will get comfortable with our new egalitarian role. Most likely, they'll decide it's a good deal.

## HONESTY

Being reasonable and being consistent are the first two elements of egalitarian parenting. The third is essential if any of the other elements is to have meaning: being honest. We can list a lot of reasons for doing or not doing something, but if they are going to mean anything, they must be our true reasons.

If Johnny calls and asks his parents for a loan or for a favor they feel is inappropriate because of his recent and lengthy history of adult adolescent behavior, they may feel that giving him what he wants will just set up another round of fighting. Since he has not lived up to his earlier promises to repay loans or meet other commitments, he has shown himself untrustworthy. His parents don't want to enable his behavior, but they may have a hard time articulating any logical reason for not giving him the money he wants.

Mom or Dad might respond as follows: "Johnny, I love you and I care about the improvements in our relationship; I think we're making good progress in overcoming some of the problems we've had the last few years. But I believe we need to keep taking it slowly. I don't believe that giving you this money would be a good idea. Recently, we've ended up in a fight every time I've loaned you money. Maybe in a year or two, you and I will be at a different point. But right now I'm afraid I won't be helping you grow, and we'll most likely end up angry with each other again. Let's just take things one step at a time. Why don't you come over, and we'll try to figure out another way to handle this problem."

The advantage of this honest communication of feelings is that, while Johnny may be disappointed or hurt, he will understand where his parent stands. If Mom or Dad had given false reasons for not wanting to loan the money, like, "We can't afford it," or, "My money's tied up right now," the parent would have left himself open to being caught telling a lie. If Johnny had challenged them by saying "You've got enough money to take a vacation," they would have had to either get into an argument over whether their vacation plans were more important than Johnny's needs (an impossible argument to win) or backpedal and give another, also false, reason for not giving the money. Johnny may have then tried to overcome that problem, only to be given yet another excuse. Or the parents, feeling guilty for being caught in their own lies, might have given in. They would then have been angry at themselves and at Johnny.

"Reasonableness" without honesty is not reasonable at all. It only leads to misunderstandings, hurt feelings, manipulation, and low self-image on the part of at least one of the players. It is certainly not egalitarian parenting. When feelings, even if they're unpleasant, are communicated honestly and with diplomacy, there can be understanding. Without honesty, real understanding between equals can *never* occur. Every person will play guessing games, trying to figure out what the other "really means." Thus, any apparent reasonableness becomes meaningless, because it is a lie.

Dependability, like reasonableness, can be rendered useless without honesty. What security is there in knowing a parent will consistently lie or withhold the whole truth? "Dependability" in the sense of predictability may be present. But dependability in the sense of being worthy of *trust* requires consistent honesty.

Thus, the first three elements of egalitarian parenting are interdependent. For any of the three to be meaningful, all three must be present. For the first three to be appreciated, a fourth element is necessary: communication.

## COMMUNICATION

The point where most human relations fall apart is in the communicating. There may be love, reasonableness, honesty, and dependability, but if the parent can't demonstrate those qualities through two-way communication with the adult adolescent, the value of these traits is greatly diminished or even lost.

The most obvious area of communication is verbal. If we make good reasonable decisions but don't explain them, they lose their impact. If we love someone and try to show that love, but never say "I love you," we've lost an important vehicle for expression. So, along with being reasonable, dependable, honest, and loving, we need to communicate—verbally and nonverbally.

What we say to each other often carries less weight than what we do, because our nonverbal messages can conflict with our verbal messages. Have you ever heard someone say, "I'm fine" with a snarl on his face? What do you believe? The verbal "I'm fine," or the nonverbal snarl? Most people would believe the snarl.

What you do—things like smiling, laughing, hugging, and touching—is a crucial communicator. Listening with an open body posture, eyes focused on the speaker, and hands still shows that you are really paying attention—valuing the words being spoken (and thereby valuing the speaker). Actions such as being willing to compromise on an issue you disagree on also communicate love and value to the other person.

To be effective, communication must make use of both verbal and nonverbal messages, and it must be two-way. Good speaking must be accompanied by good listening.

Communication also needs to be given priority, and that

means giving it time. It means one other thing—a willingness to be open and vulnerable. Sharing true feelings can be tough. But we can't expect our adult adolescents to bare their souls if we never return the favor. Sharing our deepest being shows we trust the other person to use that information carefully. Few things make any of us feel more valued than having someone really listen to our verbal and nonverbal messages and at the same time trust us enough to share part of their innermost selves. In these ways, good communicating is really the beginning point of love.

## LOVE

Volumes have been written about the mysteries of and misconceptions about love. While we cannot hope to unravel all its facets in this book, we can say a few words about what love is and is not.* Love is *not* infatuation or dependency. It is *not* "sacrificing yourself" for another. It is *not* a glowing, tingling feeling. It *is* a deep appreciation for the beauty of another human being. It *is* a desire to see that other person be healthy and to grow. It *is* a desire to be neither a crutch nor an obstacle to that person.

Love is hard work. It requires doing what is best for another person's growth and emotional health, to the extent that it doesn't stunt our own growth and health. Doing what is best for another requires putting ourselves in his shoes. And that's where the work comes in. Actively choosing to leave our prejudice and perspectives behind so that we can place ourselves in the situation of another goes against our normal tendencies. But truly loving another demands that we do this.

Love is risky. For us to succeed at seeing the world from another's perspective, we must be willing to accept that our own view may not be the right one, or even the only one. We must be humble enough, and flexible enough, to be willing to reform our own views. Putting ourselves in another's situation will frequently endanger our preconceptions about the world or about

---

*One of the best explanations of love is contained in Section II of *The Road Less Traveled* by M. Scott Peck (New York: Simon & Schuster, 1978).

that person. Love requires that we be willing to take the risk that we might need to change.

Love is a commitment. It's not always fun to love someone. Sometimes, especially with an adult adolescent, it can be agonizingly difficult. We may have to allow an adult adolescent to suffer some of the consequences of his own behavior and to put up with his wrath for failing to rescue him. Watching him suffer and dealing with his fury can be very painful. But because we truly want to see him grow, and we know that any other behavior on our part would be enabling his dependency and unhealth, we must have the strength to stick with our love. This is our commitment to him, to hang in there even when there's an easier way out.

And finally, love is joy. It is the joy that comes from taking the pain and the fun in stride and knowing that, to the greatest extent we can, we are encouraging growth in another person— that we are valuing him and trying to communicate our love. It is the joy of seeing the beauty in his soul, even when he says, "I hate you." It is the joy of giving. And, sometimes, our love is returned in kind.

Love is what makes the "parenting" in egalitarian parenting have any impact. Being reasonable, dependable, and honest, and being a good communicator, carries little weight without love. But with love, the results can be miraculous.

## EGALITARIAN PARENTING IN ACTION
It's one thing to talk about egalitarian parenting philosophically. But how do you deal with real situations with an adult adolescent? Following is one scenario, along with some possible egalitarian responses.

This is a conversation between an egalitarian mother and her daughter, Kim. Kim is twenty-four and living in an apartment on the other side of town with her roommate, Sarah. Kim has a history of adult adolescent behavior.

KIM:   [talking very fast] Mom, Sarah wants to throw me a party to celebrate my promotion! But our apartment is too small, and she can't afford to rent a place. She doesn't have any family nearby, so she wanted to know if you and Dad would let us use your place.

MOM: [*not being rushed*] That's very sweet of Sarah to want to throw you a party. I don't blame her for being proud of you. Your dad and I are proud, too. That's a big accomplishment, getting promoted after only one year with the company.

KIM: Thanks, Mom, I still can't believe it! [*A pause, as Kim is still waiting for an answer to her question, but is enjoying the praise and is no longer rushing along like a runaway freight train*]

MOM: Well, I can, and I'm very proud. [*slight pause*] Now, I'll need some more information, and some time to think about things and talk it over with your father. When does Sarah want to have this party?

KIM: Two weeks from tomorrow. That will give us time to invite everyone.

MOM: [*still gathering the facts*] And how many people do you think you might want to invite?

KIM: Twenty or thirty.

MOM: What time, and what kind of party?

KIM: Oh, it would go from 7 P.M. until 1 or 2 A.M. I thought we'd have a couple of kegs of beer, and Sarah was going to bake some of her lasagna and garlic bread.

MOM: Would everyone be of legal drinking age?

KIM: Gee, let me think. Yeah, I think so.

MOM: *If* we say OK to the party and to the beer, you'll need to be *positive* on that point, Kim.

KIM: OK.

MOM: Would the party be out in the yard, or inside?

KIM: I thought it would be nice to let people wander in and out. You know, eat dinner inside, but otherwise let people be wherever they want. What do you think, Mom? Can we do it?

MOM: I need some time to think about this and to talk with your dad. I can give you an answer tomorrow night.

KIM: Come on, Mom. Sarah and I need to call everyone. Can't you tell me now?

MOM: [*still refusing to be rushed*] Well, I can give you an

answer right now, but it would have to be no. Otherwise,
I need time to think this through. I understand your
enthusiasm, and I think Sarah's a good friend to want to
have a party in your honor. But this is a favor you're
asking of your dad and me. I want to talk with him, and
I need time to think through all the details. Can you
understand that?

KIM: [*resigning herself to being a little more patient*] I guess so.
Can I call you tomorrow?

MOM: Why don't you let me call you tomorrow. I promise I'll
call before 8 P.M. OK?

KIM: OK. Thanks, Mom. I hope you'll say yes. This means a
lot to me.

MOM: I know this is important to you. We're very proud of
your promotion, too, Kim. You worked very hard this
past year. Your dad and I will call tomorrow, I promise. I
love you.

The mother in this scenario did several important things. She
showed that she values the daughter's accomplishment and
cares about her feelings ("I know this is important to you"). She
reinforced her love for her daughter. She communicated that
she also values Sarah's good intentions ("Sarah's a good friend").
She took a firm position that showed she is part of a parenting
team and that she values her spouse as an equal ("I need to talk
with your dad"). She did not immediately acquiesce, which
would say that Kim's requests are her commands (thereby
making Mom less than equal). And she showed a desire to make
an informed, carefully considered decision. She showed this by
asking good questions and by insisting on a reasonable amount
of time to think through the implications of the request.

Whether the eventual answer was yes or no, Kim would know
that her request received plenty of attention. And, since both
parents would have participated in the decision, she would not
be able to play any games by turning to her dad for sympathy if
she didn't like the answer. Angry or happy, Kim would know
(even if she wouldn't admit it) that her parents care about her.

Let's look at a scenario where Mom and Dad have decided to
say yes:

DAD:   Hi, Kim. Your mom is on the extension phone. We
       wanted to talk to you about the party Sarah wants to
       have for you.

KIM:   Great. Can we have it?

DAD:   [*not getting rushed or pinned down*] Well, yes, condition-
       ally.

KIM:   Super! I really appreciate this! [*not interested in the
       conditions*]

MOM:   Well, we love you dear, and we're very proud of you. We
       want to help you and Sarah celebrate. But before you
       get too excited, don't you want to talk about the condi-
       tions?

KIM:   OK. What conditions?

DAD:   Well, we've wrestled some with what's reasonable. This
       is the list we've come up with. But we want to hear your
       opinions about it. [*indicating their concern for the effect
       on Kim, their value of her opinions and feelings, and their
       willingness to be flexible and compromise*]

KIM:   Shoot.

DAD:   Why don't you write these down, and then we can talk
       about them. [*Kim gets paper and pen. Dad and Mom
       then go through their list of conditions, including no one
       under drinking age may drink; if anyone gets intoxicated,
       he can't drive; postparty cleanup is Sarah and Kim's
       responsibility—although Mom and Dad will help; every-
       one should be gone by 2 A.M.*]

KIM:   How am I supposed to know who can't drive?

MOM:   We know that's tough to judge, and we'll be around to
       help figure that out, if you like. Our concern is that
       someone might have an accident on the way home and,
       God forbid, be hurt or killed. That's a terrible thing to
       have on our conscience. And then there's a chance
       someone might sue us for being negligent.

DAD:   Does that make sense, Kim?

KIM:   Yeah. But I don't know how I could keep someone from
       driving home. What do I do, take the keys away and
       become the laughingstock at work the next week?

MOM:   [*laughing*] Nasty old Kim, gets a promotion and starts throwing her weight around, right? [*showing that she's heard Kim's real concern*]

KIM:    Yeah. [*chuckles nervously*] Something like that.

DAD:    How about if we volunteer to be the bad guys? You and Sarah let us know who's been drinking a little too much, if anyone. Everyone may control himself just fine. But just in case, we'll be the party poopers and drive the person home or call a cab. We'll even pay cab fare. Sound all right?

KIM:    Yeah, sounds fine. [*The conversation continues in this vein as they work through the conditions. Each is talked through until all three feel they understand and can accept the compromise worked out. They agree to be flexible on the 2 A.M. deadline. Kim understands that Mom and Dad won't be able to sleep with thirty people partying in their house, but they agree that this should be a fun time for Kim and that they'll be flexible on the deadline. Kim doesn't want to ring a bell and usher everyone out the door right at 2 A.M.*]

KIM:    No sweat on the rules. I'll tell Sarah.

MOM:    Well, two of you are involved in this decision. Why don't you talk these conditions over with Sarah and be *sure* she understands them before you commit her to them? Call us back if either of you doesn't understand something.

KIM:    I'm sure she'll agree, Mom.

DAD:    She's your friend, Kim. She would probably want to decide for herself. I'm sure she'd involve you if something affected you. Why don't you talk to her and then call us back—as a courtesy to her, OK?

KIM:    OK.

This conversation showed Kim that her parents had agreed to the conditions together and supported each other in that decision. It showed that they were willing to trust her to have a party there as long as she and Sarah were willing to agree to certain reasonable conditions. They showed Kim the decision-making process they'd gone through up to that point. And they allowed her to have an impact on that process by listening to her thoughts and feelings, and compromising where possible. They also encouraged her to value Sarah's right to decide on those conditions as an equal party, as opposed to Kim deciding on her behalf.

How would egalitarian parents have told Kim no? Here's one possible conversation, where the reason for saying no can be explained logically:

DAD:   Kim, your mom's on the other phone. We want to talk to you about the party you and Sarah want to have.

KIM:   Great. Can we have it at your place?

MOM:   We've talked about it for a long time, but we don't think it's a good idea to have a party here anytime this month.

KIM:   Why not? Don't you trust us?

DAD:   [*refusing to get defensive, or be made to feel guilty*] We love you, Kim, and we're proud of your promotion. And we'd like to participate in your celebration. But we don't want to have a party at our house that weekend for insurance reasons.

KIM:   What's insurance got to do with anything?

MOM:   We're between insurance companies. We've just cancelled a policy with one and are starting one with another. We talked with our insurance agent, and she said we could be legally liable if someone fell and hurt himself or got into an accident on the way home. Since we're just activating a new policy, she thought it would be risky to have a party before we got confirmation back from the new company that they'd received our payment and our policy was in effect. The same thing is true about any damage that might accidentally happen to the house.

KIM:   I promise, no one will get drunk and have an accident. And no one will damage anything.

MOM:   I know none of your friends would deliberately do anything to put us at risk, but you can't guarantee these things. It may seem silly, but it worries us. Can you understand that?

KIM:   I guess so. [*sounding disappointed*]

DAD:   Well, don't give up on your party yet. We've got some
       other ideas. How fixed are you on that weekend? Would
       you be willing to wait a month? [*They discuss several
       options: waiting to have the party, having it somewhere
       else like at a local restaurant that charges no fee if they
       can guarantee thirty people, having it at a rented facility
       if Mom and Dad help pay the rental fee.*]

KIM:   I need to think about this and talk with Sarah. Thanks
       for the ideas. I'm sure we can figure something out.

MOM:   That's great, honey. And I'd be happy to make some
       appetizers if you think that would help with your ex-
       penses.

KIM:   Like those stuffed mushrooms?

MOM:   Whatever you like. Just let me know.

KIM:   Super! Thanks a lot. I'll call you back soon.

DAD:   Great. Thanks for understanding us old folks. We love
       you.

KIM:   I love you guys, too.

The result of this conversation was that Kim didn't get a flat
no. She got a "no because . . . ." She also got some options. Her
parents showed her that they are rational, considerate decision
makers. They also encouraged her to participate in the process
of decision making by increasing the options she could consider.

While Kim might be annoyed that her parents didn't do what
she wanted, she could not reasonably feel unvalued. She would
feel as though she had been treated as an adult, and as though it
was assumed that she would act responsibly and participate in
the reasoning-through process. She also knew that her parents
were being honest with her. They stated their one concern and
were willing to work around it.

As mentioned in the section on honesty, Kim's parents might
not have wanted to grant her request, but might not have been
able to give a "logical" reason. Kim might have abused their
trust continually for years. She might have failed to live up to
almost all her promises, with the resulting hard feelings and
arguments.

Because Kim's parents value her feelings equally with their
own, they would *not* have said anything like, "You can't have

the party here. After the way you've behaved lately, I can't believe you'd even ask." But they would know that giving Kim another opportunity to hurt and disappoint them, without any negative consequences for her, would be encouraging her adult adolescent behavior. It would also be damaging to the health of their marriage and peace of mind, since Mom and Dad typically get upset with each other each time they have a fight with Kim. For all these sound emotional reasons, they may choose to say no. How does a loving, egalitarian parent communicate such a no? Honesty is essential. Take this example:

MOM:   Hi, Kim. Your dad's on the other phone. We wanted to talk with you for a few minutes.

KIM:   Sure. You're gonna let us have the party, right?

DAD:   We love you, Kim, and we're very proud of your promotion. But we don't feel that we can have your party at our house.

KIM:   Why not? Don't you trust me?

MOM:   [*not taking the bait*] Kim, you are very, very important to us. And we've anguished over this. But we feel that it would not help our relationship with you to say yes right now.

KIM:   What are you talking about?

DAD:   Well, things have been rough the last few years between us. And that makes us sad. We don't like to fight with you or have hard feelings exist.

MOM:   That's right. And we think things have been improving recently. Would you agree, Kim?

KIM:   Yeah, I think so.

DAD:   I'm glad you think things might be improving. Do you also feel better about things when we're not always fighting?

KIM:   Sure. No one likes to fight. [*This may be a blatant lie. Kim may have proved by her years of game playing that she loves to provoke a good fight. But the parents let it go.*] But what's that got to do with not having the party at your house?

MOM:   We're just afraid that situations might arise that would undermine the progress in our relationship.

KIM:  [*not missing a chance*] You're saying you don't trust me.

DAD:  We're saying that we don't have a good track record together recently. Our arrangements, for whatever reason, seem to lead to arguments and hard feelings. We love you, Kim, but we really feel that the right answer now, for everyone, is for us not to have the party at our house. Can you see our point of view?

KIM:  Not really.

MOM:  I'm sorry if it seems unreasonable. But we've talked about this a lot, and we really believe this is best. We've thought up some other ways you might be able to still have your party, without any risk of the three of us getting angry with each other. Do you want to hear them?

KIM:  I guess so. [*She sounds put-upon and misunderstood. Her parents again refuse to rise to the challenge to rescue her. They proceed, with enthusiasm for the possible party, to explain the ideas they've had. Eventually, Kim decides to participate in coming up with ideas. She starts to feel more in control and responsible for working on her own problem.*] Great. I can't wait to talk to Sarah about these ideas!

DAD:  Wonderful, honey. Let us know if you want help with decorations or anything.

MOM:  And I'd be happy to provide some appetizers if you'd like.

KIM:  That would be great. We'll call you back after we figure out what we're doing.

DAD:  Super. Thanks for understanding, Kim. We love you.

KIM:  I love you guys, too.

Here again, a no became a "no, because ... ," and options were created that made more positive solutions possible. Kim felt valued and a part of the process. She had no opportunity to manipulate her parents, since they participated together in the decision and in the communicating. They were also honest in their explanation of their feelings. Kim had no room to catch her parents in a partial truth and manipulate them.

Whether the adult adolescent problem is mild or severe, an

appropriate egalitarian response is possible. Of course, it's easier in these situations because the parents are acting as a team—which brings us to our final point.

## TEAMPLAY

At this point, you might be wondering, "Great, I know how to be an egalitarian parent. But what do I do if my spouse is unwilling to change? What do I do if he insists on continuing to be authoritarian, or overprotective, or permissive?"

Adult adolescents love to play one parent off against another. If they don't get an answer they like from one, they'll try the other. Thus, the most effective way to deal with them is to work together as an egalitarian team. Realistically, this isn't always possible. The parents may have philosophical differences, or a divorce may have separated the parents. These complications can make teamplay difficult to achieve. Does this mean you should give up and not even try to be egalitarian? Absolutely not.

All that any of us can hope to control is our own behavior. We cannot force someone else to conform to our ideal. So if the other parent refuses to change in his unhealthy relationship with the adult adolescent, we must let go of that. We must accept that we cannot change that person, and that he must live with his choices and their impact on the adult adolescent. We may feel hurt that the other spouse is behaving in a way that encourages unhealthiness in the adult adolescent. But that is the spouse's choice.

Chapter 11 will give more advice about having diplomatic conversations with your spouse regarding parenting your adult adolescent. If you are living with the adult adolescent's other parent, and you cannot agree on how to parent him, you'll need to work out an understanding on who makes the parenting decisions (and this may require getting the help of a counselor), resign yourself to the status quo, or decide whether continuing to live together is a good idea.

Divorces are rarely caused solely by differences in parenting philosophy. But severe differences typically reflect deeper divisions in the relationship. And while we do not recommend threatening each other with divorce every time you disagree, there are times when, for the health of everyone involved, divorce may be the best option. If you and your spouse seem irretrievably at odds over how to parent Johnny or Mary, and you're not willing to live with the status quo or designate one parent as the one in charge, then we recommend seeking marital counseling. A good counselor can either help you reach a compromise with your spouse or help you decide to go your separate ways.

Whether or not you are living with the other parent, your energy should be directed toward agreeing on how to respond to requests—should you consult as a team, alternate taking answers, or have one "primary" parent? Parenting as a team is by far the most effective way to halt the extended dependency. Thus, we strongly recommend that you make every effort to achieve a united front.

## CHANGE IS TOUGH

Whether you and your spouse are working on becoming more egalitarian as a team or you are working on it alone, one thing is sure: change is tough. Your habits will tend to sneak up on you when you're tired, and you'll snap back with a canned answer from your old pattern. You'll need support from your spouse, a friend, a counselor, a religious leader, or a support group to keep going when you hit a bad moment. Chapter 11 will show you how to create and nurture the support systems you need.

You"ll also need support in dealing with the backlash from your adult adolescent. He or she is used to the old you: the permissive, authoritarian, or overprotective you. When you stop playing the game by the old rules, the most likely first reaction from your adult adolescent will be to escalate the game. Whatever his behavior was before, it will probably get worse—at first. The next chapter will show you how to deal with this initial backlash.

# 10

# What to Expect from Your Adult Adolescent After You Change

As parents of adult adolescents, we can all make a commitment to become more egalitarian in our parenting. We can do this because we love our children and want them to be healthy, independent adults. But there is one person who is going to be unhappy with the change in our behavior—at least at first. That person is the adult adolescent.

If we have been in a rescuer mode with the adult adolescent and have come to see that rescuing him every time he gets into trouble is enabling his dependency, we will choose to not rescue him. The first time we make that choice and allow the adult adolescent to suffer the consequences of his bad decisions, we're likely to get a negative reaction.

Since forewarned is forearmed, this chapter is designed to help you anticipate the likely reactions. If we as parents of adult adolescents persevere in egalitarian parenting , the great majority of adult adolescents will work through their negative reactions. They will come to accept our new role—and their own new and less dependent selves!

## DISBELIEF, DENIAL, ANGER, AND SELF-PITY

The most common initial response is disbelief: "Come on Dad. This is a joke, right?" "Mom, this doesn't sound like you. What's going on? What's the matter?"

If we persist in our egalitarian behavior and refuse to enable the dependency as the adult adolescent expects, the next step will be denial: "This can't be happening." "This isn't real." "This is a dream or something."

This response can frequently progress into anger or a sense of self-pity. Anger's immediate expression is usually verbal and may contain threats: "How dare you treat me like this?" "You son of a bitch. I'll make you regret this!" "You'll be sorry!" "Well, see if I'm around when *you* need me!" Self-pity can be voiced in comments like, "Well, I guess I'll figure *something* out" (said with a sob in the throat and tears in the eyes).

Some adult adolescents will react as if they were martyrs, suffering with the least caring parents in the world. These are usually the guilt throwers. Adult adolescents are skilled at the use of guilt. They frequently use guilt when parents try to change behavior patterns. "Don't you love me anymore?" "Don't you care what happens to me?" "But what if I'm thrown out of my apartment?" Often, they will use a combination of techniques: anger and tears, or self-pity and guilt.

As parents, our challenge is not to feel apologetic for changing. But how can we respond to such statements in a healthy way? There are five steps to remember in responding to an adult adolescent:

1. Acknowledge that we hear and understand the feelings of the adult adolescent.
2. State our own feelings—especially of love and support—but do *not* apologize for refusing to enable.
3. Remain firm in our convictions not to enable the dependency, and be willing to discuss why we feel that way. (See the section on reasonableness in Chapter 9).
4. Keep ownership of the problem with the adult adolescent. (It's his problem, not ours!)

5.  Help the adult adolescent reason through options for solving his problem.

Let's look at an example. Tom had a long history of needing money for routine bills. He never repaid the money he borrowed, and he did not attempt to budget himself. His job paid enough to more than cover his base expenses, but he would spend his money as whimsy dictated. He had an old sports car that was constantly breaking down. His parents told him that they wouldn't be helping him out financially any longer.

In this scenario, the car had broken down again. His parents had paid for the repairs in the past, leading Tom to expect this as normal. As a result, he hadn't seriously thought about whether he should budget to buy another car, or whether he could improve his maintenance practices to reduce the breakdowns. Repairs, as far as he was concerned, were free.

Tom approached his father for the money for the repair. If both parents were involved in parenting Tom, Dad would probably take time to talk with Mom first. Let's assume only Dad was involved. He was trying to become more egalitarian in his behavior toward Tom, and refused to pay. Tom was shocked.

TOM:   Funny, Dad. Real funny.

DAD:   I'm serious. I love you, Tom, but I'm not going to pay for this repair.

TOM:   But if you don't fix my car, I won't be able to get to work. I'll lose my job. And it'll be your fault! [*using indignation and guilt*]

DAD:   I know you're upset and want to get the car fixed. [*acknowledging Tom's feelings*]

TOM:   Damn right!

DAD:   And I understand your concern about getting to work. You'd really be in a pinch if you lost your job.

TOM:   I'd lose the apartment . . . everything. I'd be out on the street.

DAD:   It would be tough, that's for sure.

TOM:   [*totally puzzled now*] So, you're gonna fix the car, right?

DAD: I love you, son. I want you to be able to keep your job. I think it's great that you've got a way of taking care of yourself. I'm really proud of you for the way you've struggled to become independent. [*emphasizing the positives, stating his feelings*]

TOM: Cut the mushy stuff, Dad.

DAD: Well, I *am* proud of you. And, because I care about helping you grow and be independent, I don't think it's a great idea for me to pay for your car repair.

TOM: But you *always* help me out. You want me to lose my job? I thought you wanted to help me be independent!

DAD: I do. Your car not working doesn't mean you're automatically gonna lose your job.

TOM: [*getting mad now, he senses he's not going to get the usual "Dad will make it better" response*] The hell I won't. I don't get there, I get fired, period. Even *you* can figure that out.

DAD: That's true. [*determined not to rise to the temptation to get angry back or get defensive*] If you don't get to work, you'll probably lose your job. And neither one of us wants that. But there might be other ways for you to get to work until you can find a way to get your car fixed or replace it. [*giving ownership of the problem back to Tom*] I'd like to help you figure out some other solutions. [*staying concerned*]

TOM: Yeah, I can hitchhike and get killed. [*trying guilt again*]

DAD: Yes, you could hitchhike. It's your choice, of course. [*keeping ownership with Tom*] But that *is* dangerous. I would be very sad if you got hurt. [*keeping his concern apparent*] You could try carpooling with some of your coworkers, or take the bus.

TOM: *Nobody* rides the bus, Dad!
[*Dad holds firm, continuing to list out the options. He encourages Tom to add to the list. He may compromise with Tom and agree to drive him to work the next morning, to give him a day to figure out an option he can live with.*]

In this example, the father showed he understood Tom's feelings, communicated his own feelings, held firm in his convictions, kept ownership of the problem where it belonged (with Tom), and helped Tom think through other ways he could solve his problem. Tom might still be angry. But whether he would admit it or not, part of him knew that he had been heard. And if his father was sincere in his concern, Tom would also know that he was valued. Also, he'd have some idea of how to handle his own problem.

Sometimes this straightforward approach, repeated each time an incident arises, causes the frequency of adult adolescent behavior to diminish. In that case, it is important to encourage the positive developments in behavior, as discussed at the end of this chapter. Unfortunately, changes are frequently not that simple.

## THE SECONDARY ASSAULT

"If at first you don't succeed . . . ." Many adult adolescents believe that if they didn't get the desired enabling response from the parent the first time, it's because they failed to get the parent's attention. For some reason, Mom or Dad is being especially dense. Or, they believe, this new "parenting philosophy" is just a straw house, waiting for a good strong wind to blow it over. Thus comes the secondary assault.

This is typically the most painful time in dealing with an adult adolescent. As parents, we've made a commitment to doing the right thing. We've figured out what we were doing that was unhealthy, and we've decided to change it. Deep inside we hope that this will quickly "fix" the problem with our child—that Johnny or Mary will miraculously grow up.

Just when we're the most hopeful, and the most nervous and insecure in our new role, Johnny will often strike back. If we know it's coming, we can prevent ourselves from falling apart at the blow. But what shape does this assault take?

It depends to a large extent on what type of behavior your adult adolescent has typically exhibited. If her favorite misbehavior is to run out of money, she may get herself in a debt many times larger than she ever has before. She may overload her credit cards, let all her bills lapse, write bad checks, and other-wise create a crisis extraordinaire.

If Johnny has been prone to minor tussles with the law, he may assault a police officer. If he has come home every time he's lost his job, he may deliberately get himself fired—or quit due to circumstances "beyond his control." If he knows you hate it when he drinks and gambles, he may run away to Las Vegas . . . calling you collect just so you know he's there.

Sometimes it's not the seriousness of the misbehavior that escalates, but its frequency. If the typical crisis schedule was one every two or three months, the crises may become monthly or even weekly. This is the "keep it up until they give in" strategy.

Frequently, you can predict the type of crisis based on earlier patterns. Just as often, however, it is a surprise. When they come face to face with their fears of responsibility, of failure, and of change, adult adolescents can be frighteningly creative.

The best we can do as parents is to brace ourselves for the possibility of a significant retaliatory crisis. It helps to develop a good support system (as discussed in the next chapter). Because the secondary assault is the toughest time for parents, every ounce of flesh can seem to be crying out to do things the old way, to "fix" the problem, to make the crisis go away. We may start to believe that we really are the unloving, hateful parents our adult adolescents accuse us of being. That's when we need someone more objective to tell us to hang in there—to ride out the storm—and to keep giving Johnny or Mary the *healthy* love he or she really needs.

Sometimes it's a good idea to list out all the things you think your child might be capable of. Then list a few you would normally think of as "too far out," things like running away; denying access to your grandchildren; cutting off all communi-cation (pretending the parent is dead); deliberately wrecking a car, taking drugs, or attempting suicide; or exercising violence against others, including you. Thinking through how to handle the worst possible scenarios can help you make sure you have your responses prepared. It can also make whatever the actual crisis is seem a little less frightening.

No matter what type of secondary assault the adult adolescent chooses, you must be determined to persevere. How do you respond when the secondary assault hits? The same five steps apply: Acknowledge the adult adolescent's feelings. Admit to your own feelings (with total honesty). Hold firm in your convictions. Keep ownership of the problem(s) with the adult adolescent. And help the adult adolescent figure out how *he* will deal with the problem *he* caused.

There is also a sixth "step": use your own instincts, and get help when you need it. Whether it's professional counseling for yourself or your adult adolescent, or calling the police if your child gets violent, or calling social services or a religious leader—when you sense you're over your head, or your adult adolescent is headed for a life-threatening situation, *get help!* The next chapter will tell you how to select a mental health professional or find other types of help. The point is, don't risk anyone's life or safety.

## A Sample Secondary Assault

We'll use a possible scenario to illustrate a secondary assault and a healthy response from the parents. This example is deliberately extreme. Chances are that you will not face anything this difficult, but this scenario shows you that even in a worst-case situation, an egalitarian response is possible.

In this hypothetical situation, we'll call the adult adolescent Rita. Rita has tended toward the "couch potato" syndrome. When she got out of high school, she never "got around" to applying for college, or for a job. She parked herself on the sofa, slept and watched television all day, and then went out with friends at night. Once the friends left for college in the fall, Rita got bored and finally agreed to get a job. She found a part-time night shift position, and spent all her free hours shopping, sleeping, eating, or watching TV.

She did not save any money, and made no effort to contribute toward expenses or chores at home. Anytime she needed something, from shampoo to dental work, she expected her parents to pay the bill. And they did. Both parents, lonely at the thought of their only child moving out, were permissive. They never said anything to Rita about leaving home or paying rent.

After a year of this, Rita's parents realized that something had gone wrong. They understood that they were enabling an unhealthy dependency. And they decided to change, to become more egalitarian.

Their first step was to talk with Rita, to tell her that they loved her and wanted the best for her. They explained that they felt they had room to improve as parents—and that, in particular, they could improve when it came to helping her become a healthy, independent adult. They explained their beliefs about what an egalitarian parent should be, and made a commitment to her to try to treat her more as an adult.

Rita wasn't sure what all this meant, but being treated "like an adult" sounded OK—that is, until her parents explained the impact. They wanted to come up with an agreement they felt was reasonable for all three to abide by while Rita resided with them. They discussed their ideas with Rita, allowing her to contribute her ideas. She was hostile and refused to participate in drawing up the agreement. Her parents discussed it all anyway, and laid out their ideas. The first was that Rita would pay a small amount of weekly rent, which would increase gradually over a four-month period until it was half of the prevailing rate for an inexpensive one-bedroom apartment in their area.

Rita would begin to be responsible for purchasing her own toiletries immediately. After one month of phase-in time, she would be expected to contribute to the cost of groceries. She would also be expected, effective immediately, to do her own laundry and clean her own room. Her parents agreed that she could keep her room as clean or dirty as she chose. They would not interfere, but they would not clean it for her.

Rita's parents suggested that her rental payments could be suspended if she was in college or training school full-time, working toward a degree or certification program and maintaining passing grades. Rita's parents agreed to pay for all tuition, books, and registration fees. They explained that they felt this was reasonable because they loved her and wanted to help her get the best job training or career preparation possible. But they also explained that going to school was her choice, and that they would love her and be proud of her whether or not she ever changed jobs.

Rita listened with disbelief. She had come to expect permissiveness from her parents. This could not be true. So she ignored the agreement. When the first week's rent came due, she didn't pay it. Her parents had a difficult time confronting her with this, but they did it. She promised to pay them from her next paycheck, and she went to her bedroom and slammed the door. Denial was turning to anger.

The next payday came, and there was no rent payment. Her parents began going out to eat or preparing food for only two. No rent, they explained, meant no food. Rita made due with crackers and peanut butter she got out of the pantry. The next paycheck came, and she made a partial rent payment. When asked why she didn't make full payment, she flew into a rage.

She accused her parents of being selfish, of not caring about her, of not understanding how hard it is to get a good job or get started as a young person. She told them they didn't know how difficult it was for her, watching all her friends leave for college and being left "in this boring town" all by herself. Rita's mother lost control and broke down in tears. Her father told her she was a selfish, inconsiderate brat and told her to go to her room.

This was the first setback: falling into the old mode and letting Rita regain control of the situation. They regrouped, called Rita out, and apologized.

DAD:   Rita, I am sorry I yelled at you. [*Rita is silent, gloating.*] Please sit down; we need to talk. [*Rita sits.*]

MOM:   A few weeks ago, we drew up an agreement.

RITA:   *You* drew up an agreement.

DAD:   No, *we* drew up an agreement. We offered you an opportunity to participate in the conditions as we outlined them. You chose not to talk with us about them. That was your choice, Rita.

RITA:   Hum. Some choice. How about I tell you what I think now?

MOM:   Fine. What do you think?

RITA:   I think they suck!

DAD:   I'm sorry you don't like them. We'd like to hear your thoughts. But let's try to keep the conversation civil, OK?

RITA: Sure. Civil. Like anybody really gives a damn about my feelings anyway.

MOM: We do care about your feelings, as I'm sure you care about ours. [*emphasizing the positive*] If we're going to live together like adults, we need some adult understandings. You're not a child anymore.

RITA: Then why do you treat me like one? All these stupid rules. None of my friends would treat me like this.

DAD: Well, I'm not sure I agree. If you and your friend Joanne shared an apartment, don't you think she'd expect you to pay your part of the rent on time?

RITA: That's different.

MOM: Why? That's adult to adult.

RITA: Because you're my parents. You're supposed to help your kid get started. That's what every other parent does.

DAD: We love you, Rita. We do want to help you get started. And we think this agreement will help you grow and learn about the world.

RITA: Bullshit. You just want my money.

MOM: That's not the point at all. How about we agree to give every penny you pay in rent to charity? [*forcing Rita to face the reality of her accusation*]

RITA: What a waste. Why can't I just keep it?

The conversation continued in this vein, with Rita being belligerent and her parents refusing to give in. They stuck by the terms of the contract. Rita refused to discuss the terms rationally or to offer realistic alternatives. She finally gave them her ultimatum:

RITA: Tough, I'm not paying.

DAD: I'm very sad to hear that, Rita.

MOM: We love you, honey, but we truly believe this agreement is important for you. We believe it will help you grow.

DAD: You can't just ignore it and expect us to do nothing, Rita.

RITA: Yeah, throw me out into the street. Show the whole

> neighborhood what great parents you are. Well, screw
> you. I don't need you! [*She storms off, slams her door,
> and turns her radio up to top volume.*]

Rita's parents then conferred and agreed that Rita would need to move out for a while.* They called a relative who lived on a bus route that Rita could take to work. They worked out an arrangement where Rita could live there for one week while she thought things over. The conditions were that she could use their sofa bed as long as she cleaned up behind herself and tried not to wake anyone when she got home from the night shift.

Rita's parents gave her the news. She told them explicitly what she thought of them and turned her radio up again so she couldn't hear them. They left her a note on her door giving her twenty-four hours to move over to the relative's apartment, or they would move her belongings out. Rita ignored them.

When the deadline passed, Rita's parents packed up her clothes while Rita was at work and delivered them to the relative's apartment. They put a note on the front door telling Rita where her belongings were. They included the phone number and pointed out that the relative would come and pick her up if she would call and say where she was. They then bolted the door and went to bed. They did *not* answer the door when Rita rang the bell, knocked, and screamed obscenities at them.

This was the crucial point. Rita could get furious, go to her relative's, cool off for a week, and start to grow up. Or she could decide she was going to "show them" and escalate the crisis.

The most common case would be for Rita to go to the relative's home and spend the week trying to drum up support for her cause. If she could find a friend or another relative who agreed that she was being mistreated, that person might take her in rent-free. But typically those scenarios don't work for very long. Eventually, that person would expect help with the rent

---

*The authors strongly recommend the books TOUGHLOVE by Phyllis and David York and Ted Wachtel and TOUGHLOVE Solutions by Phyllis and David York and Ted Wachtel (New York: Doubleday, 1978 and 1984) for additional information regarding how to set down rules and live by them, and how to respond to adolescents (adult or not) who "act out."

and the chores, and Rita would be back into the same agreement, only with different players.

Once she realized that the real world demands certain things, and that her parents weren't being totally unrealistic in their conditions, she would reevaluate her options. She could get a full-time job and pay her expenses at home or with a roommate of her choosing. Or she could go to school and live at home rent-free. No matter which choice she made, Rita would have begun to grow up. She would be making progress toward being self-sufficient.

Accepting her options and wrestling with them might happen quickly (in a month or so) or slowly (over a couple of years). And once she had accepted them, Rita would probably still "test the water" occasionally, just to see if her parents would return to playing the permissive game with her. But if her parents held firm, Rita would gradually grow up.

Less often, Rita would not begin to grow after this one crisis. Rather, she would escalate the situation. A possible scenario would be that Rita, after exhausting the goodwill of the relative, would decide she can't live with her parents and run away. Or she might move in with someone whose values conflicted with her parents' values (for example, someone known to take drugs). Or she might get a job at a topless bar and let all the neighbors know that her parents "forced her" into this job.

Let's take the last example. How could the parents respond to Rita? (We'll deal with the neighbors in Chapter 12.) After hearing about Rita's new job from a neighbor, the parents might call Rita at the friend's apartment she is sharing. Here's the conversation:

MOM:   Hi, Rita. How are you?
RITA:   What do you care?
DAD:   [on the extension phone] We do care, Rita. We both love you.
RITA:   Yeah, sure.
MOM:   We miss you, sweetheart. And we'd really like to have some time to talk with you.
RITA:   You can't miss me too much. You threw me out. Why should I want to see you.

DAD: Maybe you don't want to see us, but we're concerned about you. We want the best for you. And we'd like to help you, as best we can, work through this tough time.

RITA: I don't need your help.

MOM: You're probably right, Rita. You're too old for that. But I hope you might choose to talk with us a little while. We'd love for you to come over for dinner tomorrow night.

RITA: I'm working tomorrow night.

DAD: [*dying to jump in and say, "yeah, we heard about your new job," but holding off*] We'd like to talk soon, Rita. What's a good time? How about tomorrow afternoon? I can take a half-day off work.

RITA: [*unable to stand it anymore, wanting the emotional crisis to begin*] If this is about my new job, forget it. I'm not talking about it.

MOM: Well, we did hear about your job. And we understand that it's your choice. But we think you might have some other options to think about.

RITA: Like what? [*She wants to avoid a face-to-face conversation, especially on her parents' turf.*]

DAD: We'd rather talk about them face to face. Can you give us a couple of hours tomorrow? It's really important to us, honey. You name the time. And we can meet at your apartment or in the park, if you prefer.

RITA: OK. The park at 3 P.M.

It is almost always preferable to have tough conversations, like the impending discussion of the job in the topless bar, face to face. Facial expressions and touching can express love and concern so much more effectively than words and tone of voice alone. It's also harder to be cruel to someone in person than it is over the phone. Hence Rita's preference for the emotional crisis over the phone. She can inflict maximum pain on her parents with minimum feelings of guilt. It's easier to pull the trigger when you can't see the victim.

Having tough conversations in person is also preferable because there's a greater chance that the people involved will hang in there long enough to talk through the problem. It's too easy to hang up a phone. Walking away from someone who has love written all over his face is much more difficult.

So Rita's parents met her the next day. Here's the possible conversation:

MOM: *[hugging her daughter, who does not reciprocate]* Hi, honey. It's great to see you. *[Rita says nothing.]*

DAD: *[tries to hug Rita, who backs away]* I'm happy to see you, too, Rita. I understand that you're angry with me. I don't blame you for not wanting to hug me right now. *[Rita is embarrassed by this frank acknowledgment of her pulling away and the understanding of her feelings.]*

RITA: What do you want to talk about? *[changing the subject]*

DAD: We heard you'd moved in with Joanne. We're glad you've got a place to live. Is it working out OK?

RITA: Fine. No sweat. No dumb rules.

MOM: Good. I'm glad you're comfortable there.

DAD: It's probably tough on you, buying all your own food and stuff. Are you having financial difficulties?

RITA: I'm managing just fine, not that it matters.

MOM: It matters a great deal to us. We love you.

RITA: *[with a sarcastic snarl]* Right.

DAD: *[letting it pass]* We thought you might want to discuss some alternatives for making ends meet.

RITA: I'm doing fine without you.

DAD: I'm sure you are. But we heard about your new job. While we agree it's your choice, we wanted to be sure you understood what you're getting into. *[Parents outline the risks of working in a topless bar. Rita argues that she knows all of that but needs the money.]*

RITA: Besides, all you care about is not being embarrassed with the neighbors. You don't want them to know how you threw me out or that your daughter is working in some topless bar.

DAD: *[again, not rising to the temptation to be defensive]* Mrs. Jones does take great delight in gossiping about everyone else, and that makes us sad. But we're proud of you, honey. And whether she likes what you're doing or not doesn't matter. We'll deal with her nastiness. What does really matter is your happiness and your health. And we're very concerned about your safety if you keep working at this bar.

MOM: We've come up with a list of ideas—different ways you can afford a place to live. [*hands a list to Rita*] It's just a start. You may be able to add a bunch more.

DAD: [*explains the list, including other jobs she has the qualifications for but that are safer, other living arrangements, including living at home rent-free if she goes full-time to school*] Do you have any comments? Any other ideas?

RITA: [*picks at the list, makes negative comments about the options*] I like my new job just fine.

MOM: Well, it's your decision, Rita. [*keeping ownership with Rita*] But we're concerned about your safety. We felt we owed it to you to make sure you knew what other options existed. You can probably think up some better ones. This is just the best we've come up with so far.

DAD: Whatever you decide, Rita, just remember that we love you. We know you're probably pretty mad at us right now. That's understandable. But I hope you also know that we love you very much and want the best for you. We're very proud of you, honey. And I hope we'll still hear from you and see you often—no matter where you decide to live or work.

RITA: [*The love is starting to break down her walls just a little, but she's still very angry.*] I know you believe this stuff. But I don't agree with you. I think you were wrong to throw me out.

MOM: I'd be angry, too, if I were in your shoes. But do you believe we love you?

RITA: I guess so.

DAD: Do you believe we're trying the best we can to be good parents?

RITA: Yeah.

MOM: That makes me so happy. We're not perfect, sweetheart. We're trying hard to be better and better parents. Give us a chance? Keep in touch? Let us help you talk through things?

RITA: Maybe. I guess so.

DAD: Take your time. Think about your options. Do you mind if we call you in a few days and see what you're thinking about doing? And see if you've had any ideas about other possibilities?

RITA: OK. But I'm not saying I'm going to quit my job.

MOM: We know that. Just agree to think about all the possibilities and about the safety hazards at your current job, OK?

RITA: All right.

DAD: Thanks, sweetheart. I'm so proud of you. [*hugs Rita, who doesn't pull away this time*]

MOM: I love you. [*hugs her too, getting a little teary, brushes her hair affectionately with her hand*] You've grown into such a wonderful young woman.

RITA: Aw, Mom. Cut it out. [*embarrassed and loving the attention at the same time*]

DAD: How about I buy everyone some coffee at the doughnut shop?

RITA: [*laughing*] Only if you get me one of those enormous chocolate éclairs.

DAD: You've got a deal.

The parents in this sample situation have done some enormously important and difficult things. First, they refused to fall into old patterns, even though rescuing Rita from her potentially risky job would have made them feel more at ease about her safety. Letting go of their need to control her life, they were able to give the decision back to Rita. Being permissive by nature, they had to conquer their fear of losing her love: she might not like them for not fixing her problem and allowing her back in their house rent-free. They knew it was more important to give her the support to become independent, even though it was painful.

They dealt with the pain of her anger and their own hurt, and gave back love. They didn't get defensive, or point out all the things Rita had done to prove how inconsiderate or immature she was. They stressed the positive and encouraged her.

They showed in many ways that they truly value her. Dad and Mom took time off of work to meet at her convenience.

They took the time to come up with a list of options (including other jobs and how much they pay, and likely monthly expenses of living alone), and they made the effort to truly hear what Rita felt. They gave their OK to her feelings ("I'd be angry, too, if I were in your shoes"). And they gave her hugs as well as "I love you's."

No matter what choice Rita eventually would make, she would be in control. She would be responsible. Her parents refused to be blamed. But they also encouraged her to expand her options. And she will continue to know she is loved and that her parents are proud of her efforts.

## SIGNS OF GROWTH

No matter how bad the adult adolescent behavior is during this period, there will almost always be signs of growth. Dr. Stockman has never seen a case where there wasn't something positive about the adult adolescent that could be a source of praise—something that he is successful at or has a talent for. And every effort at growing up, no matter how small or tentative, should be praised.

Few things nurture our sense of self-esteem more than praise from our family and friends. It's extremely important, as parents of adult adolescents, that we help our struggling young adults to redefine themselves as they work at growing up. Instead of seeing themselves as children, they must learn to see themselves as responsible adults. We can help by catching them in the act of trying to grow and then telling them how proud we are. The more reinforcement they receive, the faster their growth can be. By becoming egalitarian in our parenting, we can stop encouraging dependency, and spark growth in our adult adolescents. The final step is to encourage the tentative efforts they make at becoming adults.

### How to Give Praise

What may seem like a routine accomplishment for some twenty-year-olds may be a minor miracle for another. Instead of comparing our adult adolescent's efforts to the accomplishments of others in his age group, we need to compare him to where he started. For example, Tom may decide to sell his car, put the money in a savings account, and take the bus until he can save enough to buy a better car. Another young man the family knows may already be married, own a house and two cars, and have an impressive title to go with his large income. Obviously, comparing Tom to this young man would tear down Tom's significant efforts at taking control of his own life.

Thus, the first rule for encouraging growth is don't compare your adult adolescent to anyone else. If he gets discouraged, or you want to praise him for his growth, show him how far he's come in the last few months or years. Point out his personal progress. Tell him how proud you are that he's working hard and saving his money—or whatever it is that he's doing. Do *not* compare him to another person (especially a brother or sister).

The second rule is to praise often. Anytime something is worth recognizing, do it right away. Don't save up your praise for occasional bulk deliveries. Make it a steady diet. Say it directly: "Son, I'm so proud of you." Add a lot of statements of love: "Mary, I love you. I'm so proud that you're my daughter." And say it in writing. A letter or a note can be treasured and read again and again. If you're sincere and loving with your praise, your adult adolescent will thrive—even if he pretends not to have heard it or not to need it.

Third, show your praise in actions. If Johnny has finally shown progress in managing his money, and truly seems to be budgeting himself, you may want to break the rules a little. For example, when Johnny was dependent, you chose to not enable his dependency by giving him money for basic expenses. Now that he's paying for his basic expenses but leading a fairly Spartan lifestyle, you may want to show your faith in him by helping him kick up his heels a little. If it's too soon to give him cash, you may want to buy him a packet of gift certificates to a movie theater, or a dinner for two at a local restaurant. Or, if he really loves to spend money on records, tapes, or compact discs, you might give him a certificate for a local music store. Sometimes just baking a cake and taking it over is all that's needed.

The point is, give both words and actions. Think creatively about what you can do to show your pride and affection. And do things that are not going to foster the dependency, but that show how proud you are of his progress.

One word of caution: don't overpraise or praise falsely. Some parents, with good intentions, start praising Johnny for remembering to eat with his fork instead of his fingers, or praise Mary for remembering to comb her hair. To someone at twenty or thirty years of age, that's insulting. Or, feeling that there cannot be too much of a good thing, some parents will say, "I love you," so many times in one conversation that it sounds likes a nervous tick. Or it may sound like they're trying to hide something— namely, that they really *don't* love the adult adolescent.

You are trying to emphasize love and trust in your relationship with your adult adolescent. Overpraising or false praise sounds like a pitch from a used-car salesman—it raises suspicions and devalues the words spoken. This harms your relationship. Even worse, too much praise, or seemingly insincere affection can harm the adult adolescent's self-image: "If Mom or Dad can't say nice things and mean them, maybe it's because I'm not worth saying nice things about."

Thus, give praise and affection as frequently as it is deserved. Give it sincerely. Give it in words and in actions. If you do this regularly, the adult adolescent will trust in your love, and in his worthiness of love.

## DON'T GET DISCOURAGED

The secondary assault, if it comes, is the toughest time for almost all parents. You may doubt yourself, dissolve in tears and self-doubt, or want to quit the "egalitarian-parenting nonsense." That's perfectly understandable, but take heart. Dr. Stockman's work with hundreds of such cases shows that egalitarian parenting works. It's not easy, and sometimes the results are very slow in coming. Once in a very long time, an adult adolescent will come along who refuses to grow up despite all good efforts by his parents. That is his right and is outside the control of the parents. But in most cases, there will be growth.

So, when things get tough and you want to fall apart, know that it's normal. Don't be afraid to turn to your support systems. These can include your spouse, friends, religious leaders, parents' networks, and others. How do you find or foster a support network? That's our next subject.

# 11

# Support Systems

By this point, you are probably convinced of the need to become more egalitarian and of the fact that becoming egalitarian will be hard work. The negative reactions of your adult adolescent are sure to make you want to backtrack—to go back to the familiar, codependent mode of behavior. We say things to ourselves like, "Well, it may not have been great the old way, but it was sure easier than this."

In our efforts to become egalitarian, it is inevitable that we will come upon moments when we want to give up, times when we're tired, hurt, frustrated, depressed, and don't know what else to do. These are the times when we desperately need a reliable person or network to help us, to say, "Hang in there. It really is worth it."

A spouse (or "significant other") is the likeliest first line of support. It's important that you know how to support each other when the going gets tough. But if you're parenting together, your spouse may want to cave in at the same moment you do. So it's a good idea not only to know how to support each other, but also to expand your support system beyond the two of you.

## SUPPORTING YOUR SPOUSE

If the two of you can agree to work together to become more egalitarian, then you can also agree to help each other stay on track. A few ground rules will help you get through the disagreements over what to do or say in each situation:

- Use "I" statements instead of "you" statements (for example, "I feel angry" rather than "You make me mad").
- Always acknowledge your own feelings to your spouse, as well as your thoughts: "I feel sad, too, honey. It makes me want to cry when he does this."
- Acknowledge that you understand your spouse's feelings: "I don't blame you for being angry with her." "I can feel how hurt you are."
- Repeat your mutual goal of being egalitarian and of doing the best thing for your adult adolescent.
- Do *not* create a win/lose environment over who's right and who's wrong or who's the better parent.
- Avoid discussing the past except for your adult adolescent's behavior patterns.
- Accept responsibility for the compromise of solution *together*: "There's no guarantee that this will work, but I agree we should give it a try." Do *not* blame in advance: "If we do it your way, and Mary gets in trouble, it'll be your fault."
- Whenever possible, expand the time frame you have available for response. Rushed decisions are frequently regretted decisions.
- List as many different options for responding as you can both think of. Keep an open mind as you both talk through them and figure out which is best.
- Say "thanks" a lot. When your spouse keeps you from backtracking, you may be mad at that moment. But later, when you realize he was right, be sure to say it: "Thanks, honey. I almost blew it yesterday. I'm glad you had the courage to tell me before I made a mistake."

The time of change will be tough for both of you. As long as you both understand that and act as a team, it will be much less stressful for your marriage. And you will be more effective as a parenting team.

## Single-Parent Alternatives

If you are a single parent, and the other parent is either not involved in parenting the adult adolescent or refuses to change his enabling behavior, you may feel terribly alone. A spouse or another participating egalitarian parent can be available for support at all hours of the day or night. But what is a solo parent to do for that kind of support?

One alternative some such parents have found useful is to form a parenting team. Two or more single parents who are trying to be egalitarian can agree to be there to listen and talk through problems regardless of the inconvenience. They can even decide to talk to the adult adolescent(s) together. Some even decide to share households to create the stability of a two-parent home.

Needless to say, as many problems are inherent in this arrangement as there are in parenting by married partners. There is the additional complication that the two are not in love, nor are they committed to sharing the rest of their lives together. But if they are strongly committed to a shared goal—namely, doing the best at parenting their children—then it can work.

Another alternative for a single parent is the buddy system. In scuba diving, no one ever dives alone. Everyone takes a "buddy," who keeps an extra breathing apparatus available to supply oxygen to the partner should the partner's run out. The same can be true in parenting. While "shared parenting" may be too strong a commitment to each other's children, committing to be "buddies" may not be too much to ask.

Buddies can agree to be available at all times to talk, but their commitment is one step removed from the parenting team. It's more of an "I'll listen to you and give you my opinion" kind of arrangement. Buddies are great for providing a shoulder to cry on. They can tell you you're doing a wonderful job just when you need to hear it.

How do you find a buddy? Neighbors, coworkers, members of

your church, and other members of self-help groups can be good candidates. Relatives, if they're not too determined to get you to do it "their way," can be good buddies also, since you usually already have affection for one another. What is required is a common philosophy of parenting and a steadfast commitment to always listen and encourage, and to argue when it's appropriate.

The rules for interaction between parenting team members, or between buddies, are the same as those listed for spouses. There is one extra rule, however. Ultimately, it is the parent's choice. The team member or buddy must not *tell* the parent what to do. He may advise, argue, cajole, or discuss at length. But, ultimately, the parent must decide how to handle each situation and must retain full responsibility for the decision.

One final note. As a single parent, you should remember that the selection of a team member or a buddy is not irrevocable. Should you decide to use this type of support system, and later realize that the other person doesn't have your own or your child's best interest at heart, then it's time to politely say, "Thanks for the advice," and, "I think I can handle this myself from here on." It is also a good idea, whether you are married or a single parent, to diversify your support system. Sometimes you and your buddy will be too tired, sick, or distracted to be of much use to each other.

## OTHER PLACES TO FIND SUPPORT

The more different people you have supporting you, the easier the tough times will be. Someone can always listen to you, or argue with you when you start rationalizing why it wouldn't hurt to give in "this one time."

It's helpful to remember that you are not unique. Dr. Stockman estimates that no less than 40 percent of all young adults suffer from adult adolescent behaviors. It's the embarrassment of the parents that keeps this problem hidden. Everyone feels that his own inadequate parenting is responsible, and that no one else has this kind of child. So silence becomes the enemy.

Shedding your embarrassment can be an enormous relief, and can help you to find others in similar situations. At almost any dinner party, you can find others in the room with similar problems. Someone else on your block or in your building is suffering as you are. Most likely several of your friends, co-workers, and members of your church are in your boat.

When you're with people who have children over eighteen, and they ask you how your kids are doing, you can say, "Just great, thanks," or—if you feel inclined to be more trusting with them—you could say, "They're good kids. But Tommy's having a tough time growing up." The latter response will almost always elicit similar feelings: "Yeah, my Alex is driving me nuts." There is support just in the comfort of knowing you're not alone.

But such conversations can be more than just gripe sessions. They can be networking opportunities. Just as you would net-work at a cocktail party to find potential business contacts, you can network at gatherings to find potential parenting support. If you offer to listen to the concerns of other parents, and if they are also interested in working to become egalitarian, you may find valuable allies this way.

Most of the parents who have come to Dr. Stockman for help with adult adolescents have found that as they work on becom-ing egalitarian, they just "naturally" tend to find people they know who are struggling with the same problem. We believe that this experience is primarily due to the loss of embarrassment. When you start revealing your concerns, you'll find many who share them.

Relatives can also be a source of assistance and encourage-ment. If your own parents, sisters, or brothers are reasonable people, you may want to enlist them in your effort. This can be particularly effective when the adult adolescent turns to relatives for sympathy and finds a loving but unified front. If you have understanding family members, make use of them.

Perhaps you're not yet ready for one-to-one chats with friends or relatives—you're looking for a "safer" place to turn for support. There are quite a few, including social services and religious organizations, self-help groups, and mental health professionals.

## Social Services and Religious Organizations
Any phone book contains listings for all sorts of charitable and

government organizations that can help parents deal with adult adolescents, or refer them to places that can. Most cities have crisis hot lines. The operators on such lines typically have extensive lists of people or groups that can help. So do agencies such as the United Way and the YMCA/YWCA. Local hospitals and churches also usually have such contacts. They may even have groups meeting at their facilities.

Your city, county, or state probably has a mental health services agency listed in the phone book. The agency may have help available at no cost or at reduced cost. It can certainly also provide information about other support networks. Other places you can call to get started finding help are child welfare agencies, offices of the federal Department of Health and Human Services, and even the local high school guidance counselor.

Finally, religious leaders are frequently involved in family counseling. If you are a member of a church or temple, you may want to approach your religious leader to see if he or she does such counseling. Of course, his philosophy of parenting may turn out to conflict with your goal of egalitarian parenting. If this is the case, you can thank him for his time, and move on.

The result of these calls may be that you find someone within an agency or religious organization who is willing to help, or who puts you in touch with some of the excellent self-help networks that have formed across the country.

## Self-Help Groups

Self-help groups have the advantage of being free, composed of people with a common problem and goal, and composed of peers. Rather than having an "expert" give answers, these groups figure them out together.

One nationwide movement that has resulted in hundreds of local self-help groups is TOUGHLOVE. Founded by Phyllis and David York, the groups apply the principles laid out in their books *TOUGHLOVE* and *TOUGHLOVE Solutions*. (These are listed in the Bibliography and are highly recommended.) While many of the parents in the TOUGHLOVE groups are dealing with irresponsible, acting-out teens, the problems are often very similar to the adolescent behavior of adult adolescents. Especially for permissive or overprotective parents, a TOUGHLOVE group could prove invaluable.

Another very effective self-help group is called Co-Dependents Anonymous (CoDA). A relatively new movement, this self-help organization recognizes that breaking the extended dependency is a two-way problem. Both the parent and the adult adolescent have to give up the old patterns. While this group also deals with other forms of codependency, such as can occur in marriage or other relationships, a large portion of those attending usually have parent/child codependency problems. And while the manifestations of codependency can be seen in other relationships, tackling the problem starts at the same point: with the group members themselves. Thus, these groups, while not specifically focused on parenting, have proved extremely helpful to many of Dr. Stockman's clients.

Since extended dependency problems frequently run in the same families where there has been alcoholism, the self-help groups named after the book *Adult Children of Alcoholics* (see Bibliography) can also be useful. The premise of the ACOA groups is that the children of alcoholics, whether or not they become alcoholic themselves, will bear emotional scars. These scars predominantly take the form of codependent behavior, and these codependent behaviors pass from one generation to the next. Thus, while the alcoholic person in your family may have been your grandfather who died before you were born, the chances are good that your parent was affected, and that you and your adult adolescent were, too. If you suspect alcoholism to be a factor in your family tree or your spouse's, this group can help you become aware of the impact of that alcoholism on your life and how to work on the resulting problems.

Local self-help groups are also usually available. The agencies listed earlier, such as the United Way, or local religious organizations can put you in touch with these groups. See the Appendix for further ideas on how to contact sources for support.

## Mental Health Professionals
Sometimes, whether or not you have other forms of support, it is

advisable to consult a mental health professional. This is true if you believe anyone's life or health is at risk, or if you find yourself suffering from extreme anxiety or prolonged depression. It is also advisable if you feel the other support systems you have are inadequate or are giving you bad advice, or if other support does not exist.

But how do you find such a professional? As we mentioned earlier in the book, we do *not* recommend calling a local psychiatric hospital first unless the situation is truly life-threatening. Such hospitals have proliferated recently and are competing aggressively for business. They have high fixed costs and a predisposition to recommend inpatient evaluation in most cases. Such evaluation is expensive and usually leads to a recommendation for inpatient treatment or residential care—which is even more expensive. It is also frequently ineffective, because there is too much focus on the adult adolescent as "the patient." The problem is almost always a family problem, and rarely requires inpatient treatment for significant progress to occur. Additionally, the older the adult adolescent, the less likely he is to agree to participate in inpatient treatment. Typically, it is the parents who have to create change in the relationship.

This is not to say that such hospitals don't serve a useful purpose. They do. And they can provide referrals to self-help groups in the area. However, they sometimes use their position as a "hospital" and as "experts" to convince people that the best first-choice treatment is often inpatient treatment. The authors don't doubt that these facilities believe what they say. However, we disagree with the results and the high cost. For these reasons, we recommend against such institutions as a first choice.

Instead, consult a family counselor first. Such a counselor may be psychologist, psychiatrist, social worker, or licensed layperson. Psychiatrists are typically the most expensive. However, they are medical doctors as well as counselors and are trained to look for possible physical as well as psychological sources of the problem.

A family counselor, whether a psychologist, social worker, or licensed layperson, should be able to determine fairly quickly if it is advisable for a psychiatrist or inpatient facility or residential treatment center to become involved. In the great majority of cases, this is not necessary.

A good family counselor is best found through someone you know who has had a good experience with that person. If you can't get a referral, many cities have set up medical referral phone numbers and can provide a list of family therapists who meet your needs (cost, location, type of education, family therapy orientation). Many employers now provide Employee Assistance Programs, which may have counselors available to you at no charge or may be able to refer you to a family counselor in your area. There are also listings in the yellow pages under headings such as psychologists, doctors—psychiatrists, and mental health. Agencies such as those listed earlier (like the United Way) can usually help you find counselors.

No matter how you get a counselor's name, call and ask for a no-charge introductory meeting. The purpose of the meeting will be to find out more about the counselor, his credentials and philosophy about parenting and extended dependency, rates, and also to get a feeling about whether or not you want to work with that person. If the counselor strikes you as cold and unfeeling, you'd probably better keep looking. You need to have some fundamental, instinctive trust, or you'll be wasting your time and money.

If the counselor will not agree to a ten- or fifteen-minute no-charge introductory meeting, we recommend finding another referral. If you do get a meeting, ask where the counselor was educated, and if he is licensed. You may want to call your state licensing board and verify the license. Ask your questions without embarrassment. You are preparing to purchase a service. You have the right to know what you're buying.

Remember, if you choose to begin counseling, you do not have a lifelong commitment to the counselor. There are usually times when a counselor will challenge you to grow, thereby making you mad or defensive or depressed. At those moments, you will wonder if you made the right choice. We don't recommend quitting counseling the first time you get mad. If what your counselor says consistently feels wrong, tell him. Attempt to resolve the issue directly. But if you cannot accomplish this, it is usually best to seek another therapist.

## YOU ARE RESPONSIBLE
As in all things, it's important to retain responsibility for your parenting decisions. Do not abdicate responsibility to a group, a spouse, a minister or rabbi, or a mental health professional. Talk through things with your support network, but ultimately, you must commit yourself to the decision that you make.

There are no guaranteed right answers. No one can see into the future. If things don't work out as you hoped, it doesn't mean you made a bad choice. If you'd chosen a different response, things might have been worse—or they might have been the same. All any of us can hope to do is our best. If you work at making the most egalitarian decisions you can, then you can do no more except give lots of love. The rest is up to your adult adolescent.

## I'M DOING MY BEST,
## BUT MY FRIENDS THINK I'M NUTS
Sometimes we make decisions affecting our adult adolescents that may seem harsh to the rest of the world. Yet we know that any other choice would enable the dependency. It's an unfortunate reality that many people feel free to comment on our decisions, even though it's none of their business. They may tell us we're being too harsh, or too soft, or too *something*. Whatever it is, we're not getting it right. How do we deal with these antisupport types? We can let them tear down our morale and defeat our purpose, or we can stand up to them.

Dealing with the interferers and know-it-alls is the subject of the last chapter.

# 12

# Learning to Deal
# with Others

One of the difficulties of parenting an adult adolescent is that we
sometimes get "assistance" from others that we'd really rather
not have. Some people will give us advice. Others cast blame.
Others will try to control our decision making, forcing us to do
things their way. Dealing with such people is not easy. It is made
harder by the fact that we may feel tired and vulnerable already.
But there are a few things we can do to respond to such people
in a way that is kind, but firmly discourages future repetitions of
the unwanted behavior.

The first step toward a healthy response is to control our
anger, defensiveness, or feelings of hurt. We can start defusing
those feelings by remembering that we're not perfect either.
Being human, we all have a tendency to believe that we are a
little bit wiser, a little bit smarter than almost everyone else. A
healthy sense of self-esteem encourages us to feel that way.
When we take our opinion of our own wisdom too seriously,
however, we may try to convert the rest of the world to our way
of thinking. Or we may feel happy sitting in our living room
passing judgment on how others choose to run their lives.

The authors have never met anyone, themselves included, who didn't sometimes indulge in too much advice giving or who wasn't judgmental occasionally. Admitting that about ourselves can help us be more forgiving when we see those habits appear in others. Being forgiving can diffuse anger toward those people and help us react more reasonably and more effectively when confronted by unwanted advice or blame.

The second step in controlling our emotional responses to such people is to remember that we do not have to explain our parenting to anyone except the other parent, the stepparent (if involved), and our children. Well-intentioned or not, other people's involvement is by our permission only. We have the right not to involve them. When we feel we have to justify ourselves, we immediately get defensive. Thus, if we can remember that no one else is entitled to an explanation, we can feel more in control of whom we *choose* to explain ourselves to.

This is typically the most difficult area where grandparents of the adult adolescent are concerned. Most of us do choose to explain our parenting to the grandparents. We do this because they are usually very close to us and our children, and care deeply about what happens. But even with grandparents, it is a choice that we make. It helps to remember that.

Once we gain some control over our immediate reactions— such as defensiveness, anger, and hurt—we can then give some thought to what the best response is to the various advice givers and judgment pronouncers we encounter. Because the nature of our ties to these people affects how they speak to us and how we may choose to respond to them, they are divided into five categories: friends, neighbors, and coworkers; church or temple members and spiritual leaders; grandparents and other family members; and ex-spouses. These are ordered by the increasing difficulty of responding appropriately. Finally, we will address how to handle parenting with your spouse when that person is the adult adolescent's stepparent.

## FRIENDS, NEIGHBORS, AND COWORKERS

Friends, neighbors, and coworkers can become afflicted with the "keeping up with the Joneses" disease. To distinguish themselves, they can become obsessed with comparisons—whether it be of cars, houses, front yards, or children. They believe that their value as a person is somehow tied to how nice their home looks, or how much money they make, or how well their kids behave. For such people, cocktail parties and neighborhood picnics are important opportunities to prove that they are "worthy" or "better" by comparing as many things as possible.

This type of person will leap joyfully into conversation with you with all manner of self-serving questions. If he just got a promotion, his first question will concern your job. After pretending to listen to your answer, he'll wait for your polite return of the question. To which he'll respond, "Well, I just got a promotion. It's a lot more money. Jean and I will be going to Peru this year to celebrate." Notice that this provided him with three "triumphs": I got promoted, and you didn't; I got a big raise, and you didn't; and I'm taking an expensive overseas vacation, and you aren't.

This is a different type of conversation from the one with a person who is truly your friend and who calls you up, excited as can be. Rather than manipulating you into asking the right question, he or she just honestly shares the good news. "Hi! You won't believe it! I'm so excited! I finally got that promotion!" This is straightforward sharing, not a contest. There is no implied challenge of "Can you top that?"

The person who implies a contest is insecure. He is saying, "I need to be better than you, and I'm only better if I can one-up you."

How do you handle such a person, especially when the conversation turns to comparing kids—and therefore the successfulness of your parenting? Take this example. Your friend says, "My little Mary just won the district spelling bee, and Susan got accepted by Stanford University—with a scholarship! How are your kids?" Like most conversations with such a person, the conversation contains the challenge: Can you do better than that? And if not, I am proved to be the better parent. How do you respond?

First, to control your emotional response, remember that he or she must be very insecure to behave so immaturely. This is something to be sad about, but not angry about. Second, remember that in all of us is a desire to be "better"—and we all struggle with the tendency to prove ourselves at someone's expense. The humble acknowledgment of this fact puts aside our tendency to judge our friends. Third, remind yourself that the behavior of your children is none of his business and does not prove or disprove the value of your parenting. It's easy for parents of a bright child who graduated number one from Harvard Law School to try to take credit for the child's accomplishments. But they could have had a brain-damaged child just as easily, or a child who decided that his purpose in life was to sleep on the streets of New York City.

If you remember these things and feel sad for your friend, but not angry or hurt, you still have to figure out what to say. Well, you should *not* rise to the challenge and compare anything. That would be playing his game and be demeaning to you.

Give compliments and praise to the speaker. If he is bragging about his perfect children, tell him how happy you are for him. Then be pleasant but noncommittal when he asks how your job or kids are doing. Something along the lines of, "Fine. Thanks for asking," is all that is needed. Add a smile and a steady, self-confident gaze, followed by silence. Your failure to play his game may either get him off track and cause him to talk more like a real friend, or it may help him decide you're boring, and he'll go bother someone else.

There is another, much crueler game that some insecure people play. It's a combination of wanting to embarrass you and forcing you to justify yourself. People who play this game want you to beg for understanding or sympathy or approval. Take an example where you recently chose not to bail Mary out of jail, at age twenty-nine, when she was arrested for the third incident of shoplifting. You and your spouse agonized over the decision but felt it was the right answer, given Mary's continuing adult adolescent behavior. Somehow a coworker named Tom discovers this. He mentions this to you in private by saying, "I heard a nasty thing about you yesterday, but I defended you. I knew it couldn't be true. I heard that Mary was in jail—again—and that you refused to bail her out."

What do you say in this private setting? That depends on your relationship with Tom. If you want to preserve a superficially friendly working rapport, you could say something like, "Thanks, Tom. I appreciate your defending me. We have some tough decisions to make about Mary, and we like to keep them private. I'm sure you can understand and respect that." Notice this does *not* directly answer the question, which is none of Tom's business. It also closes the door on the conversation.

If Tom is insensitive enough to go on and ask, "But you didn't leave her in jail, did you?" your response could be, "Thanks for your concern, Tom. I really appreciate it. There are no easy answers in parenting. You're a good friend. I know you'll give me the space to work on this alone." This makes Tom feel that you have ascribed to him only the purest of motives and expect him to be a "good friend" and shut up. You can then change the subject or leave the room.

If Tom is a real jerk, he may have brought this subject up in front of the water cooler or the coffee machine, so that everyone else can watch him drag the skeleton out of your closet. The essential thing to do is to not believe it's a skeleton! Since so many of today's young adults go through a period of adult adolescent behavior, most of the people listening have had or will have someone in their family with this problem. They may even be adult adolescents themselves! You are doing your best to correct the extended dependency. You are working hard at being a good parent. Your methods are none of these people's business, and you have nothing to prove to them. Laughter is the strongest and best defense in such a situation—along with *not* answering the question.

The ideal response is something like, "Ha ha ha ... Tom, you are such a card!" followed by walking away chuckling. This leaves people with several impressions: that they can't get your goat by raising the subject, that you're pretty self-confident, that there may be nothing at all to Tom's story, and that Tom looks silly for bringing it up at all. Another approach, if you're not a good enough actor to pull off the laughter, is to shake your head and commiserate with Tom—making him a part of your "inside circle": "It's truly amazing, isn't it, Tom, what some people will waste their time talking about." Then walk away or ask him something about his work (not his family—you don't want to get into a tit-for-tat).

All of these approaches have important results. You have not demeaned yourself or hurt your friend or coworker. You have not participated in comparing your child to another's child, or to some unspoken ideal. This means you have not demeaned your child by making him a tool to prove your own self-worth. If your friend was bragging, you have shown true pleasure in the accomplishments of the friend's child. You have not, in the case of Tom, allowed anyone the right to tell you how to parent. You have established, pleasantly, that your parenting is your business—period. In each of these scenarios, you have turned a win/lose into a win/win situation.

## CHURCH OR TEMPLE MEMBERS
## AND SPIRITUAL LEADERS

Dealing with a similar conversation between yourself and a fellow church member can be one degree more difficult. This is because an implied third party is judging your parenting: God. Fellow church members can use the win/lose technique to prove not only their superiority as parents, but also as religious or spiritual persons. Thus, they can marshal to their side all the expectations and rules in your religion to prove their superiority. "Keeping up with the Joneses" is changed to "I'm holier than thou."

Let's take an example where your church believes that children should obey their parents at all times, and that disobedience should be punished. Please note that we are not going to discuss the merits of any religious or spiritual belief. Our only concern is helping you to deal with parenting advice that is wrapped in a religious belief—a belief you may be choosing to disagree with or interpret differently.

For example, you may have been a severe disciplinarian for most of Mary's life. You may have, however, determined that your severe authoritarian behavior is part of the problem of extended dependency. You may be working now to give Mary's decisions back to her, instead of always giving orders. You are trying to let go—to love, but not to control.

To use the shoplifting example again, Mary was twenty-nine and in jail, and you were letting her deal with the consequences of her decision. You did not bail her out. You also did not wield any physical or psychological "rod" of punishment. She is her own person, accountable to herself and to the community for her infraction of the law. You were not going to take responsibility for her misbehavior and punish her. Neither were you going to rescue her. When she called you, you told her you were sad and felt sorry that she had to be in jail. You told her you loved her, but because you loved her, you were choosing not to bail her out. In your heart, you explained, you truly believed it was the best choice. You stated your feelings, but you did not scold.

Word of Mary's situation got back to the church group. Here's a sample conversation with "Sally":

SALLY:   I heard that Mary was in jail again. I just couldn't believe it. But I really couldn't believe it when I heard you left her there. No decent parent would do a thing like that.

YOU:   Thank you for your concern, Sally. I know you have our best interests at heart.
*[Sally will most likely not stop there, although changing the subject or staring her down may work.]*

SALLY:   I do. That's why I think you should go get her right this minute. Take her home, and teach her some respect. That's the way we raised our kids, and all four of them turned out just fine.

YOU:   You are truly blessed, Sally. I'm very happy for you.
*[You are still not answering the advice with any defenses or promises. Sally may quit or press on.]*

SALLY:   Well, what are you going to do?

YOU:   I'm sure Martha [your spouse] and I will continue to struggle over this. We'll just keep praying and doing our best. We both appreciate your concern for us and for Mary.
*[Most of the time, Sally will be tired of the conversation by now. Assuming she has no sense of tact, she may go on.]*

SALLY:   Are you going to leave her in jail?

YOU:   [*still refusing to answer the question, which is none of her business*] Parenting is awfully tough, isn't it? We wrestle with it constantly. You may be right about what to do— I don't know. Keep us in your prayers, please.
[*Now Sally is really at a dead end. She's been told she may be right—although no commitment has been made to take her advice. And her help through prayer has been requested. She can't really say anything except . . .* ]

SALLY:  Of course, I'll keep you in my prayers. [*She might add a parting shot.*] You must be firm with her, though.

YOU:   Thank you, Sally.

Sally will probably conclude that you're unreachable and beyond help. She may moan about your incompetent parenting to others and ask them all to pray for you. She will continue to feel superior, but she will be frustrated in her efforts to get you to play the game with her. Since you're no fun, she'll most likely find a new target. If she tries again another time, just keep thanking her for her concern until she's ready to scream.

This conversation may be even more difficult if it takes place with a spiritual leader who feels there is only one right answer to your parenting dilemma, and it is different from what you believe to be right. You may use all the polite techniques just outlined to thank him for his concern, and it may not work. The leader may feel a sincere moral imperative to save you from a horrible mistake. If it comes to an impasse, you will need to decide who is in control. If you wish to turn over the parenting decisions to your spiritual leader, that is your right. You are still responsible for their impact on your adult adolescent, however, because you are *choosing* to hand the reigns to someone else.

If you cannot live with the advice of your leader, you may want to see if there is another leader in your organization from whom to obtain a second opinion. If that is not available, or of no help, only you can decide what your vision of God is and whether or not you can live within the demands of your church or religious organization.

There are no easy answers in egalitarian parenting. There can be wrenching moral or spiritual choices. Egalitarian parenting means that we believe that the struggle is worth it, and that as parents we are accountable for the choices we make. They will not always be "perfect" choices, but they will be our own.

You can only hope your religious leader will allow the latitude for sincere disagreement. If not, you alone can decide whether or not you can remain in that organization.

## GRANDPARENTS AND OTHER RELATIVES

Grandparents and relatives can be a wonderful source of advice, support, and consolation. They can also, unfortunately, be the source of much heartache. Parents can use guilt against their children—even when those children are independent adults raising their own families. Their best advice can be mixed in with a sense of "if you were a good daughter/son, you'd do what I'm telling you."

You know whether your parent is the kind you can talk a problem through with, but still be left with the freedom to choose your own answer, or whether the parent will try to take away your freedom to handle the situation and will try to give you orders or manipulate your choice down to only one—his or her recommended course of action. If your parent is the kind who treats you like an equal in the discussion of your child's problems, then you don't have anything to worry about. But if he makes you feel angry, guilty, frustrated, confused, and trapped when talk turns to how to handle your adult adolescent, then you need a better way to manage that parent.

We are assuming that you yourself are an independent adult—that you are not financially or emotionally dependent on your parent(s). In this case, there is no reason you can't improve on a difficult relationship with your parent. If you are not yet independent of your parents, the first and crucial step is to get some counseling to help you break those ties. You can't help your son or daughter break their ties to you until you have broken your ties to your parents.

When dealing with a difficult grandparent, the first thing to remember is that your children are *your* children. You most likely have different values, religious beliefs, and a different lifestyle than your parents. Your children are probably different from you. The world is certainly quite different from the one in which you were raised. All this is to say that things *are not the same*. You and your spouse must do the best you can within your own value system to help your children cope with the pressures of the current society. While your parents may believe that the way they raised you was better than the way you're raising your own kids, and they may believe it with great love and sincerity, it is not their choice to make. You must stand up for your right to do what you feel is best.

Kindness, firmness, love, and tact are the best way to make a grandparent understand that you (and your spouse) must make the decisions regarding how to handle your children. How can you be kind and loving to someone who's driving you nuts? As in the other examples, be sure to thank them for their concern. But go one step further . . . thank the grandparents for their love. Remind them that you love them and are very happy for the love they have for your child.

Here is a sample situation where you and your spouse have taken some action in response to some misbehavior by your adult adolescent. Your father disagrees with your action and lets you know it:

GRANDFATHER: He's not too old to respect his parents. Somebody's gotta teach him self-discipline. [*Often criticism is just this vague. "You're not doing it right, but I can't tell you exactly how to do it. . . ."*]

YOU: We're doing our best, Dad. I'm really grateful for your concern. I know how much you love Mark. That means a lot to all of us, but we've got to handle these problems as best we can. I hope you can understand that.

GRANDFATHER: [*if he's really a tough nut*] No, I can't. I don't know why you don't come down harder on him.

YOU: I'm sorry you can't understand our point of view, but we have to do what we believe to be best.

GRANDFATHER:   *[after proclaiming the general inferiority of the "younger generation," the decline in American moral values, and the lack of respect that young people—meaning you—have for their elders, makes a final pronouncement]* Well, if he gets in trouble, don't say I didn't warn you.

YOU:   I won't, Dad. We're not going to agree on this one, so why don't we change the subject?

Much will depend on how inflexible and controlling the grandparent is. He may be completely inflexible in his views but still give you the freedom to differ. But if he is also controlling, needing to have the final say, then real trouble can arise. Grandparents are an important part of the extended family. Having ones who care and want to be involved with your children is usually a blessing. But it is essential to control their involvement so that it doesn't cause you to make bad decisions. This can usually be done without permanently alienating the grandparents, although the process of drawing boundaries can cause some rough going at the beginning.

Compensating for their feeling of being disenfranchised by including them when it's possible—in birthday parties, holidays, or a Sunday afternoon picnic—can help ease the pain of not being able to direct the parenting of their grandchildren. You may at first hear words like, "In my time, we showed more respect for our parents." The response is, "I do respect you, Mom, but Gina and I are doing what we feel in our hearts is best for the kids." You won't win them over quickly. Be patient and firm, and always try to be kind and loving. Repeat your appreciation and love, but don't surrender your right to disagree and take a different course of action.

If both your parents are alive, and they are able to communicate with each other reasonably well (that is, they are not divisively divorced or living together in a state of constant warfare), you may try talking openly to the most rational or least controlling parent. Explain that you and your spouse feel that you are responsible for the decisions regarding your children. State that you appreciate the involvement of the grandparents, but that advice is only advice. You will not always follow it. Ask the noncontrolling parent to help you in getting the controlling parent to understand. If he agrees to help, you may want to have an open conversation with the other parent, or with both of them together.

If none of this helps, and the grandparent(s) are still a problem, you may want to find a good counselor who can help you deal with your day-to-day circumstances. At a minimum, you should try to find a support network of friends or neighbors who can help you stand your ground when the grandparent seems to be wearing you down. In the very worst case, a temporary break in communications may be necessary. Sometimes a short "cease-fire" can help everyone put things into perspective. You can allow them to see the grandchildren, but just put a moratorium on advice. Even if it's just for a week or two, the relief can be all that is needed to cool tempers and allow more productive conversations afterward.

Once you've learned how to deal with grandparents, the other relatives will be easier. Intruding aunts, uncles, or cousins will most likely be less resistant to a change in your relationship. Your parents may feel that they have a God-given right to tell you what to do. Sisters and brothers are usually more easily broken of such a habit. Tell them you love them and appreciate their concern, but stand firm on who is in charge. Eventually, they should get the message. If they don't, tell them straight out that either they quit pushing advice on you, or you feel it's best to correspond only at holidays.

What about the relative who doesn't give advice but rather gives blame? For example, upon hearing the latest misbehavior of your adult adolescent, a relative might call you and say, "Well, if you all hadn't been so interested in money that you spent all your time working, Johnny would have had more supervision," or, "I always said a child needs to grow up in a small town. You two insisted on living in a city. This is what happens." Such comments are obviously meant only to make the speaker feel better, not to be any real help to you. It's the same as the "holier than thou" church member or the "keeping up with the Joneses" neighbor.

There are two responses. First, if the person is generally reasonable and/or truly cares about you, and you think he might be willing to listen, tell him that his behavior is hurtful to you. If you have a basic affection and trust in your relationship, this is the preferred approach because it is honest and open. You are showing him the impact of his hurtfulness and giving him a chance to change.

If that approach doesn't work or isn't possible because there is no true affection, or if you just plain don't want to work on a better relationship with that person, the alternative is to tell the person how happy you are for him that his life is so wonderful, and then wait him out with silence.

One final tip on dealing with relatives: Remember, unless you live in a very small town where nothing is left undiscussed, you can control what your relatives hear about your children's behavior. If a particular relative is intrusive, and kindness and tact have not slowed him down, then you can quit sharing so much information. When asked how your son or daughter is doing, just say, "Very well. Thank you for asking." Then drop it. If you tell an advice-prone relative about your problems, you are inviting his advice. So don't give him the opening.

## EX-SPOUSES

When the adult adolescent's other parent is your ex-spouse, parenting decisions can be difficult to make or enforce jointly. You may have very different perspectives on the correct response to Johnny or Mary. As we mentioned in the section on teamplay, it's very important to do the best you can to create a unified front. When you agree on your responses to the adult adolescent, he has less chance to manipulate the situation.

Relationships with ex-spouses fall anywhere along a spectrum of a fair degree of cooperation to a total inability to communicate. The bitterness of the divorce can find its way into arguments, and a contest can result along the lines of who can make whom feel worse. Blaming statements are a big part of this game: "Johnny wouldn't be doing this if you hadn't. . . ."

The nature of your relationship with your ex-spouse will determine how effectively you can parent as a team. So, to the extent it is reasonable, it's time well invested to try to improve that relationship—at least where the kids are concerned. We recommend adhering to the ten ground rules laid out in Chapter 11 for dealing with a spouse. In addition, if at all possible, try to reach the following three agreements:

1.  Agree to communicate the jointness of the decisions to your adult adolescent. Avoid the "Your father thinks we should do it this way" statements.
2.  Agree to write down your joint decisions when they are particularly important, or all the time if you feel it's necessary. This clarifies understanding and avoids later disagreements about what was really said.
3.  Agree that if you repeatedly can't reach joint decisions, you will seek assistance from an objective and trained third party (a counselor, social worker, or other person or group).

If the two of you cannot live within most or all of these ground rules and agreements, then it may not be possible to parent as a team. This is a regrettable situation, since it will make it easier for the adult adolescent to remain codependent.

However, all you can control is your own behavior as a parent. Do the best you can to be egalitarian, and courteously allow the other parent to do what he feels he must. Don't run the other parent down in the eyes of your adult adolescent. Use simple statements like, "I am choosing not to give you that money, because in my heart I believe it would not be right for me to give it." If the adult adolescent points out that the other parent thinks you should give it, reply, "Well, I know he loves you, and he wants the best for you, just as I do. But we don't agree on what the best is. We each have to figure that out. It's not easy to decide. In this case, my choice is to say no."

Whatever your relationship with your ex-spouse, that person is your adult adolescent's parent. You owe both the ex-spouse and your adult adolescent an explanation of your parenting philosophy. Maybe several repetitions will be necessary. If at some point you've explained and explained, and your ex-spouse is not listening, then you may have to terminate discussions, at least for a while. You can do this while leaving the door open for future change by saying something like this:

"I'm sorry we disagree. I believe we both love Johnny and are trying to do what is right. But it is clear that we are not going to understand each other's perspective, and neither of us wants to change our view. From here on, I guess we'll just have to parent Johnny as separate people. That makes me sad. Maybe it'll change somewhere in the future. But for now, let's not discuss this anymore."

In most relationships with ex-spouses, it's a good idea to put a lot of your discussions (not just your decisions) in writing—or at least—follow them up with letters to confirm understanding. Spoken communication contains tone-of-voice elements and innuendos that can make it less clear than the written word. Having things in writing can also provide a clear history of your decisions over time. Keep copies of your correspondence. You can learn what didn't work by going back over your letters. You can also see how far your adult adolescent has come when, at some point, you go back and see your earlier letters and compare the behavior described there to his behavior in the present. That's a good way to remind yourself to pat yourself and the adult adolescent on the back for making progress in breaking the codependency.

## STEPPARENTS

With the large number of blended families now, the role of stepparents is a significant and widespread issue. If your adult adolescent is acting up, what right does your spouse, the stepparent, have to be involved in decision making?

When stepparents are involved, issues of who's in charge become delicate. On some issues the stepparent clearly has a right to a voice, for example, anything involving use of the stepparent's property, anything affecting the stepparent's children, behavior in the home the stepparent shares with the parent, and anything that *directly* affects the stepparent.

How do you determine what "directly" affects the stepparent? It's not always easy. Take money issues, for example. If an adult adolescent asks his parent for a loan, does the stepparent have a right to a voice in the decision? The answer depends on how the two partners have decided to share responsibility for other financial matters. For example, it is very common now for both partners to work full-time. In such a marriage, there may be a joint checking account, into which each contributes either equally or according to income. From this account, all household expenses are paid. In addition, each partner may have separate checking and savings accounts. Decisions on how to spend the joint money are typically shared. Decisions regarding how to spend the separate monies may not be.

Before you can know who should participate in the decision regarding the adult adolescent's loan, you must determine how you normally make financial decisions within your marriage. If both your incomes are pooled and everything that is earned is "ours," then the stepparent should be a part of the response to the adult adolescent. However, if a hands-off policy exists regarding your private accounts, the parent alone can decide to grant or not grant the loan from his personal account. This is not to say that you can't seek the advice of the stepparent. Frequently the stepparent is a more objective observer and can be a great help in making this type of judgment.

When an adult adolescent becomes a chronic problem, it is a good idea for the parent and stepparent to outline areas of responsibility. Two areas in particular must be covered. First, who is parenting? Who will deal directly with Johnny or Mary? The answer depends on the stepparent's relationship with the adult adolescent. The more recent the marriage, the less likely it is that the adult adolescent will accept any discipline or interference from the stepparent. But if a good relationship exists, or if the stepparent has in fact actively raised the child for quite some time, he or she may want to be involved in some or all interactions with the adult adolescent. If the adult adolescent is hostile or the stepparent is unwilling to be involved, then it is better to leave the parenting to the natural parents.

The second area where responsibility must be defined is on what issues the stepparent wants to be involved in the decisions regarding the adult adolescent. To what degree will the two of you work together to wrestle through things? This may range from none ("He's your son, I don't want to interfere") to almost all ("I feel like I'm his other dad"). Where the stepparent wants to be involved in some but not all decisions—the most common case—it helps if the partners make a list of areas the stepparent feels should definitely involve him. Examples might include anything involving time spent in the house, use of the stepparent's belongings, and schedule changes that affect the stepparent.

The parent should be sensitive to the fact that this list may not be all-inclusive. The adult adolescent may think of new and interesting requests that will affect the stepparent. When faced with such a request, the parent should defer answering. "Let me think about it," is all that needs to be said. Then ask the stepparent if he wants to be part of the decision.

When communicating a decision to the adult adolescent, it may be appropriate to say, "Helen and I talked about this . . . ," to indicate that the stepparent was involved. This is especially important when the adult adolescent knows that the decision affects the stepparent directly. It may even be advisable for the stepparent to participate in communicating the decision to the adult adolescent, if that relationship is strong enough.

At other times, when a request does not obviously involve the stepparent, it may be wise for the parent to take responsibility for the decision. "I've thought about this and . . . ," and leave it at that. Even though the stepparent may have been an important part of the decision making, it might be better to leave it unsaid.

At all times, however, the natural parent is ultimately responsible for the choices involving the adult adolescent. The nature of the marriage and of the stepparent's relationship with the adult adolescent may make that person an almost-equal partner in the decision-making process. But in the final analysis, if there is no agreement on the right choice, the choice should be the natural parent's.

Where the parent and stepparent frequently disagree on parenting technique, the three agreements outlined for ex-spouses can be helpful in negotiating differences with spouses who are or are not the other natural parent.

## CHOOSING OTHERS TO BE
## A SOUNDING BOARD

As mentioned in Chapter 11, it's crucial that each of us have someone to turn to who can help us stay on the egalitarian path when we're tempted to go astray. Those people are ideally not advice givers. They don't tell us what we should do. Rather, they talk through options with us, helping us to see the advantages and disadvantages of each. They help remind us of the goals we have chosen for ourselves. They act as a sounding board. Most importantly, they do not allow us to push the decision onto them. They refuse the responsibility because they know it must remain our own if we are to be healthy. Anything else is codependency.

When you need someone to help you clarify your thoughts and talk with you while you wrestle with the best thing to do, look for those who do not give advice. Look for people who are concerned, who share your understanding of egalitarian parenting, and who are good listeners. They should also be good questioners.

As for anyone who tries to intrude unasked, telling you how to "fix" the problem, don't be intimidated. No one knows all the answers. Parenting is too difficult. Don't let anyone convince you otherwise. Have faith in yourself and in your efforts to love your adult adolescent and to be healthy in your relationship with him. As for the rest of the world . . . just remember to say, "Thanks so much for asking," and move on.

# Conclusion

Few things in life are as challenging as parenting. With the exception of marriage, most of us encounter no other relationship that is potentially more trying or more rewarding. How great the reward depends solely on our response to the challenges presented. The greater the challenges, the more enormous our opportunities for personal growth.

As a parent of an adult adolescent it helps to remember the opportunities your troubles offer. Your troubles are your own Mt. Everest—just waiting to be conquered by health and growth. They are not insurmountable. Many parents have successfully adopted egalitarian parenting and the principles of letting go. With their support systems helping, these parents have learned to give healthy love to their adult adolescents.

You can only control or change yourself. Make yourself the goal. Be the best person and the most egalitarian parent you know how to be. The impact will not be felt only by the adult adolescent. Such a philosophy of parenting invariably spills over into better communication techniques between spouses, co-workers, friends, and relatives. Egalitarianism and empathy grow together. And where empathy goes, love also goes.

Miracle after miracle has taken place in families who adopted egalitarian parenting and being emotionally healthy as their goals. We believe you'll be proud of the healthier you. Eventually, so will your adult adolescent. And in the process of breaking your codependent relationship with your adult adolescent, you will discover a renewed sense of love for your offspring—and for yourself.

# Appendix

## LOCAL PHONE NUMBERS

In your phone directory, you can look up in the white pages numbers for:

- Crisis hotline (most cities have one or several)
- Red Cross
- Salvation Army
- YMCA/YWCA
- United Way

These agencies can usually help you locate whatever referral numbers you may need. In addition, you can check the blue pages (or government pages) for your city, county, state, or federal mental health services or social service agencies.

Although we encourage you to obtain mental health professionals through a referral of someone you trust rather than a random selection from the phone book, you can also get started by looking in the yellow pages under such headings as Doctors—Psychologists, Doctors—Psychiatrists, or Hospitals—Mental Health.

Many cities now have doctor referral phone numbers. You call a phone number and tell the person answering what you need and receive a list of doctors who meet your criteria. For example, you might ask for a licensed psychologist who specializes in family therapy, who works within ten miles of your home or office, and who will provide free introductory meetings. Note that the doctors listed are those who agree to participate in the network, so the list may not be all-encompassing.

Some self-help groups may be listed in your white pages. These include:

- TOUGHLOVE—for parents of acting-out adolescents
- Co-Dependents Anonymous (CoDA)—for anyone involved in a codependent relationship
- Parents Anonymous—for parents who have abused their children and want to stop
- Alcoholics Anonymous
- Al-Anon—a self-help group for families and friends of alcoholics

If your local phone book is particularly unhelpful, you can call your own church or look in the yellow pages under Churches and call various church offices. Most larger churches keep referral lists and will be able to refer you to the agency, group, or professional who can help. You do not have to be a member of a church to call their office and ask for a referral.

## TOLL-FREE AND NATIONWIDE REFERRAL NUMBERS

The following list provides some toll-free numbers you may find helpful. These were current as of publication. If any of them are out of order when you call, you can call toll-free information at 1-800-555-1212 to obtain the new listing. Where a toll-free number is not available, we have listed the toll number.

**Adult Children of Alcoholics (ACA)**
*See* Al-Anon

**Aids Hotline** 800-342-AIDS
National hotline, twenty-four hours a day.

**Al-Anon Family Group/Alateen** 800-344-2666
Designed to help the families and friends of alcoholics, this
group will assist you in locating a group near you. Adult Children of Alcoholics information available. Monday to Friday, 7:30
A.M. to 5 P.M. Eastern Time. For brochures and other information, call 1-800-359-9996, twenty-four hours a day.

**Alcoholics Anonymous** 212-686-1100
Access to local chapter phone numbers. (Also try your local
phone book.) 9 A.M. to 5 P.M. Eastern Time. Or you may write
to: Alcoholics Anonymous, P.O. Box 459, Grand Central Station,
New York, NY 10163.

**Child Abuse Hotline—Childhelp** 800-422-4453
Twenty-four hours a day. Purpose is to provide information and
referrals. Can provide crisis counseling.

**800-Cocaine** 800-262-2463
Twenty-four hours a day. For the user or his friends or family.
Primarily for information and referral. Crisis intervention avail-
able.

**Co-Dependents Anonymous** (CoDA) 602-944-0141
For information regarding contacting a group near you. 1 P.M. to
5 P.M. Central Time. Answering machine available during off
hours. Or write to CoDA, P.O. Box 33577, Phoenix, AZ 85067-
3577.

**National Domestic Violence Hotline** 800-333-SAFE
Twenty-four hours a day. Sponsored by the National Coalition
Against Domestic Violence. Provides information, options, and
shelter referral. Primarily for battered women, but can provide
referrals to protective services agencies if you are being abused
by your adult adolescent.

**National Drug Information and Treatment Referral Line**
800-662-4357
Monday to Friday, 9 A.M. to 3 A.M.; Saturday and Sunday, 12
noon to 3 A.M. Eastern Time. Forty-five percent of their calls are
from the friends and family of addicts. They provide information on drugs, addiction, how to get counseling for yourself or

the addict, and how to find support groups. Free literature available.

**TOUGHLOVE** 800-333-1069
An organization dedicated to helping parents deal with acting-out adolescents and similar problems. This number provides referral to local groups. Printed information available. Monday to Friday, 9 A.M. to 5 P.M.

# Bibliography

The readings listed here are ones we particularly recommend. Considering the volume of books available in print and through your library, this is only a small portion of what is available on these subjects. However, we believe these to be among the best.

To make your selection easier, books are grouped by subject area with a brief comment on each. The books are listed with the most highly recommended first.

## The Nature of Love and the Purpose of Human Existence

Peck, M. Scott. *The Road Less Traveled: A New Psychology of Love, Traditional Values and Spiritual Growth*. New York: Simon & Schuster, 1978.

In this bestselling book, Dr. Peck tackles a large number of difficult subjects in an easy-to-read style. These include love, dependency, and the interwoven nature of mental health and spiritual growth. If you read only one book from this bibliography, make it this one.

Peck, M. Scott. *The Different Drum: Community Making and Peace*. New York: Simon and Schuster, 1987.

Being healthy as an individual is only the first step in being happy. Ultimately, to be truly joyous, we need to come to terms with our fellow humans—be they family, friends, coworkers or others. This book addresses the difficulties we all have in extending ourselves to truly understand another person and make loving compromises.

## Understanding and Working with Your Adult Adolescent

York, Phyllis and David, and Ted Wachtel. *TOUGHLOVE*. New York: Bantam, 1978.

York, Phyllis and David, and Ted Wachtel. *TOUGHLOVE Solutions*. New York: Bantam, 1984.

These two books and the companion self-help manual should be required reading for all parents. These books discuss the difficulties of parenting "acting-out" teens—children whose behavior is unacceptable or even destructive. While the children mentioned are teenagers, the principles also apply to adolescents who are over the age of eighteen.

Okimoto, Jean Davies, and Phyllis Jackson Stegall. *Boomerang Kids: How to Live with Adult Children Who Return Home*. Boston: Little, Brown and Company, 1987.

For parents of an adult adolescent who manifests his dependency by returning home, this is a helpful guide to setting limits and dealing with the difficulties of coexistence.

Littwin, Susan. *The Postponed Generation: Why America's Kids Are Growing Up Later*. New York: Morrow, 1986.

Susan Littwin writes about why and how many young people are postponing the responsibilities of adulthood. This book is helpful to a parent trying to understand the adult adolescent's viewpoint.

Elking, David. *All Grown Up and No Place to Go*. Reading, Mass.: Addison-Wesley, 1984.

Although this book appears to be about teenagers, it is relevant to the struggles of adolescents of any age. It provides good insights into the adolescent's stress as he searches for his own identity.

Miller, Gordon Porter, with Bob Oskam. *Teaching Your Child To Make Decisions: How to Raise a Responsible Child*. New York: Harper & Row, 1984.

In their own minds, adult adolescents typically feel their problems are "unsolvable." This is most often because they have not learned how to make ordinary decisions. This book is a great tool for teaching parents how to lay the groundwork for healthy decision making.

Johnson, Spenser. *One Minute Father*. New York: Morrow Press, 1983.

Johnson, Spenser. *One Minute Mother*. New York: Morrow Press, 1983.

These straightforward and simple handbooks teach parents to help their children build self-esteem and self-discipline. Good books for parents of children of any age.

## Codependency

Schaef, Anne Wilson. *Co-Dependence: Misunderstood—Mistreated*. San Francisco: Harper and Row, 1986.

Ms. Schaef's book is outstanding. She has a deep understanding of the varied manifestations of codependency.

Woititz, Janet Geringer. *Adult Children of Alcoholics*. Pompano Beach, FL.: Health Communications, Inc., 1983.

Children raised in alcoholic families suffer a particularly difficult form of codependency. Dr. Woititz explains in simple language the nature of that dependency, and how people can break out of their unhealthy family behavior patterns. If someone in your family tree was an alcoholic, even if it was several generations before you, we *strongly* urge you to read this book.

Beattie, Melody. *Codependent: No More*. Hazelden Foundation, St. Paul, 1987.

This book both explains codependency and helps the reader to break free of it in his or her own life.

Black, Claudia. *It Will Never Happen to Me*. Denver: Medical Administration Company, 1981.

This is another very good book on the children of alcoholics.

## Balancing Your Own Rational (Logical) and Emotional Life

Ellis, Albert. *Humanistic Psychotherapy*. New York: Institute for Rational Living, Inc., 1975.

Dr. Ellis is recognized as one of the world's foremost teachers and psychologists. This is his text for teaching rational-emotive therapy, and is highly recommended both for mental health professionals and for lay readers.

Viscott, David. *The Language of Feelings*. New York: Pocket Books, 1976.

Many of us have difficulty acknowledging how we really feel about things. Since we don't tell ourselves, we really have trouble telling anyone else! This book, written in an easy, conversational tone, helps the reader to appreciate the importance of honest communication of feelings and provides advice on how to get started.

Walen, Susan R., Raymond D. DiGiusseppe, and Richard L. Wessler. A *Practitioner's Guide to Rational-Emotive Therapy.* New York: Institute for Rational Living, Inc., 1976.

Another important text related to balancing the rational and emotional sides within each of us.

Young, Howard S. A *Rational Counseling Primer.* New York: Institute for Rational Living, 1974.

An easy-to-read booklet on the ABCs of emotions. The author discusses how you can get in touch with your feelings.

## Articles
These articles are the recently published ones about this subject.

Curran, Dolores. "What to Do When Your Kids Won't Leave the Nest." *U.S. Catholic* 53 (July 1988), p. 6.

"Can You Go Home Again?" *Glamour* 86 (Aug. 1988), p. 272. Survival Strategies for Moving Back in with Mom and Dad.

"You Can Go Home Again." *USA Today* 117 (Aug. 11, 1988), p. 5.

"Should You Lend Money to Your Adult Children?" *Prevention* 40 (Jan. 1988), p. 96.

"When the Kids Come Home to Roost and How Long They Should Stay." *Better Homes and Gardens* 66 (Feb. 1988), p. 60.

"Back to the Nest: Grown-up Children Who Move Back In." *New York* 21 (Feb. 1, 1988), p. 24.

"Kept Kids." *New York* 21 (Feb. 1, 1988), p. 28.

Toufexis, Anastsis. "Show Me the Way to Go Home." *Time* 129 (May, 1987), p. 106.

Smith, Harold Ivan. "When Jenny Comes Marching Home (Again)." *Christian Herald* 110 (Sept. 1987), p. 46.

"I Moved Back into My Parents' House: My Problem and How I Solved It." *Good Housekeeping* 205 (Aug. 1988), p. 24.

"Parenting the Downside: Being Parents to Grown Children Living at Home," Letter to the Editor. *U.S. News & World Report* 101 (Aug. 25, 1986), p. 63.

"Hi, Mom, I'm Home . . . Again." *Redbook* 167 (July 1986), p. 86.

"Going Home Again." *Newsweek* 106 (Dec. 16, 1985), p. 72.

Leavitt, David. "The New Lost Generation: It's Post-Sixties, Pre-Eighties and Forever in Between." *Esquire* 103 (May 1985), p. 85.

# Index